# THE CRECY WAR

## DATE DUE

# THE
# CRECY WAR

❖

A MILITARY HISTORY OF THE HUNDRED YEARS
WAR FROM 1337 TO THE
PEACE OF BRETIGNY, 1360

*Lieutentant-Colonel*
## Alfred H. Burne
D.S.O., F.R.HIST.S

*"Such a breed of mighty men"*

## WORDSWORTH EDITIONS

TO GLADWYN TURBUTT
who took me to Crecy

First published in 1955
by Eyre & Spottiswoode

This edition published 1999
by Wordsworth Editions Limited
Cumberland House, Crib Street, Ware,
Hertfordshire SG12 9ET

ISBN 1 84022 210 7

Printed and bound in Great Britain
by Mackays of Chatham plc, Chatham, Kent.

# CONTENTS

# LIST OF MAPS

# PREFACE

THE Hundred Years War was, in all but name, four wars. The first was the invasion of France by Edward III; the second saw the almost total expulsion of the English; the third was the war of Henry V; the fourth resulted in the loss of all our territories in France except Calais.

This book chronicles, in its military aspect, the first of these wars, from 1337 to 1360, terminating in the Peace of Bretigny. This war possesses no name, so I have been obliged to coin one, and have fixed upon *The Crecy War*, which at least is self-explanatory, as every historical title should be: the word CRECY conjures up in the public mind the great war of Edward III in France better than any other.

Yet, though it enjoys no name, this war is in all essentials self-contained. It is only because historians when writing of it have presumed the future, that it has been merged in the war that followed it. The peace that ensued was, it is true, of short duration, but this was solely because of the premature and unexpected death of the French king. It lasted for nine years—not a long period, but longer than the interval between the War of the Austrian Succession and the Seven Years War.

The fact remains that the Crecy War has an individuality, a coherence, a continuity, and a central theme that gives it ample claim to be considered and treated as a single whole. That central theme is the struggle carried on for twenty-one years by one dominant personality for one over-riding purpose —to extirpate, once and for all, the root cause of the abiding enmity between England and France—namely the homage due by the English king for his French dominions. That was the aim which Edward III kept ever before him, in good times and in bad, and that aim was secured and sealed by the Treaty of Bretigny, as the direct result of the most continuously successful war that England had ever fought.

9

England was a young nation, only recently moulded into one, and the cement was still damp. Mainly as a result of this war the cement hardened rapidly, and such a spirit of pride and national consciousness was engendered in its people that, long afterward, Jean Froissart noticed and recorded the proud mien of Englishmen everywhere. This may or may not be a good thing–I am not arguing the point–but it was at least an important result of the war, and for this if for no other reason the Crecy War deserves to be rescued from anonymity.

There are other reasons too. For the soldier and the military student the war will repay study, as it marks a step in the progress of the military art, in the age-long contest between mounted and dismounted troops, between "missile" and "personal" weapons, and in the emergence of a third arm–the artillery. It is thus all the more surprising that no soldier, French or English, has hitherto written a history of this war. A few, a very few, battles have been dealt with by military writers, but the grand strategy has been left, for the most part, to civilian historians. These men seem to compete with one another in deriding the strategic ability of Edward III and their verdict may be summed up thus: "He was a good tactician, but he did not understand strategy." I was brought up on Victorian accounts of his campaigns (for practically nothing has been written on the subject during the past half century) and I was therefore prepared to endorse this adverse verdict on Edward III. But the deeper I studied the subject the more firmly I became convinced that the English king, so far from not understanding, was a master of strategy, and that he never showed it more strikingly than in his last and much criticized campaign of 1359.

Thus I came to the conclusion that a military study of the war of Edward III was overdue. That king has been hardly treated by historians. Not only have they failed to eradicate from their minds the ultimate sequel to Bretigny, but they cannot forget that Edward died in his dotage. What of that? Other great men have done the same, Marlborough for example, but what possible bearing has that on events that had taken place 30 years earlier? There has also been a tendency to judge him from the standpoint of Victorian morality, by which criterion there is of course much to reproach in his character and conduct. He was not so judged by his contemporaries: he was everywhere regarded as in all respects a great and gifted man. He was indeed described by an opponent as *le plus sage guerrier du monde.* It is one of the objects of this book to justify and establish this contemporary assessment of one of our greatest kings.

No one can study this war for long without becoming conscious of the fact that England in those days bred a race of masterful men: both leaders and led were men mighty in spirit. Well did Henley sing of them:

> *Such a breed of mighty men*
> *As came forward, one to ten . . .*

Yet their reputations and their very names have been forgotten (for Shakespeare never wrote *The Life of King Edward III*). Let these resounding names therefore be set down at once: Henry of Lancaster, Northampton, Warwick, Oxford, Salisbury, Stafford, Lord Bartholomew Burghersh, Sir Thomas Dagworth, Sir William Bentley, Sir James Audley, Sir Robert Knollys, Sir John Chandos, and the Black Prince. Only the last two of these names are now widely known, yet never did such an illustrious band of English soldiers take the field. When the paragon of them all, Henry of Lancaster, was buried in the Collegiate Church at Leicester (his grave has now vanished) the greatest in the land came to do him honour, for his passing was looked upon as a national disaster.

The Hundred Years War as a whole is a sealed book to most Englishmen, apart from Crecy, Poitiers, and Agincourt, and this may in part be due to the strange fact that no English professional historian–let alone professional soldier–has ever written a history of the War or of any of its phases, although it looms so large in our history. Nor has the task been attempted

by a French soldier. Recently there has appeared a single-
volume history of the war (*The Hundred Years War*, by Edouard
Perroy) brilliant in its own way, and particularly under the
circumstances in which it was written, but the author is a
French civilian and the book is confined mainly to the political
aspect of the war. It was indeed the appearance of this book
in Paris in 1946[1] that inspired me to tackle the task from the
military point of view.

\*             \*             \*

The reconstruction of all history is largely conjectural, and
this applies more to military than to any other branch of
history. It should therefore be clearly understood that there
is this element of the conjectural in all the events described
in this book, but it would become wearisome to the reader
were I to qualify almost every sentence with such expressions
as "It would seem that", "In all probability", or "The evidence
points to the fact that. . .". When in particular doubt or
difficulty, I have applied the test of what I call Inherent
Military Probability to the problem, and what I.M.P. tells
me I usually accept. All military historians to some extent do
this–they are bound to–but they do not all admit it.

\*             \*             \*

This book is designed primarily for the general reading
public and I have not cumbered it with voluminous notes
and references,[2] nor have I interrupted the narrative appreciably in order to discuss controversial points. But for those
who wish to delve into such matters there is an appendix to
each chapter in which the principal sources are also listed,
and controversial points are discussed in greater detail. This
appendix can of course be skipped by those who wish for
narrative, pure and simple.

The space devoted to political considerations is confined to

---

[1] English edition published by Eyre & Spottiswoode.
[2] In footnote references I have only included the specific page reference in cases
that I consider particularly important.

a minimum in order to allow greater space to the military operations, but the political side cannot of course be completely omitted: for instance the effect of shortage of money upon the operations must be mentioned, but not the cause of that shortage, or the means taken to remedy it; the strength of armies must be gone into, but not the method of providing the men. (The latter subject is dealt with in the Appendix to Chapter I.)

On the political side I am much indebted to Professor Lionel Butler, of All Souls, Oxford, and to Mr. Robin Jeffs, of Trinity College, Oxford, for reading my MS with such eagle-eyed care, and for pointing out slips and errors of which I had been guilty and pitfalls into which I should have fallen but for their help. On the military side, for the reason given above, I have no acknowledgements to make.

ALFRED H. BURNE.

# THE CRECY WAR

# CHAPTER I

# PRELIMINARIES

THE seeds of the Hundred Years War were sown as far back as A.D. 1152 when Henry Plantagenet, count of Anjou, married Eleanor, the divorced wife of Louis VII of France and heiress to the duchy of Aquitaine. Two years later Henry succeeded to the throne of England and Normandy and thus found himself in possession of the whole of western France from the English Channel to the Pyrenees. For all this vast area—a good half of France—he was the nominal vassal of the king of France and thus the unnatural position was established of a king in his own right being also the vassal of another king. What made it worse was that the vassal was often more powerful than his suzerain. It is therefore not surprising that for the next 300 years every king of England was at some time or another at war with the king of France.

The situation was aggravated in 1259 by the complicated Treaty of Paris which made various adjustments and new enactments and reaffirmed the vassal status of the English dominions in France. No king of France enjoyed the sight of a rival monarch in occupation of a large portion of the land of France, and no king of England could stomach the thought of having to do homage to another monarch whom he regarded as his equal. It made matters worse when the two were blood relations. The Treaty of Paris produced so much confusion and conflict that some historians have dubbed the ensuing 80 years "The First Hundred Years War".

Edward III was only 14 years of age when, in 1327, he succeeded to the throne of his luckless father, Edward II. Although he had a French mother, the notorious Isabella, he was born and brought up in an atmosphere and tradition of enmity with France; his ears were filled with stories of

French insolence and bad faith and he smarted with humiliation at having to travel to France and do homage to his rival.
The seeds of war had been so well sown that it would have
been little less than a miracle if the peace had been maintained
throughout his reign. In fact we need look no further than the
duchy of Aquitaine to explain the outbreak of a conflict that
was to last off and on for over 100 years.

But wars are seldom the effect of a single cause. Like most
events in life they are the result of several causes or factors.
In this case there were at least three minor and predisposing
causes: the wool trade with Flanders, the relations between
France and Scotland, and the succession to the throne of
France.

The county of Flanders, occupying roughly the areas
between the sea and the Lower Scheldt, was a fief of the French
crown. The count of Flanders had to do homage for his
domains in just the same way as the English king had to do
homage for his French possessions, but, unlike Edward, he was
on friendly terms with his suzerain. But the Flemish merchants
and the lower classes were favourably disposed to England for
there were close trade links between the two countries. English
sheep provided the wool for the cloth mills of Flanders. Without
this wool the artisans of Flanders would starve—just as the
cotton operatives in Lancashire starved when American cotton
was denied them during the American Civil War. The great
cloth towns realized that their true interests resided in an
English alliance, and they appealed to Edward for help against
the exactions and harsh treatment of their count and their
suzerain. Thus began the long era of community of interests
and friendship between England and the Low Countries.

The relations between England and Scotland had been
unhappy for half a century and they were destined to remain
unhappy for a further 100 years.

Young Edward, at the outset of his reign, had one over-
ruling ambition—to restore the ascendancy established by his
grandfather, Edward I, over Scotland, and to give the island

of Great Britain a single government. Yet when he invaded Scotland, and seemed on the verge of complete success, the French king, Philip VI, twice intervened diplomatically, and secretly helped the northern country by all possible means. Thus was induced in the minds of both the English king and his parliament a deep feeling of suspicion and distrust of the French king and the belief steadily grew that war between the two countries was inevitable. This suspicion of Philip was not fully justified, but it became ingrained nevertheless. The damage was done.

The third predisposing cause of the war was the disputed succession to the French throne on the death of Charles IV, the last of the Capetians, in 1328. When in 1314 Philip IV ("the Fair") died, he left a younger brother, Charles of Valois, three sons and one daughter. Each son wore the crown in succession, none of them having surviving male issue. When the last of them died the French barons selected his first cousin Philip, son of Charles of Valois, thus passing over Isabella, the sister of the late Capetian kings. It was understandable that Isabella should be passed over; there were two precedents for it, and a woman had never been sovereign of France. But Isabella had a son, who was thus nephew of the late kings, and a nephew is nearer in kinship than a cousin.[1] Isabella's son was in English and in some French eyes the lawful claimant to the throne. Why then was he also passed over? The answer is because he was born and bred in a foreign country, and was moreover the king of that country, for the name of this son was, of course, Edward III of England. Philip was thus a natural choice on the part of the French barons. England was at the time a hated rival, and it will be easy for us to appreciate their motives when we think of Philip II of Spain as king of England when he married Mary Tudor.

The selection of Philip VI did not create much stir at the time,

---

[1] "*Neveu des derniers rois et leur parent au troisième degré, Edouard III leur était plus proche que le Comte de Valois, qui n'était que leur cousin germain et par conséquent parent au quatrième degré.*" PERROY, ÉDOUARD. *La Guerre de Cent Ans*, p. 54 (1945).

and indeed within a year Edward III crossed to France to do homage for his French possessions, thereby recognizing his rival as sovereign. It is true that he added some qualifying words which became afterward the subject of argument, but there is no evidence that he at the time wished for the French throne. Scotland was much nearer his heart.

Even when he eventually broke with France, he did not officially put forward the claim. The war had been in operation nearly two years before he officially advanced it, and then only at the request of the Flemings whom he was trying to bring into active alliance against France.

The assertion made in so many history books that Edward III went to war for the crown of France is thus incorrect. Confusion has been induced by the intrusion of the "Salic Law" into the controversy. It is alleged that the so-called Salic Law prevented Isabella or her son from sitting on the throne of France. But the truth is that this law was not mentioned or thought of by the French jurists till over 30 years later. The truth of the matter can be summed up in a sentence: the legitimate heir was passed over because he was a foreigner.

In any case, it was a wise decision. The law of female inheritance has been responsible for much misery in European history. We have seen how disastrous in its effects was the marriage of Eleanor of Aquitaine with Henry Plantagenet; almost equally unfortunate was the marriage of another French princess, Isabella, to Edward II.

\*            \*            \*

Though the dynastic seeds of discord were powerful, the overriding cause of the war was, as we have seen, the fact that Aquitaine was a fief of the French crown and this fact alone would have been sufficient cause for war to break out, or rather for the "First Hundred Years War" to be resumed. When we add the further predisposing causes which we have listed, it becomes clear that the war was not only natural, but practically inevitable.

\*            \*            \*

PRELIMINARIES                                21

We pass now from the fundamental causes of the conflict to
the events that brought matters to the breaking point. The first
move that led to the final breach came from the French side. In
the spring of 1336, when Edward was on the point, as it seemed,
of clinching his Scottish war, Philip sent his fleet round from
the Mediterranean and settled it threateningly in the ports of
Normandy. Both Edward and his parliament interpreted this
as a threat to invade England, and it is difficult to see what other
interpretation they could have placed on it. They seem to have
decided from that hour that war was unavoidable and they
started to make methodical preparations for it. Subsidies were
voted, funds and military stores were sent to Gascony, and
troops both naval and military were moved to the south coast.

War now looked imminent, in spite of the efforts of the pope,
Benedict XII, to avert it. The fact that Benedict was a Frenchman told against him in English eyes, though he seems to have
been sincere in his efforts.

Both sides now looked round for allies in the coming struggle.
On the English side one soon came to hand unbidden. Robert
of Artois, the dispossessed lord of that county, a thoroughly
disgruntled man, took refuge at the English court late in 1336,
pressed the king to lay formal claim to the throne of France,
and promised his personal support in a war with his hated
suzerain.

Before we follow Edward in his search for allies we must
glance at the composition of the Low Countries at that epoch.
For it was to the Low Countries that Edward's eyes naturally
turned. What is now modern Belgium was then occupied by
the three provinces of Flanders, Brabant, and Hainault.
Flanders, as we have seen, was a fief of France, and occupied
the seaboard from the estuary of the Scheldt to Dunkirk, its
southern boundary running along the river Scheldt almost as
far as Cambrai. Brabant stretched in a rather narrow belt from
Antwerp to Mons and Namur, while Hainault formed a sort of
buffer State between Brabant and France. Both Brabant and
Hainault were provinces of the German Emperor. The boun-

dary of France proper ran much as it does today as far as Tournai
and along the upper Scheldt (spelt Escaut in modern French).
The county of Artois lay, as it still does, round Arras, which was
its capital.

It was, as we have said, natural for the English king to look
to the Low Countries for allies. They were the nearest communities to our shores; there was a tradition of friendship and
commerce between them and us, and through his wife, Philippa
of Hainault, Edward had many connections by marriage with
these parts. Above all, the Low Countries formed the best
jumping-off point for an attack on France. Gascony, an English
possession, was threatened, but Gascony was a long way off. In
the days of sailing ships it might take weeks before troops or
military stores could be landed there, whereas the prevailing
westerly wind ensured that the Low Countries could be reached
in a few days at the most. Moreover the Low Countries were
nearer Paris, the French capital, than was Gascony. Edward
saw, as clearly as did the duke of Marlborough four centuries
later, that a threat to the capital from the Low Countries was
the most effective way of conducting a war with France.
Edward would save Gascony on the plains of Flanders, just as
Pitt four centuries later "conquered Canada on the plains of
Germany".

Of the three communities comprising the Low Countries,
Flanders was the most eligible as an ally. She was the nearest,
direct access could be obtained to her by sea; she was a traditional friend and she had commercial and trade interests in
common with England. If it had been left to her burgesses, she
would gladly have joined in a war against France. But unfortunately her count was a Frenchman, Louis of Nevers, and
although he probably had little love for Philip VI he retained
considerable fear of him and he dared not risk open revolt
against his suzerain. Flanders therefore was not responsive to
Edward's wooing, and in retaliation for this cold attitude,
Edward took the drastic step of cutting off all imports of wool
to the Flemish towns. Where Flanders lost, her neighbours

stood to gain–in particular, Brabant and the Dutch principalities. Where Ypres and Ghent lost, Brussels and Amsterdam
gained. Partly by this means, and partly by lavish expenditure,
Edward built up an imposing alliance comprising Brabant,
Hainault, and a number of towns and counties. Against this, the
king of France–apart from his Scottish alliance–had few
allies outside his own vassals, some of whom displayed little
zeal in the cause of their suzerain.

Furthermore, the duchy of Brittany inclined to the English
cause, and best of all, the Emperor, Louis of Bavaria, who was
married to the king's sister-in-law, signed an offensive and
defensive alliance with Edward in the summer of 1337.

On May 24, 1337, Philip took the decisive step; he solemnly
confiscated all the territories of his English vassal.This, in the
view of a modern French historian,[1] was tantamount to a
declaration of war, and we may conveniently accept this date
as the official beginning of the war. As if to clinch matters,
French troops, who were already stationed on the border,
invaded Gascony and the French fleet raided Jersey, following
up with a raid on Portsmouth and the south coast. The war
was on!

Edward III responded in October by repudiating his
homage and addressing his rival as "Philip", describing himself
as "king of France". He declared that he was the rightful
occupant of the French throne, though he did not proclaim himself king. That claim was not put forward for nearly two years.

The English king followed up words with deeds: in November
he sent a small expedition under Sir Walter Manny (a compatriot of his queen) to raid the Flemish island of Cadzand.
This was accomplished successfully, largely because of the
striking action of the archers, who put down what would now
be described as a barrage of arrows to cover the landing of
the infantry. The English troops then drew up in a formation
that was afterward to become familiar–the men-at-arms in line
and the archers massed like two bastions at the ends of the line.

---

[1] Edouard Perroy, in *The Hundred Years War*.

During all this time the pope was striving to avert the conflict, but was trusted by neither side. All he succeeded in doing was to delay the outbreak of serious operations for six months. But in the summer of 1338 naval operations began again in the English Channel and the French fleet made itself again uncomfortably familiar off the south coast of Hampshire, burning Portsmouth and other towns.

Meanwhile Edward carried on his preparations steadily for an invasion of the Continent, and on July 12, 1338, he set sail from Orwell, with a considerable fleet and army, his flagship being the *Christopher*, of which we shall hear later.

### THE YEAR 1338

When Edward III of England landed at Antwerp amid scenes of pomp and pageantry on July 22, 1338, his first object was to complete and cement his grand alliance against France. Hitherto he had had no practical experience of working with allies. The task was to tax all the power, patience, and talents of the 26-year-old king. He found his new allies slippery, tepid and timid. They were hesitant and dilatory and the months passed without anything being effected.

The immediate task was to meet the Emperor in person. Louis of Bavaria, Emperor of the Holy Roman Empire, some-times loosely called the German Empire, or even Germany, came to Coblenz, 160 miles from Antwerp, on the Middle Rhine. After careful preparations the king of England set out with an immense retinue and arrived at Cologne on August 23. Here he was received with enthusiasm, which was intensified when he made a handsome contribution to the building fund for the great new cathedral that was then slowly rising. From Cologne he went to Bonn, where the scenes of welcome and rejoicing were repeated: thence by water to Coblenz, cheering crowds greeting him at every halting place. It was a royal progress, the like of which had not been seen within memory.

When the king reached Coblenz on August 31 all the world seemed gathered to meet him. The emperor's train was even larger and more magnificent than that of the king, and included all the imperial electors save one. A few days were spent in preparation; then the king and emperor took their seats on two thrones that had been erected in the market place, the emperor with crown, orb and sceptre. The market place was packed with a huge throng, upward of 17,000 in number, of the nobility of western Europe and their trains. None could recall such a scene of pomp and magnificence. The emperor opened the proceedings by proclaiming that Philip of Valois had forfeited the protection of the empire because of his perfidy. Next, he bestowed on the English king the gold wand, symbolizing his appointment as the emperor's vicar, or vice-regent in western Europe. Edward then spoke, declaring that Philip had usurped the crown of France, which was his own by right. The impressive ceremony passed off without a hitch, and on the morrow the nobles of the empire did homage to Edward III as their vicar for the next seven years. In fact "all went merry as a marriage bell".

The season was too far advanced for a campaign that year, so Edward summoned the princes to attend him in the following July in a campaign for the recovery of Cambrai, which belonged by rights to the empire. This was a shrewd move, for it did not necessarily involve an invasion of France, a course to which some of the principalities were averse. This accomplished, Edward returned to Antwerp where, surprisingly, he spent the winter, instead of returning home. As the result of over a year's labours he had built up a grand alliance, as it might well be called, against France, almost as wide in its scope as the more famous Grand Alliance of the duke of Marlborough. Though the month of July was distinctly late for the opening of the campaign, the prospects appeared bright. But before describing Edward's first campaign in the Low Countries we must glance briefly at the respective strengths and natures of the rival countries.

THE RIVAL FORCES

Though conditions and numbers on the two sides necessarily varied from time to time, the following general statement for the whole period of the war, omitting allies, will never be very far from the mark.

The population of England was between three and four million, while that of France was well over ten million. It may thus be supposed that the French armed forces normally outnumbered those of England by three or four to one. This was not the case, for two particular reasons. England's methods of recruitment were better developed than those of France, and she had at command from time to time both Welsh and Irish troops. These were only slightly offset by the Scottish contingents that from time to time fought under the French colours.

Fairly exact estimates can generally be made about the English strength in the great battles, but that of the French must always remain in doubt because of a marked absence of official records. This book, being primarily a military history, is not directly concerned with the method by which armies were raised and maintained, but rather with the way they operated and fought. The subject is however dealt with in some detail in the appendix to this chapter. Here it will suffice to epitomize the system that obtained in the army of Edward III.

The old English army, inherited by Edward, consisted of two categories: the feudal array or levy, and the national militia. Under the feudal system the barons were obliged to provide retinues of mounted men-at-arms for the service of the crown.[1] But feudalism was decaying and Edward III, shortly before the outbreak of the war with France, had started substituting for it a system of indenture which produced a body of paid professional soldiers and gradually replaced the old feudal levy.

[1] The French had a similar feudal array, called "Hosting", but though every knight in theory was liable for service, in practice vassals were no longer obliged to provide more than one-tenth of their number. PERROY, E. *The Hundred Years War* (Eng. trans.), Eyre & Spottiswoode (London, 1951), p. 44.

The national militia (the old fyrd) was raised from the able-bodied male population between the ages of 16 and 60, selected by Commissioners of Array in each shire. It consisted of hobilars, or mounted lance-men (corresponding to the dragoons and mounted infantry of later ages) and foot soldiers who were subdivided into bowmen and spearmen (later billmen).

To complete the army, there were some foreign mercenaries and Welsh spearmen (for the longbow was by now used exclusively by Englishmen).

The French system of raising and organizing armies was much the same as the English, that is to say the core of the army was made up of the feudal levy of mounted men-at-arms and this was supplemented by the national levies, whose organization and composition was very loose and vague. Broadly speaking the French knights reckoned to win their battles without much assistance from the "communes" or common, base-born men.

But the feudal retinues were only obliged to fight for 40 days outside their own provinces. To induce them to extend their service they had to be paid, but as the royal treasury was generally almost empty the number who could be so paid was very small. Even so the armies that were raised invariably exceeded in number the English armies against which they were pitted.

The French also engaged mercenaries, who in their case were almost exclusively Genoese crossbowmen.

ARMS AND EQUIPMENT

Arms and equipment in the two armies were very similar. Knights and men-at-arms were armed with lance, sword, dagger, and occasionally battle mace. They wore mail armour for the most part, but it gradually gave place to plate armour in the course of the Hundred Years War. A helm, shield, and spurs completed the full outfit. It became customary for each knight to have with him some armed attendants, the usual number being three, two mounted archers and one *coutillier* (swordsman), the whole constituting a "lance". Thus when a certain number of lances is mentioned we must multiply by about four to arrive at the total of effectives.

The English archer, whether mounted or dismounted, carried a longbow and sword, and usually a dagger. The long-bow could be discharged six times a minute: it had an effective range of 250 yards and an extreme range of about 350 yards. The French archers, on the other hand, carried a crossbow. This weapon, though more powerful than the longbow, could only discharge one bolt to four of the longbow. Moreover it was more inaccurate and had a shorter range.[1]

But though both armies were armed and equipped in sub-stantially the same way there was a considerable difference in their efficiency. For over a generation the military exper-iences of the French army had been limited to occasional operations against their vassals, notably in Gascony, whereas the English army was fresh from its successes in the Scottish campaigns. These successes had gone far to expunge the memory of Bannockburn and to link up with the victories of Edward I, who was remembered as the Hammer of the Scots. Edward III had also, by the introduction of the indenture system of service, in effect transformed his army into a body of long-service professional soldiers, highly trained and disciplined. Nothing like it existed on the Continent at the time and it may be compared to the British Expeditionary Force which landed in France in 1914.

As for the third arm, the artillery, at the opening of the war, there is no reliable evidence for the presence of cannon in the English fleet in the battle of Sluys in 1340, nor is it likely that Edward III took any with him to Flanders; and though the French did undoubtedly use cannon in the defence of Tournai in 1340 the first occasion that artillery was used in the field was at Crecy, six years later. Until that date, then, we may ignore its existence.

[1] For further details of arms and armour see the article under that heading by Sir James Mann in the new edition (1950) of *Chambers' Encyclopaedia*.

Of the rival fleets there is not much that need be said. Each country had a small nucleus of royal ships of war, the exact number of which is unknown. The bulk of the fleet was collected in an emergency by the simple means of requisitioning ships, so many from each port. In his efforts to raise a large fleet against the increasing activity and threatening moves of the French fleet, Edward went as far afield as Bayonne, demanding and begging in turn for a contingent of vessels from that distant port. The French had in addition a number of war-galleys which had been rowed round from the Mediterranean.

But naval warfare was at a primitive stage, and the only big engagement at sea approximated to a land battle.

# APPENDIX

## The Army of Edward III

RAISING THE ARMY

From the time of the Norman Conquest to the accession of Edward I a medieval army was raised from two sources: the national militia (fyrd), and the feudal levy. Regarding the first, every able-bodied man between the ages of 16 and 60 was liable to serve if called upon, and to provide himself with suitable arms. Service was, in the first instance, for 40 days (unpaid) and the summons was for the repelling of invasion. The feudal levy or array came in with William I, who allotted lands to his barons on the stipulation that they provided military service for the crown with their own tenants and retinues. The lands so allotted were called fiefs of the crown. The tenants-in-chief could, and did, enfeoff their lands on sub-tenants who thus owed fealty to their immediate lords in the first instance and then to the crown. The size of the contingent that each lord was required to produce varied. Later, tenants were allowed under certain conditions to pay "scutage" to the crown in lieu of military service.

Such, in broad outline, was the military system in vogue at the time of the accession of Edward I. Sixty-five years later, when his grandson embarked on the first campaign of the Hundred Years War, the situation had been transformed. The army, for all practical purposes, consisted of long-service professional volunteers and was based on the indenture system introduced by Edward III himself. The explanation of this almost startling change was that the feudal system was in decay and had ceased to function satisfactorily as a troop-raising medium. The causes of this decay of feudalism form an interesting constitutional study, but one outside the province of this military history. Suffice it to say that the system was no longer providing the crown with the number of men-at-arms required. To give an example: In 1277 only 375 knights answered the summons, out of a possible total (as calculated by Dr. J. E. Morris)[1] of about 7,000. Thus the number had been whittled down to less than one-eighteenth of the available figure.

Edward I set about alleviating this weakness by issuing pay (confined to the mounted troops). "The key was the systematic use of pay. The paid squadron under the professional captain could be combined, and was more efficient than the incoherent units of a feudal host."[2] The earliest example of such pay contracts was in 1277. Other such payments followed, but the contracts remained merely verbal, so far as is known, throughout the reign, and indeed until 1338. The first crack in the old feudal system had appeared, and Edward III extended it. But only gradually. In his first campaign against the Scots he seems to have relied mainly on the impressed national militia. He summoned the whole force of the country; but the results were so disappointing that he resorted to the tentative methods of contract applied by his grandfather. But he went further; he instituted a system of written indenture and gradually extended it throughout his army till the biggest and most important part of it consisted of indentured soldiers. Of this innovation A. E. Prince writes: "In the history of the English army in the

[1] *The Welsh Wars of Edward I*, pp. 41 and 45.          [2] Op. cit., p. 68.

middle ages there is no more significant development than that of the indenture system of recruitment."[1]

By this system a commander contracted with the king to provide a specified force for military service. The indenture laid down precisely the size and composition of the force, rates of pay, place of assembly, length of service, and obligations and privileges such as "regards" (bonuses) to which the men would be entitled. Such a force was generally one of all arms; i.e., men-at-arms, mounted and foot archers, hobilars, foot spearmen, and even miners, artificers, surgeons, chaplains, and interpreters. (This system was, no doubt unconsciously, followed in the British army of the eighteenth century when a colonel contracted with the king to raise a regiment for his service.) The terms of service varied, the shortest being the traditional 40 days, and the longest normally one full year,[2] though in exceptional cases this term was exceeded. For instance, in the army that the Black Prince took to Gascony in 1355 the engagement was "during the king's pleasure" – which was just as well, for the men had little chance of returning home by any specified date. The indenture system had other advantages. It was found to be a convenient method of providing regular garrisons for certain of the royal castles; and foreign mercenaries could also be obtained by this means.

It also became quite common for captains to resort to sub-contract on the same principle as sub-tenancy. The effect of this system was that a long-service professional army was produced. The transformation that had taken place is vividly expressed by Carl Stephenson: "The English army . . . had definitely ceased to be feudal. Rather it was a mercenary force, in which the mounted noble, as well as the yeoman archer, humbly served at the King's wage."[3]

[1] Morris, (Edited) W. A., and Willard, J. F., 'The Army and Navy' in The English Government at Work, 1327-1336 (Medieval Academy of America, 1940), p. 352.
[2] Prince, A. E., 'The Indenture System under Edward III' in Historical Essays in Honour of James Tait (1937), p. 291.
[3] Medieval Feudalism, p. 100.

THE MILITIA

The National militia was raised in the following manner. When the force was to be mobilized, writs were issued to the sheriffs of counties giving the quotas to be provided by them. The county quotas were then subdivided between the hundreds and large towns. The selection of the men to fill these quotas was made by Commissioners of Array, normally one per county, appointed by letters patent by the crown. These commissioners were sent round with instructions to pick out "the strongest and most vigorous men". The men selected received pay from the central government from the date they marched out to the rendezvous appointed.[1] As the numbers raised by indenture increased, so the number of impressed men diminished. This leads Professor Prince to declare: "It was the retinue, based on an indenture contract, rather than the man impressed by commission of array, who superseded the feudal levies and formed the backbone of the Hundred Years War armies."

ORGANIZATION AND EQUIPMENT

Each member of the nobility[2] from the king downward possessed a retinue. These retinues consisted of two categories: the men-at-arms (sometimes loosely called cavalry, though in the reign of Edward III they almost invariably fought on foot), and the mounted archers. There were three degrees in the hierarchy: first came the earls (with whom we must include the Prince of Wales and the duke of Lancaster); second came the bannerets; and third the knights bachelor (so called to distinguish them from the knights banneret). Banneret was not a degree of nobility but a purely military term[3] denoting an officer who was entitled to carry a banner (rectangular); knights bachelor could be promoted to this rank. The knight

---

[1] Before the reign of Edward III the first 40 days had been done without pay.

[2] And some knights. For example, Sir John Chandos in the 1359 campaign had a retinue of seven knights, 54 esquires and 34 archers. PRINCE, 'The strength of the English armies of Edward III' in E.H.R. (1931), p. 362 n.

[3] PRINCE, The Army and Navy, p. 337.

bachelor carried a pennon (triangular). What we might term the rank and file of the men-at-arms were the esquires. These were usually the younger sons of the nobility or others who were aspirants to knighthood.

But the term men-at-arms comprises the whole body, including the officers. Thus a knight was a man-at-arms, but a man-at-arms was not necessarily a knight. The retinue, as mentioned above, also included the mounted archers. To king Edward must be given the credit for the creation of this corps. Before his reign the only mounted troops outside the men-at-arms had been the hobilars, or light-armoured mounted infantry. The technical difference between the hobilars and the men-at-arms was that their horses were unprotected whereas those of the men-at-arms were "covered", i.e., they wore a coverlet of mail or stuffed material. Usually the hobilars carried lances. They had been found very useful in the mountains of Scotland in pursuit of the agile inhabitants whom the heavy cavalry could not reach. J. E. Morris states that the mounted archers were first formed in 1337.[1] But Prince has shown that it can be antedated by three years.[2] As the numbers of the mounted archers rose, those of the hobilars fell, till by the end of the War they had reached negligible proportions. Similarly the numbers of foot archers fell.

The proportion of mounted archers to men-at-arms was consequently variable. Nominally a banneret was expected to find one archer for every man-at-arms, but naturally this provision was not strictly complied with. Even in the king's last campaign, that of 1359, when conditions might be expected to have become standardized after 21 years of war, it is impossible to descry any fixed proportion between the two. Some of the retinue figures for this campaign will repay examination. Thus, the Prince of Wales's retinue consisted of seven bannerets at 4s. a day, 136 knights at 2s., 143 esquires at 1s., and 900 mounted archers at 6d. On the other hand the duke of

[1] 'Mounted Infantry in Medieval Warfare', in *Transactions of the Royal Historical Society*, 3rd Series, vol. VII, p. 94.
[2] *The Army and Navy*, p. 341.

Lancaster's retinue consisted of six bannerets, 90 knights, 486 men-at-arms, and 423 archers.[1] These figures show the rates of pay at a time when they had become reasonably standardized, but they also show that the proportion of archers to men-at-arms was still far from standardized. From the above figures we see that in the Prince's retinue a banneret commanded on an average 210 men, whilst in that of Lancaster he commanded only 130. (These figures omit some Welsh levies in the retinues whose numbers are unknown.) A banneret, it would seem, can be equated with a battalion commander of the present day. It should be noted that the headquarters staff of the army was provided by the bannerets of the king's own retinue of the Household.

Each knight possessed three or four horses, including two destriers (heavy chargers). He also had one or two pages whose duty it was to clean and polish his armour and help him into and out of it, and to assist him to mount his charger.[2] A page also acted as horseholder and groom to his master.

## THE INFANTRY

Thus far we have dealt with the cavalry. The infantry in medieval days consisted of archers and foot spearmen, but since the introduction of mounted archers, who may be designated mounted infantry (as well as the hobilars) we should confine the term infantry, pure and simple, to the foot archers and spearmen. These consisted principally of "the men impressed by the Commissions of Array" as thus described above by Professor Prince. The remainder of the infantry was made up by foreign mercenaries, Irish, Gascons, etc. (though it is likely that many of the Gascons were genuine volunteers and would not have appreciated the term mercenaries).

The foot archers, except that they drew less pay (2d. a day was the basic wage), were almost indistinguishable from their

[1] Tout, T. F., *Chapters in Administrative History*, vol. IV, p. 144, n. 3, as amended by Prince's *Indenture System*, p. 308, n. 2.
[2] The scene in the film *Henry V* depicting knights being hoisted by winches into the saddle may be disregarded.

mounted comrades once the battle had commenced, being similarly armed, though devoid of armour except for a steel cap.

The foot spearmen were drawn mostly from Wales. Although the longbow originated in the Principality, it had soon crossed the border, and first the Cheshire men and then the archers of the other counties were armed with it. In fact, all the archers in Edward's armies were Englishmen.

Though the pay of the army varied from time to time there was one basic rate that was invariable–the pay of the foot archer. That, as we have seen, was fixed at 2d. a day. It remained stationary–just as the basic wage of foot soldiers of later days remained fixed at one shilling a day for over a century. As long as feudalism remained strong the earls scorned to accept any pay, but by the beginning of the Hundred Years War not only the earls, but even the Prince of Wales, accepted pay.[1] A soldier drawing regular pay for his services is naturally more amenable to discipline than one who is not dependent upon it. This was an important factor in building up the cohesion of the English army.[2]

## TACTICAL ORGANIZATION

Chronicles and records alike are reticent on the details of organization in the field. What was the tactical unit? How did it deploy? What was the formation on the march? Did the troops march in step? What non-commissioned officers (as we should now call them) were there? What was the system of picquets and outposts? These and suchlike questions we cannot answer with any degree of certainty. Chroniclers were generally monkish clerks, sequestered in distant monasteries, devoid of practical knowledge of war and dependent upon the tales of old soldiers.[3] Hence they failed to record or explain details of routine which we nowadays are so avid to learn about. It is however known that men-at-arms were grouped in "con-

[1] The Prince's pay was one pound per day.
[2] "Pay produces discipline", writes Morris tersely (op. cit., p. 68.)
[3] Froissart, and still more le Bel, who served under Edward in the Scottish campaigns, were of course exceptions.

stabularies" and that impressed men were formed into units of 1,000, 100, and 20, which may be termed battalions, companies, and troops.[1] Further than this we cannot safely go. No doubt both organization and drill were tentative and fluid, varying according to the character, will and whim of the local commander. A strong man, in command of a small force, such as Sir Thomas Dagworth in Brittany, could weld his force into a remarkable and well-disciplined body of men, as we know by the results.

EQUIPMENT

The best guide to arms and armour carried at any period is provided by the effigies and brasses of knights to be seen in churches all over the country. Perhaps the best example of a knight in armour during the reign of Edward III is that of the Black Prince in Canterbury Cathedral.[2] It was a transition period: the days of mail armour were ending, and it was being replaced by plate armour. The Prince is shown wearing plate except for his gorget, which is of mail; but the ordinary knight may be presumed to have worn a bigger proportion of mail—still more the esquires. Over the breastplate or hauberk was worn a loose-fitting surcoat, emblazoned with the arms of the knight. This, besides being spectacular, had practical advantages. For example, in an emergency, such as an ambuscade, or night attack, the knight would hastily don his surcoat, which became the rallying point for his men, who would automatically gather round his person.[3]

It is interesting to note that as the strength of armour increased the need for the additional protection of a shield diminished. Consequently its size decreased, till eventually it was discarded altogether—just as portions of the body that have ceased to have a function gradually wither and eventually

---

[1] PRINCE, *The Army and Navy*, p. 340. Morris speaks vaguely of "brigades", but without citing his authority.

[2] See article 'Arms and Armour', by Sir James Mann in *Chambers' Encyclopaedia* (1950 edition), p. 608, for a photograph of this, and also for general information.

[3] A good example of this occurred in the battle of Auberoche. See chapter V *infra*.

disappear.[1] The spur, on the other hand, so far from diminishing, tended to increase in size with the introduction of the rowell.[2] Archers, both mounted and foot, wore a steel cap, and breastplate or padded hauberk, and spearmen were similarly attired except that they seldom wore a breastplate.

Rudimentary forms of uniform can be traced at this time. Thus, some Welsh levies raised for the war in Brittany were ordered to be clothed in uniform clothes.[3] And other local authorities were frequently enjoined to dress the impressed men alike.[4]

## WEAPONS AND THEIR EMPLOYMENT

Men-at-arms carried swords, lances, and daggers. The lance was an inheritance of the days of mounted charges. It was the *arme blanche par excellence*. Although it could also be used dismounted we do not hear much of its use in the bigger battles of the war. The sword was the main stand-by of the knight in Edward's army. The lance was unwieldy and out of place in a mêlée, and even the sword often gave place to the dagger in such engagements. Effigies of knights are invariably shown armed with daggers. For a set battle the knights would dismount and hand over their horses to their pages, who would lead them to the rear[5] and establish themselves in the baggage leaguer, for which they formed the guard or garrison during the ensuing battle. Meanwhile the men-at-arms were deployed in line by the two marshals, after which, if the enemy was still motionless, they would be allowed to fall out and refresh themselves. Normally each division[6] of the army (of which there were three) would form up in a single line, flanked by the archers. On the rare occasions when a pursuit was undertaken

---

[1] It would not be surprising if many of the knights in this war discarded their shields just as our troops discarded their gas-masks in the 1940 campaign.

[2] Sir J. Mann, op. cit., p. 608.

[3] EVANS, D. L., 'Some Notes on the Principality of Wales . . .' in *The Transactions of the Honourable Society of Cymmrodorion* (1925), p. 48.

[4] WROTTESLEY, THE HON. G., *Crecy and Calais*, p. 1.

[5] Just as did the artillery horseholders in pre-mechanized days in England.

[6] Many are the Latin and early French words all denoting the same formation, which I translate division.

the pages brought up the chargers, assisted their knights to mount, and probably followed them in the ensuing charge (for there would be no one to restrain them). The archers also dismounted, as stated above. We hear little about the disposal of their horses, but clearly a proportion of the men, perhaps one in ten, led them away to the wagon leaguer. The bowmen then formed into "herces", or hollow wedges, in conjunction with the archers of the next division. These were easily and simply constructed: each body inclined diagonally forward, pivoting on the flank of its own men-at-arms; where the two contiguous lines of archers joined up an apex was formed. The effect was that a bastion-like formation was created in the intervals between the divisions, and the flanks of the army were similarly enfiladed. Thus:–

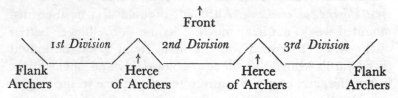

The obvious advantage of this formation was that the front of the men-at-arms could be enfiladed by the archers. Each archer carried two quivers; each quiver contained 24 arrows. With this very limited supply the ammunition problem became acute. When the last arrows had been discharged, three possible courses were open to the archer. He could await the arrival of a fresh supply of arrows; he could pick up the arrows discharged by the enemy; or he could join in the mêlée with his sword. Poitiers is a good example of the second case, Agincourt of the third. Being less encumbered with armour than the men-at-arms, the archers were more nimble and therefore more effective in the hand-to-hand fighting. Moreover they were probably more muscular; only a strong man could wield the longbow.

The few hobilars that Edward still retained with his army were employed as messengers, scouts and orderlies, and as a support to the reserve.[1] The bulk of the reserve was composed of spearmen, and they were utilized after a battle in the rather inglorious task of "clearing up" the battlefield, a task in which the Welsh found that their long knives came in handy. At Crecy some of them broke ranks in their enthusiasm and joined in the mêlée.

SUPPLY AND TRANSPORT

Regrettably little information has come down to us on these all-important subjects. In his otherwise admirable chapter on the Army and Navy in *The English Government at War*, Professor Albert Prince, under the heading "Commissariat arrangements", confines himself to the bald remark that armies mainly lived on the country except at the beginning of a campaign, and he then describes the administrative arrangements at home for procuring supplies for the army abroad.[2] These administrative arrangements concern us here but little; they do not add one iota to the better understanding of the operations in the field, with which this work is primarily concerned. We may therefore confine ourselves to recording that the official responsible for the collection and dispatch of supplies was known as The Receiver and Keeper of the King's Victuals.

As for arms and ammunition, they were stored at the Tower of London, which was the main arsenal of the country and contained, so far as we know, all the cannon in existence in the country at that time. They were under the charge of the Clerk of the Privy Wardrobe. It is from this official's journal and accounts that we get practically all the extant information about the early history of artillery in this country.[3]

On the subject of transport in the field Prince has nothing to say. Very few people have. Some of the things we should like to know are the type of carts and wagons employed;[4] the proportion of stores carried on pack, and on wheels; the number

---

[1] MORRIS, J. E., *Mounted Infantry*.                    [2] Op. cit., p. 364.
[3] TOUT, T. F., 'Firearms in England in the 14th Century', in *E.H.R.*, vol. 12, and in *Collected Essays*, II, p. 233.
[4] For the 1359 campaign the king had special wagons constructed.

and nature of roads traversed; the speed at which the transport could travel; and the extent to which it was "road-bound".

Some light is thrown on the last-named point by an incident in the Poitiers campaign. At one place in the English retreat the combatant troops left the road and pushed on across country, in order to shorten their route, leaving the wagons to continue by the road. This is a clear indication that in Poitou at any rate vehicles were road-bound. And I think there can be little doubt that this was the case in most other campaigns.

Not only were they road-bound, but road-bogged in winter operations, for roads were unmetalled, and the wagon train was often a long one. Especially was this the case in the 1359 campaign, which opened in November and continued without a break till the following April. This campaign does furnish some interesting particulars about the composition of the train. Here are some of the stores carried:—

Field-forges, horseshoes, hand-mills for "man-corn" and "horse-corn", fishing boats, a pack of hounds (60 couple), and so on, the whole carried in an enormous train of wagons, variously given as 1,000 to 6,000 in number.

But this campaign was exceptional. In his previous campaigns the king had never cut himself deliberately adrift from the home country, and the campaigns had been of limited duration. In this one the army plunged into the heart of France, and its length was foreseen and planned to be of unspecifiable duration. Nevertheless the general trend of the evidence is that the armies of Edward III lived on the country less than did many of more recent times, for example the French armies in the Peninsular War. There were some surprisingly modern features about Edward's campaigns, such as his carrying on operations in the winter season; but perhaps the most marked of them were his supply and transport arrangements. We only once hear of his army running short of food—that was in the Calais campaign. Indeed, in his first campaign in Flanders he offered to share with his allies the bread that he was carrying for his own troops in wagons. Bread was always the staple food of military life.

Marlborough's bread wagons are famous[1] and Edward's bread wagons have the right to be equally celebrated.

It should go without saying that the fullest possible recourse was had to local supplies, but they were necessarily an uncertain quantity and the king took steps not to be entirely dependent upon them. To sum up: the result of the various measures and efforts designed by Edward, and indicated above, was that during his war in France the English army became the most powerful and highly trained army of its time, and it is not surprising that successive kings of France evinced a strong disinclination to cross swords with it in the field.

[1] They still exist and are in use in Austria under the name of marlbrooks.

I. THE CAMPAIGNS OF 1339–40

# CHAPTER II

# THE 1339 AND 1340 CAMPAIGNS

KING EDWARD had fixed on Vilvoorde, six miles north of Brussels, as the rendezvous for the army, but July came round without any sign of the allied contingents. Week after week passed while the English army fumed, but the king exercised what patience he could, sending out constant letters of exhortation or reproof. It was not till well on in September that the Elector of Brandenburg, the Emperor's son, arrived at Vilvoorde and the army at length set forth.

It is impossible to make a close estimate of numbers, though it is fairly certain that the English contingent was about 4,000 strong. The allies varied from time to time, and though greatly outnumbering the English, the army total probably at no time reached 20,000. Still, that was a formidable number for those days. The king of England had, in accordance with the chivalrous etiquette of the time, sent a formal challenge of "defiance" to Philip VI in Paris, by the hand of the bishop of Lincoln. The French king thereupon collected an army, also formidable in numbers, and ordered a concentration at St. Quentin, 25 miles south of Cambrai. Three potentates joined its ranks – the blind king of Bohemia, the king of Navarre, and the king of Scotland.

The route for the allies was the shortest possible, namely that *via* Mons and Valenciennes. Sir Walter Manny led the van and his first brush with the enemy occurred at Montaigne, about ten miles north of Cambrai. Though successful in rushing the town he failed to capture the castle. Passing on, he attacked Thun, a few miles further south, and here managed to take both town and castle. A young squire of the name of John Chandos was prominent in these operations. Many engagements were these two destined to share in. Sir Walter Manny seems to have been the "maid of all work" for the king, just as Lord Cadogan was for the duke of Marlborough (though we must discount some of the claims made by Froissart for this remarkable man, both being Hainaulters). The army swept on, the English portion paying its way in the countryside, but the Germans showing themselves "bad payers".

Cambrai was reached on September 20 and its surrender was demanded. Its gallant bishop, who was in control, refused; so siege was laid. Without waiting to "soften up" the city, Edward tried to storm it. A simultaneous attack was made upon its three gates, but in spite of heavy fighting which lasted all day no impression could be made. Froissart asserted in his earliest edition (the only one translated into English) that the defenders had some artillery, but he gave no details and omitted the assertion in both the Amiens and Rome editions. I do not credit the presence of artillery in Cambrai.

Edward now changed his plans; deciding not to waste time on a lengthy siege but to push on into France proper and ravage the dominions of his opponent. At this point a curious incident occurred, illustrating the sort of difficulties with which the English king had to contend. Count William of Hainault, brother of Queen Philippa, and therefore brother-in-law of Edward, solemnly marched off, declaring that he could not enter France as that would mean fighting against his uncle, the king of France. It is surprising that he was allowed to depart without any sharp words being uttered by the king. Still more surprising, three days later he offered his services to the other king. This was more than Philip could stomach and he dismissed the traitor in a rage. As the super-cautious duke of Brabant had now put in a tardy appearance the desertion of the count of Hainault did not amount to much.

Pursuant to the new plan, the army broke up the siege of Cambrai on September 26 and the same day entered France proper seven miles to the south-west, at Marcoing (a town that figured prominently in the 1917 battle of Cambrai). Advancing another ten miles to the south, the king set up his headquarters in the abbey of Mont St. Martin, near Le Catelet. Here he remained for a fortnight whilst his army ravaged and burnt the surrounding country systematically in the hopes that the king of France would be forced to come forward in defence of his subjects and property.

Meanwhile where was Philip VI? When the allies advanced to Cambrai, he was seated in his château at Compiègne. When he heard of the hostile advance he returned to Peronne, *via* Noyon and Nesle. At the latter place he saw on the eastern skyline the smoke of burning villages. This was the work of an expedition under the earls of Salisbury and Derby. They penetrated down the Oise valley, almost to the gates of Laon, burning, among other places, Moy–the scene of a brilliant cavalry action in the 1914 retreat from Mons. Other contingents laid fire to villages further west up to St. Quentin and within sight of Peronne.[1]

It is difficult for us to understand the military object to be achieved by this systematic burning, but two things may be said. In the first place, it was a very usual custom in those days for an invading army not only to pillage but to burn a hostile country. In the second place, Edward by this time thought he knew his man; his own object was to cross swords with his rival while the great army that he had spent so much time, trouble and money to build up was under arms and in the field. Philip, he knew, was loth to fight, but surely the sight of the misery that his subjects were suffering would force him to action. But Edward did not really know his man. Philip, on arriving at Peronne, where his main army was concentrated, instead of advancing boldly against the evil invader sat still, waiting stolidly for laggard contingents to arrive or for the English to advance. So we have the curious spectacle of two rival kings and armies, 12 miles apart, each waiting for the other to advance.

After halting at Mont St. Martin for a fortnight without inducing any offensive move on the part of his opponent,

---

[1] In 1794 the Austrian invaders, in spite of the expostulations of the Duke of York, burnt the same villages. The famous Hindenburg Line of 1917 ran through the middle of this devastated area.

Edward decided to change his strategy. He would move east into the province of Thierache (the modern Aisne). This move would have the appearance of running away from his opponent, who might thereby pluck up his courage and follow him. A sudden stand might then produce the desired battle. Such a manoeuvre would have the additional advantage that the allies would be moving parallel to and near the frontier between France and Hainault, and so could easily slip across the border if need be.

On October 16, therefore, the army struck east. Leaving St. Quentin some miles on its right, it crossed the Oise near Mont Origny. But a cruel shock was in store for the English king. His lukewarm allies suddenly came to him and announced that they must go home! The army, they averred, had done enough; their supplies were well-nigh exhausted, the season was far advanced, and it was high time to seek winter quarters.

Edward must have experienced the same feelings as did Christopher Columbus when his crew demanded to turn back before they had sighted America. It was the moment for the young English king to show his true metal. He expostulated, he argued, he pleaded and finally he bargained. If they were short of supplies he would supply them from his own resources; he would scrap the huge wagon train (rivalling in size that of an eighteenth-century monarch) and mount the whole army on horseback. His allies withdrew to consult among themselves in private. Coming back, they stuck to their decision and then they went off to bed.

Edward no doubt spent a restless night, but next morning the situation was unexpectedly saved. A messenger arrived in the camp from the French lines. He carried a proposal from the French king. According to the testimony of two French chroniclers, Philip had at last been stung into action by the "scandal and murmurs" both of the army and of the unfortunate inhabitants. He thereupon advanced to St. Quentin directly his enemy had cleared off to the east. The events of the next few days are difficult to unravel from the confused mass of evidence. Dates especially are in dispute, but the general trend is clear.

From St. Quentin Philip sent his message. The exact wording of it would help us to appreciate the course of events could we be sure of it. Unfortunately we cannot. Edward himself, in a letter to his son, the Guardian, gave the import of it and Knighton in his chronicle practically repeated it. The English king was to "seek out a field, favourable for a pitched battle, where there is neither wood, nor marsh, nor river". These words are accepted by most historians, but Hemingburgh gives in Latin what purports to be the exact terms of the letter. Unfortunately, the grammar is bad and the meaning rather obscure, but it seems that no onus was placed on the English king of selecting the battlefield. Probably Philip made the message intentionally obscure, and Edward was left to interpret it as he liked.

The message, whatever its exact terms, had an unexpected effect upon the allies. Instantly their martial spirit revived and they declared that they were willing to stand and fight. But it was decided to continue the march another 24 miles to the east, drawing the French army after them. The march was accordingly resumed and on the evening of October 21 a suitable place for battle was found.

The position selected by Edward was near La Flamengerie, three miles north of La Capelle, and 30 miles east of Cambrai. A little stream runs in an east-west direction just to the north of the village and the English position was probably on the ridge beyond, facing south. The French army followed up, and halted the same night, October 21, at Buironfosse, four miles west of La Capelle. The road to La Flamengerie ran through La Capelle, and thus approached the English position from the south. Edward, on learning of the proximity of the enemy on October 22, sent a herald with a challenge to battle on the morrow, a challenge which was accepted by the French king.

In the early morning the following day, the English army drew up in its position in the following order: there were three "battles" or divisions in line, with a fourth in reserve, the foremost division being English and the rearmost the Brabanters. The order of battle from right to left seems to have been:—Derby, Suffolk, Northampton, Salisbury, Pembroke. Robert of Artois and Sir Walter Manny were present and probably held minor commands. The English archers were, it seems, on the wings, flanking the line of men-at-arms, and the whole army was dismounted. This was a repetition of the formation that Edward had found so successful at Halidon Hill six years before and the formation adopted by Walter Manny at Cadzand.

The king himself set his army in order of battle and extorted the admiration of his allies by the skill with which he did it. Then he rode along the ranks in a last review. Finally he posted himself in front of the line and awaited, with what patience he could command, the approach of the French host.

In the official report to parliament the strength of the army was given as "15,000 men and more, and people without number". Make what you can of this! Eugene Deprez, who has made the most detailed study of this campaign, does not even attempt to appraise the strength of either army.

The French army was also drawn up in three divisions in line. It probably outnumbered the English, and was extraordinarily comprehensive. All the great vassals were present, the six, dukes of Normandy, Brittany, Burgundy, Bourbon, Lorraine and Athens. Besides the three kings (of Scotland, Navarre, and Bohemia) there were 36 counts, Douglas of Scotland included.

It must have taken some hours to marshal the rival arrays. When both armies were drawn up a prolonged pause ensued. Evidently, though so much had been prepared by mutual arrangement, the question of who should attack had been omitted. Clearly Edward expected from the terms of the challenge to be attacked. But Philip made no move.

Suddenly there was a long, rolling shout in the English ranks. This was followed by clamour and excitement in the opposing

army: the English were attacking! A French vassal hastily
knighted several of his officers—a usual procedure on the eve
of a battle. But the English did not move, the shouting died
down, and the two hares which had sprung up in the English
lines, thus producing the "view halloas", had met their end.
The unhappy new knights were afterwards dubbed the Knights
of the Order of the Hare.

Meanwhile Philip was engaged in hot dispute with his
captains. They were equally divided between attacking and
standing; arguments in support of both views were advanced,
but apparently none that the English were holding an unfairly
strong position. Finally the king was informed that the
astrologer of king Robert of Sicily had seen in a horoscope that
he would be defeated if he attacked. This decided the vacillating
king, and the absurd day came to an end with the German
princes suggesting at vespers that it was time to go home. The
allies thereupon mounted their horses and moved a stage
toward home. This brought them to Avesnes, ten miles further
north. There the army halted for the night and Edward sent
to inform the enemy that he would offer battle at that place.
Next day he halted, but the French army did not appear; in
fact it was already on its way back home. "Our allies would
stay no longer" explained the English king to his son, and
the whole army returned to Brussels and afterward to
Antwerp.

Thus ended in fiasco a campaign on which so many preparations and so much good English money had been lavished.
Condensed accounts in most histories make this campaign
appear not only ridiculous but puzzling. But there is nothing
to be puzzled about. Edward's allies had no heart in the
venture; on the one hand they feared the power of France, on
the other they coveted English gold. The two forces nearly
balanced; when they had received all the gold they could
expect the latter motive disappeared, but fear of the French
remained. Hence they seized every excuse to be done with it.
Edward was as powerless to control his allies as was Marl-

borough 400 years later, and Edward probably lacked some of the patience and tact of John Churchill.

At the end of the campaign the king wrote a long letter to his son, which is particularly helpful because it provides a type of information that is almost always lacking in accounts of military operations of the period, that is, it tells us what information about the enemy the king had from time to time. Here are some extracts from this unique letter, which may be described as the first military dispatch in English history. On reaching Marcoing,

"we heard that Philip was coming towards us at Peronne, on his way to Noyon (i.e. moving south).... On Monday there came a messenger from the king of France saying that he would ... give battle to the king of England on the next day.... In the evening (after arriving at La Flamengerie) three spies were taken who said that Philip was a league and a half from us and would fight on Saturday. On Saturday we went in a field a full quarter of an hour before dawn, and took up our position in a fitting place to fight. In the early morning some of the enemies' scouts were taken and they told us that his vanguard was in battle array and coming out towards us. The news having come to our host our allies, though they had hitherto borne themselves somewhat sluggishly, were in truth of such loyal intent that never were folk of such good will to fight. In the meantime one of our scouts, a knight of Germany, was taken, and he showed all our array to the enemy. Whereupon the foe withdrew his van and gave orders to encamp, made trenches around him and cut down large trees in order to prevent us approaching him. We tarried all day on foot in order of battle until towards evening it seemed to our allies that we had waited long enough. And at vespers we mounted our horses and went near to Avesnes and made him to know that we would await him there all the Sunday. On the Monday morning we had news that the Lord Philip had withdrawn. And so would our allies no longer abide."

The first campaign of the Hundred Years War had ended in disappointment and almost in farce. Moreover, in spasmodic fighting in Gascony the French were gaining ground. But Edward III, though naturally disappointed, was not discouraged. He displayed a tenacity of purpose and a serenity of spirit unusual in one so young. The first thing he did on arrival at Antwerp, and before the army had dispersed, was to hold a Diet, or conference of nobles, to decide on the following year's campaign. For the next two months he was busied in important political and diplomatic negotiations, which can be more conveniently dealt with in connection with the next year's campaign.

## THE 1340 CAMPAIGN

Flanders had observed an uneasy neutrality during the previous campaign. But though the count of Flanders kept her faithful to her overlord, the King of France, the heart of the country was against him. The opposition was led by Jacques van Artevelde, a merchant prince of Ghent. By advancing money to Edward he had procured the removal of the restrictions on the import of wool and thus became popular with all classes. By the winter of 1339 he had become the virtual ruler of the country and the count fled to France.

The way was now open for an Anglo-Flemish alliance. The stumbling-block lay in the fact that if Flanders took up arms against the king of France, her lawful suzerain, she would incur heavy ecclesiastical penalties. But Artevelde pointed out to Edward, with cunning casuistry, that if Edward laid official claim to be king of France, then the Flemings would acknowledge this claim and recognize him as their overlord and fight for him. All that was necessary was for Edward to undertake to help them recover their lost cities of Lille, Douai, Tournai, and Bethune.

All this suited Edward's purpose admirably and in January, 1340, he made a state entry into Ghent, where, on January 24, he was proclaimed king of France with much pomp, the ceremony taking place in the market place, and the three towns of Ghent, Bruges, and Ypres swearing allegiance to him as their overlord. In order to clinch the matter Edward had a new Great Seal made, quartering the lilies of France with the leopards of England.

When all this was settled, the king took boat for England where he spent the next five months bargaining with his parliament—with some success—for fresh subsidies for the war, and strengthening the new alliance by various treaties.

Meanwhile fighting of a rather sporadic nature flared up in the Low Countries. Philip sent an army to wreak vengeance on the towns of Hainault in revenge for the ravages committed by the Hainaulters—the chief offenders—in the preceding campaign. He sent his son John, duke of Normandy, to ravage Hainault to such a degree that it should never recover. John attempted to carry out his father's behests, and certainly did a vast amount of damage, but his progress came to an end at Quesnoy, where the garrison startled his men and horses by discharges from a number of small cannon.

Flanders was also involved in these raids and Jacques van Artevelde set off from Ghent with an army to which the earls of Suffolk and Salisbury attached themselves with a small contingent. On the way to Valenciennes, near Lille, the two earls were captured in an ambush and taken in triumph to Paris. King Philip had now joined his army, and it looked as if there would be a clash between the two armies just to the north of Cambrai. But, as in the previous year, it came to nothing. This time the cause was the arrival of the news of a great naval victory by the king of England and of his landing in Flanders with a large army. On receipt of this news Philip took the course that we are beginning to expect of him. He fell back to Arras, where he disbanded part of his army, and dispersed the remainder into the neighbouring garrisons.

### THE BATTLE OF SLUYS

We must now hark back a few weeks, in order to see how this naval battle came about. It will be remembered that in the early stages of the war the French navy held the upper hand in the Channel, and there was a real danger of invasion. Right through 1339 the danger persisted, and one of the king's pre-occupations on his return to England was to strengthen his own shores. While he was gradually amassing a large fleet the French were doing the same. It was a polyglot affair, consisting mainly of Normans and Genoese. By this means Philip was able to concentrate, according to king Edward, 190 ships of war in Sluys harbour in the month of June, in readiness for Edward's expected return to Flanders. It was a shrewd selection of position, for whether the English made for Antwerp or for the ports of Flanders, the French fleet could intercept them or cut their communications.

Meanwhile Edward was collecting his new army in Suffolk, and arranging for the concentration of his fleet at Orwell, near Ipswich. At the last moment, when he was about to embark, the archbishop of Canterbury came hot-foot from London beseeching him to defer his journey as the French fleet was in waiting and the risk was too great to take. The admirals backed up the archbishop; but the king would not be deterred. "Ye and the archbishop", he exploded, "have agreed to tell the same story to prevent my crossing. I will cross in spite of you, and ye who are afraid where no fear is may stay at home."

He did, however, stay a few days longer, awaiting the arrival of a northern squadron, and at length, on June 22, the great fleet weighed anchor and set sail for Flanders.

It is impossible to compute exactly the strength of either fleet or army, but it would seem that the English fleet was inferior in numbers to that of France, while Froissart may not this time be greatly exaggerating when he estimates an army of 4,000 men-at-arms and 12,000 archers. The king commanded in person, having as navigator the veteran John Crab, who had deserted the Scottish service because of bad treatment. His chief admirals were Sir Robert Morley, the earls of Huntingdon and Northampton, and the ubiquitous Walter Manny. (It must be remembered that admiral and general were almost synonymous terms in those days, and for long after.)

The king wrote another admirable letter to his son a few days after the battle that ensued, the first naval dispatch that we possess, just as the letter on the Cambrai campaign was the first full military dispatch. Other and later accounts of the battle of Sluys are so confusing and conflicting that they can almost be ignored and the story built up round the royal dispatch, from which we are quoting. After setting out:

"we sailed all day and the night following and on Friday about the hour of noon we arrived upon the coast of Flanders, before Blanken-berg, where we had a sight of the enemies' fleet who were all crowded together in the port of Sluys. And seeing that the tide did not serve us to close with them we lay to all that night. On Saturday, St. John's Day [June 24] soon after the hour of noon at high tide [the actual hour has been computed at 11.23 a.m.] in the name of God, and confident in our just quarrel, we entered the said port upon our said enemies, who had assembled their ships in very strong array, and who made a most noble defence all that day and the night following. . . ."

It was indeed a "very strong array"; the ships were drawn up in four lines, all except the rear line being bound and clamped together with ropes and chains. They thus formed four gigantic floating platforms. Since land armies were to contest the battle, it was natural that the arena should be made as near as possible like the dry land. The first requisite of a battle is a battlefield. It is perhaps appropriate that the place where the battle took place is now land. Long ago the port silted up and there is now nothing but a flat sandy plain.

In the English fleet each vessel containing men-at-arms had on each side of it a vessel containing archers–the Crecy formation on the high sea. Fleets in those days were regarded merely as vehicles to convey armies, much as horses convey mounted infantry: neither was expected to take a part of its own in the battle. That was reserved for the soldiers. The only missiles the French fleet seem to have possessed were stones, thrown on to the English decks by soldiers perched in the rigging.

After what has been said, the reader will not be surprised to learn that the battle took the form of a land battle. The English attacked, each vessel clamping itself to its opposite number, and the chivalry of England clambered (without their horses) on board the French vessels and engaged in a hand-to-hand fight on the decks.

Early in the engagement a striking success was gained. The royal flagship, the great *Christopher*, the pride of the navy, had been captured in a Flemish harbour the previous year and the French had the effrontery to station her in the very forefront of their line. The English naturally made a dead set at her and speedily effected her recapture. They also recaptured a second great ship, the *Edward*. Hastily manning these warships with English crews they sent them back into the fight with the English flag aloft.

The English army was a picked one; the cream of the chivalry and nobility of the country was on board. The long-bowmen had "sitting targets", each arrow found its billet in the massed ranks on the French decks, and the lusty and expert men-at-arms carried on the slaughter, pushing back their opponents step by step across the decks and into the sea. It must have been an extraordinary sight. Even in France the story got about. King Philip's clown was heard to ask his master: "Do you know, Sire, why the English are cowards? Because, unlike the French, they dare not jump into the sea."

The rear squadron of the French fleet, 24 ships in number, made its escape under cover of darkness. Every other ship was captured. It must have been easy to count them and Edward's statement about numbers (190 vessels in the fleet) can be accepted as accurate. But when it comes to computing the number killed or drowned, the case is different—unless the king captured the French strength return, which is most unlikely. Therefore his estimate of 30,000 French lost is probably a wild exaggeration. More than that we cannot say.

After spending a few days on the spot and at Bruges, Edward III entered Ghent on July 10 where he was greeted by the burgesses like a conquering hero. This was gratifying, but he received another greeting which he appreciated even more. It was from his wife, Philippa, who presented him with his new-born son, John, born while the king was in England. John was, in accordance with the custom of the time, called by the name of his birthplace, John of Ghent; but as our forefathers pronounced the word Gaunt, he has come down to us as John of Gaunt.

Edward's great victory added immensely to his prestige and his vassals came flocking to congratulate him. He lost no time in taking advantage of his good fortune. He summoned a Diet to meet at Vilvoorde on July 18, and there the alliance between England and her three allies, Brabant, Hainault, and Flanders, was sealed. The Diet was then turned into a war council and plans were made for the season's campaign. This war council was numerously attended–too numerously for secrecy. A simple plan was formed. While Robert of Artois took an army of Flemings against St. Omer, the main blow was to be struck against Tournai by the remainder of the forces, under the personal command of Edward III. The king assured the Home government that there were 100,000 Flemings– probably a deliberate exaggeration, for he had contracted to pay them, and he depended upon friends in England to do so. He was, in fact, the first of a long line of English commanders who had under them a mixed army of varying tongues and nationalities, most of whom were in the pay of the English government.

Situated in the middle of the cockpit of Europe, Tournai has repeatedly figured in our military annals, and the surrounding ground has been plentifully watered by English blood. The duke of Marlborough captured it in a brilliant siege, and his armies marched and counter-marched around it for two years. Forty years later the duke of Cumberland, with another allied army, marched to its relief and fought the marvellous battle of Fontenoy under its walls. In 1793 the duke of York made it his headquarters on several occasions, besides fighting three battles in the vicinity in the area between it and Lille. In the war of 1914–18 it was taken by our 55th Division only two days before the end of the war, and finally in the Second World War it was liberated by the Guards Armoured Division on September 3, 1944. At the time of the Hundred Years War, and for long after, Tournai was the chief town on the French north-eastern border, greater even than Lille, and its fortifications were immensely strong. In the days of Henry VIII its population was, according to Cardinal Wolsey, 80,000, and it probably was nearly that size in the time of Edward III, though Wolsey's figure must be over-high.

The all too public plan of Vilvoorde had reached the ears of the king of France and Philip VI promptly sent the garrison a large reinforcement of his best troops, under count Raoul, the Constable of France. He also supplied it with "l'artillerie, engiens, espingalls, et kanons" to use Froissart's terms. Here we encounter a difficulty. When a new invention appeared in the Middle Ages it took some time to coin a word for it, and usually an old word was made to do duty. Thus "engine" may mean "cannon" or merely "mediaeval siege weapon", such as balista, trebuchet, mangonel, etc. In the same way, "artillery" may mean merely archery. "Kanon", however, can have but one meaning, as also ribaudequin, which Froissart explains as three or four guns bound together. Now from other sources we know that ribaudequins were employed by the English and Flemings, so it is clearly established that artillery was used by *both* sides in this famous siege. We will return to the subject presently.

CHALLENGE TO COMBAT

After the Vilvoorde council Edward III had sent his allied commanders to their various capitals to collect their armies for the coming campaign. It was arranged that they should concentrate for the siege on July 22. The king, with the English army, marched along the course of the Scheldt through Audenarde—later to become famous in our history (see sketch map). After a skirmish at Espierres, ten miles north of Tournai, he reached Chin, three miles north-west, on July 22, according to plan. From here he sent a remarkable letter to the king of France, in which he offered him three alternatives, first that the two of them should decide the issue by single combat; second, that they should engage each other at the head of

100 picked men a side; third, that the complete armies should engage. As he addressed the letter to "Philip of Valois" and not "King of France" the latter pretended at first not to have received it as it was incorrectly addressed. Eventually he rather astutely agreed to single combat on condition that if he won he would have the kingdom of England as well as that of France. This of course was tantamount to a refusal, and probably did not come as a surprise to the English king. We are not however warranted in ridiculing the whole affair. King Edward was the embodiment of chivalry, and he conceived himself merely to be acting in accordance with its tenets.

Meanwhile the other allies were drawing near, and the defenders of the city were putting the finishing touches to their defence measures. A vast amount of food had been collected in the town, the walls had been strengthened, as also had the gates (some which had been blocked up entirely). Booms had been placed across the river where it entered and left the town. The guns, or–to be on the safe side–the engines, had been stationed mainly at the various gates. Of the old defences, a bridge in the town and the twin towers of the Marvis still stand. The four national contingents of which the allied army was composed took up their position as follows:

*English,* opposite the St. Martin gate, on the south-west.
*Flemings,* opposite the St. Fontaine gate, on the north-west.
*Brabançons,* opposite the Marvis gate on the north-east.
*Hainaulters,* opposite the Valenciennes gate, on the south-east.

Thus the city was completely surrounded and pontoon bridges were thrown across the river in order to link up the different contingents in closer union. The siege commenced in earnest on July 31–remarkably punctually.

While the English king was thus engaged in methodically encompassing the threatened city his French counterpart appeared to be dawdling supinely at Arras, nearly 40 miles to the south-west. In reality he was concentrating an army for the relief of Tournai. But there seemed no need for particular haste; the numbers of the allied armies, reasoned Philip, were so great that it would not do to venture forward with a weak host and Tournai was well defended and well supplied.

The allies were indeed taking advantage of their preponderant force. Leaving only a fraction of their numbers engaged in the actual siege they carried out raids and forays throughout the surrounding countryside. Seclin, to the south of Lille, was captured, pillaged and fired; so was Orchies still further south; St. Amand nearly suffered the same fate. The French were powerless to prevent all this. As their enemies closed in on Tournai the garrison ejected all Flemings, English, and Brabançons within the city. Otherwise they would only become "bouches inutiles" (an expression that had been coined at the famous siege of Chateau Gaillard). With great magnanimity, Edward allowed three days for this evacuation, a sign that humanity was not entirely absent from medieval warfare.

Edward's plan for conducting the siege had a distinctly modern flavour. Instead of attempting to carry it at once by storm, he decided to do the job as cheaply as possible, sparing his infantry until the "artillery" (by which term I include both mechanical and gunpowder weapons) had effected breaches in the walls and gates, and the inhabitants had been "softened" by bombardment and hunger. It thus became largely an artillery siege. From the difficulty already mentioned of distinguishing between ancient and modern "artillery" and "engines" we will not attempt to discriminate in the following account, except in the case of the ribaudequins, which were incontestably cannon.

The besieging artillery was concentrated against the various gates, each national contingent bombarding its own sector of the defence. A number of incidents have been recorded in the local archives, and nowhere else.[1] Three "engines" were placed in action opposite the Porte Marvis, but they do not

---

[1] Fortunately for us they have been collected by the Baron Kervyn de Lettenhove and inserted as notes in his edition of Froissart's *Chronicles* (vol. III, 1867).

seem to have effected a breach. The walls of the two still existing towers are very massive and strong, and the probability is that the projectiles did little material damage. The same applies to the other gates. The English used two against the Porte Cocquerel in their sector, while the Flemings, somewhat injudiciously, placed their artillery in the camp of their commander, the famous Jacques van Artevelde. Thereat ensued the first "artillery duel" of which we have record: the French had placed an "engine" just inside the Porte St. Fontaine, which engaged the Flemish "engine" and knocked it out. The Flemings repaired and brought it into action again, only to be knocked out a second time. The French had evidently got the range to a nicety. Not to be outdone the English now took up the contest and knocked out a French gun in the Marché-aux-Vaches.

And so the contest went on. The ribaudequins were otherwise employed, being wholly anti-personnel weapons. Now in order to hit the defenders upon the battlements, plunging or at least horizontal fire was required. The ribaudequins had therefore to be raised by some means to an equal height with the tops of the walls. Wooden towers were constructed for this purpose and the ribaudequins mounted upon them. What damage they did we are not told, but it is related that at the end of the siege the towers were dismantled and the wood of which they were constructed sold to the inhabitants. The ribaudequins were then floated down the Scheldt to Ghent.

After the siege had been in progress for nearly a month a series of assaults was made upon the walls where they had been weakened by artillery fire. On August 26 the Flemings made a vigorous assault; they also endeavoured to smash the boom which had been placed across the river in their sector, with some of their own boats. But the current was against them and the attempt failed. It is even said that the French sallied forth in their own boats and that a miniature naval engagement then took place. Two days later the French took the initiative, making an attack against the English lines. This was not only repulsed, but the English followed the French so closely that they almost succeeded in getting into the town.

By this time food was running short inside the city and the garrison smuggled out a message crying for relief. It did not fall on heedless ears. Philip VI had by this time collected his army at Arras and he advanced to the relief of the beleaguered town.

Midway between Tournai and Lille flows the River Marque. It is about 15 feet wide, but boggy and deep, and in most places unfordable.[1] There were (and are) bridges at Bouvines and Pont-à-Tressin. King Edward occupied the line of river between these two bridges in what would afterwards be called "lines of contravallation". (Marlborough's army marched and fought over this ground nearly 400 years later, and again it was the scene of a victory by the duke of York in 1794.) The French king, finding both bridges occupied by the enemy, formed his camp midway between the two. This was on September 7, and the garrison of Tournai, being now in their sixth week of siege, were getting to the end of their tether, and were clamorous for relief. Philip, however, made no sign of attempting to storm the river crossings and to relieve the city.

But the king of England also had his difficulties. When a number of allies are collected together it is seldom that trouble and friction does not arise between some of them, and Edward's heterogeneous army was no exception to this rule. The Brabançons, who had no common frontier with the French, were not so zealous in the cause as the other allies, and some of them began to clamour to go home.

One day king Edward was sitting in his tent, discussing matters with Artevelde and the duke of Brabant, when the former acidly remarked that it was about time the Brabançons made an assault on the city, as had all the other allies. A Brabançon knight who was also present told Artevelde sharply to hold his tongue and get back to Ghent and get on with his

[1] The duke of York in the 1794 campaign once saved his life by fording it.

brewing—an allusion to his plebeian origin. The Flemish
leader drew his sword in fury and ran him through on the spot.
The duke of Brabant then rushed from the tent and sprang
to his horse, with the evident intention of leading his army
away. But Edward was equal to the occasion. Following the
duke out of the tent he seized the charger by the bridle before
the duke could gallop off, and used all the eloquence at his
command to mollify the outraged Brabançon leader. So
successful were his entreaties that the duke ultimately consented to patch up the quarrel. To clinch the matter king
Edward gave a great banquet to which he invited all the
leaders and he so arranged the seating that the duke of
Brabant and Jacques van Artevelde found themselves seated
next each other. The English king must have possessed that
gift of harmonizing warring elements which both the duke of
Marlborough and the duke of York afterwards exhibited with
the same sort of allies in the same sort of country.

Peace reigned once more in the allied lines, and the end of
the siege seemed near. The garrison was famished and the
French king was at his wits' end. Like Masséna before the lines
of Torres Vedras, the longer he looked at the lines of the
Marque the less he liked them. But help came to him from an
unexpected quarter—a woman, and an abbess. Philip had a
sister, the Lady Jeanne de Valois, who was also the mother
of the count of Hainault and Philippa, and therefore Edward's
mother-in-law. This good woman, leaving her abbey of
Fontenelle, came to the French camp and prevailed upon
Philip to consider negotiations for a truce. Then she crossed
over the river to the rival camp, and put the same suggestion
to the English king. The Brabançons were now seething with
discontent and Edward had no money with which to quieten
them. He called a council to consider the Lady Jeanne's
appeal. All the allies were in favour of a truce, while the king
and Artevelde alone held out against it. This was too serious
a matter to ignore and eventually Edward, though much
against his will, agreed to negotiate. His money troubles, which

were likely to grow worse, partly reconciled him to this course. A meeting was therefore held on September 25 and a truce for one year was signed – the truce of Esplechin.

By this truce, Edward's allies all acquired some slight advantages, but he gained nothing. Things were left as they were at the outset between France and England; everything remained in suspense. Thus the second campaign had ended as inconclusively as the first, and the disappointment was cumulative. The main blame for this dismal conclusion Edward placed, not on his miserable allies, but on his Home government, who had sent him no subsidies or reinforcements in spite of his urgent appeals. If he had been able to keep his allies in gold he could have kept them in the field. Such was his belief, and it was probably justified. Rage boiled up within his breast, and he took the first opportunity he could (it did not come for two months) to slip away home. He landed at the Tower unexpectedly and in savage mood. Within 24 hours he had dismissed his ministers and appointed others. But the damage was done, and it was irremediable. Early in 1341 the emperor rescinded Edward's appointment as his Vicar of the Holy Roman Empire and the grand alliance collapsed in ruins. The first round of the great war on sea was to our advantage, but on land a pointless draw. The king of England would have to start all over again.

## APPENDIX

PRINCIPAL SOURCES

The sources for the first two chapters of this book can be grouped together. They are few and straightforward, and most can be found in any standard reference library.

On the English side the usual chroniclers of the period cover most of the ground, the most useful being Henry Knighton, Adam Murimuth, Walter de Hemingburgh and Robert of Avesbury. The last two, with Rymer's collection of *Foedera*, contain all the letters referred to here. The French chroniclers

are, as throughout the Hundred Years War, disappointingly
meagre. The *Grandes Chroniques* belies its name. More reliable
are the *Continuation* of *Guillaume de Nangis* and *Chronographia
Regum Francorum* (not cited in Ramsay's *Genesis of Lancaster*
for some reason).

On the neutral side, as we must call it, there are the Chronicles of Jean le Bel, the Liégeois, and Jean Froissart of Valenciennes. Le Bel had served in the army of Edward III in
Scotland and he had an unbounded admiration for the English
king. His Chronicle attains a high standard of accuracy when
judged by the historical standards of the period. Not so Jean
Froissart, who in his first edition copied unblushingly the
chronicle of the Liégeois, and added to it–embellished it would
be a more exact expression–according to his information and
his fancy. His reckless irresponsibility is the despair of all who
search for the truth in his pages. Broadly speaking, any statement by him, except such as are inherently probable, should
not be accepted unless corroborated by another source. There
are two standard editions of his *Chronicle*, one by a Belgian, the
Baron Kervyn de Lettenhove (1866–onward) and the other
by a Frenchman, Simeon Luce (1869–onward). Though the
Belgian started publishing his colossal edition first, the two ran
simultaneously. It is essential to work on one or other of these,
since English translations give only the first edition; to read
the *Amiens* or *Rome* or the *Abrégées*[1] editions one must go to the
original French. Lettenhove's edition is set out the more
conveniently, but it contains some grave errors of transcription
(as his French rival did not fail to point out). For general notes
Luce is best, but Lettenhove prints many hitherto unpublished
or unknown MSS, such as the *Récit d'un Bourgeois de Valenciennes*,
which is useful here and elsewhere.

These remarks on the neutral chroniclers should be borne
in mind throughout this book.

The best bibliography is contained in *Les Préliminaires de la
Guerre de Cent Ans* (1902) by Eugène Deprez (who died in

---

[1] So named in Lettenhove. Luce describes it as MSS B6.

1953). Professor Deprez was fully acquainted with English writings on the period (which is more than can be said for some French writers). The most detailed account in English is that of the American, H. S. Lucas, *The Low Countries and the Hundred Years War* (1929), but the period as a whole has been sadly neglected.

# CHAPTER III

# BRITTANY TO THE BATTLE OF
# MORLAIX, 1341–42

FTER his return to England, Edward III was for a year
occupied with Home and Scottish affairs. He undertook
a short campaign north of the Tweed where the Scots
were slowly recovering the territories lost in the earlier campaigns. Meanwhile an event occurred in Brittany which was
to have a lasting effect upon the fortunes of the Hundred Years
War. In April, 1341, duke John III of Brittany died, leaving
no son to succeed him. His father, duke Arthur II, had a
second son, Guy, who had died young but had left a daughter,
Joan. Duke Arthur's second wife was Yolande, the widow of
Alexander II of Scotland. By her he had a third son, John.
Both Joan de Penthièvre and John de Montfort claimed the
succession. Thereby arose the war of succession in Brittany,
which was to last for 24 years. In this war England and
France became increasingly involved. It brought to the front a
succession of notable English soldiers and proconsuls (as we
should now call them), and produced some notable battles. (Both
soldiers and battles have alike passed almost into oblivion.)

The dispute arose in this way. Joan had married Charles,
count of Blois, who was a nephew of the French king. Joan
therefore claimed the throne for her husband, and appealed
to Philip VI for approval. This approval the French king was
anxious to give, for obvious reasons. With his own nephew duke
of Brittany, the province was more likely to remain faithful
to its suzerain than it would under John, who inclined to the
English cause. For the same, or rather for the opposite reason,
England favoured John. Charles de Blois based his wife's
claim on the fact that she was the nearest blood relation of
the dead duke, whereas John de Montfort based his on the fact

that he was the nearest *male* relation, invoking the Salic law. Thus we find the king of France supporting a claim that ignored the Salic law, whereby he himself wore the crown, and the king of England supporting a claim the principle of which he had rejected in the case of the French crown. The irony of this situation has not been lost upon historians.

But for the moment neither England nor France was drawn into the contest. John was first in the field. He entered Nantes, was well received by the citizens, and in a short campaign of two months rapidly overran most of the country. He then crossed to England where he obtained promise of support from the king, in return for acknowledging Edward as his lord, and king of France.

Meanwhile Charles de Blois was collecting an army at Angers. With it he advanced on Nantes in November, 1341. This count de Blois was a pious man with saintly habits. He put pebbles into his shoes and wore a hair shirt swarming with vermin. This may have made him irritable in mind as well as in body, for after capturing some of John's men in a sortie from Nantes, this holy man beheaded 31 of them and threw their heads into the town with his catapults. The inhabitants, fearing for the fate of their relatives outside, quickly came to terms. De Blois entered the city, and count John was captured and sent to Paris, where he lay imprisoned in the Louvre for four years.

Charles in his turn now overran most of the country, helped by a French army under the king's son John, duke of Normandy.

All seemed lost for the Montfort party, but men had forgotten the countess. This heroic woman, Joan of Flanders, took energetic measures to restore the situation, and for a time she was successful. But the Blois party advanced in overwhelming numbers, and eventually the countess of Flanders was besieged in Hennebout. This town lies at the head of an estuary on the south coast midway between Vannes and Quimper.[1]

---

[1] Lorient, the famous German submarine base in the Second World War, is lower down the estuary.

The countess naturally appealed to Edward to redeem his promise of help. This the English king was quite willing to do, and a small expedition under Sir Walter Manny was fitted out. In March, 1342, it sailed for Hennebout, but the voyage took 60 days, incredible as this may sound. Consequently it did not

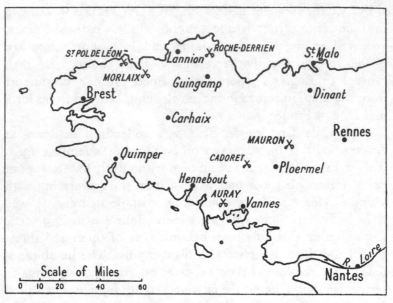

2. BRITTANY

arrive till May, by which time the countess was hard pressed and almost in despair. Froissart, in a well-known passage, describes the dramatic moment when the countess, standing on the roof of a tower and scanning the horizon anxiously, caught sight of the gleaming white sails of the English fleet, slowly making its way up the estuary.

The relieving force ran the blockade without much difficulty, and was received with unrestrained joy by the famished garrison. A great banquet in honour of the English was given that same night, while a "great engine" (doubtless a catapult) kept hurling projectiles into the town. This led Sir Walter

Manny, in the course of the banquet, to remark that he would like to capture that engine. Leave was given, and next morning he led out a sortie of English troops, drove off the defenders, seized the catapult and broke it to pieces.

This was only the beginning of a series of exploits by Sir Walter Manny and his gallant band, which we will not recount in detail. It is Froissart who relates them, and as we have said his statements about his fellow Hainaulter, when un-corroborated, must be accepted with caution. Be this as it may, the net result of Manny's activities was that the siege was raised, as was also that of Auray, 20 miles east, and Louis de la Cerda, the skilful Spanish general in the service of de Blois, was defeated at Quimperlé (12 miles to the west).

We must leave Sir Walter Manny and Charles marching and countermarching in southern Brittany, in order to follow a more serious attempt on the part of England to intervene in the war.

The strategical pattern of the war that ensued was con-ditioned by geographical and ethnological factors. Brittany is a peninsula; Upper Brittany (Haute Bretagne) is the central zone stretching from the eastern border through Rennes to Pontivy. It was French in tongue and sympathies, and the bulk of the nobility of French blood resided there. It was therefore natural that Upper Brittany should espouse the cause of the French king's nephew. The northern district of Penthièvre also came under French influence, since Joan countess of Blois was the daughter of Guy de Penthièvre. Thus the essentially Montfort regions were confined to the south and west. (This, with many fluctuations, was the line of demarcation throughout the war.) Hence, if an English army was to fight a French army on Breton soil it would have a long and precarious sea passage round Cape Finisterre, and it would be the aim of the French to cut this line of communications by naval operations. *Per contra*, the French had a short and easy approach by land from the east. Two main gateways guarded this approach, Nantes and Rennes. It was therefore the English object to seize these gateways (just as the duke of Wellington seized the two main gateways from Portugal to Spain, Badajoz and Ciudad Rodrigo).

These factors gave France a big advantage. It was like the war between England and Germany in Italy in 1944; the Germans could reinforce their armies speedily by land, whereas we had to reinforce by a long and dangerous sea route.

This strategical handicap, much greater in the days of sail than of steam, dogged the English efforts throughout the war, especially in Gascony, and should be kept in mind throughout, for attention will not be incessantly drawn to it.

In July, 1342, Edward III appointed the earl of Northampton, whom we last met in Flanders, as his lieutenant in Brittany, assisted by the earls of Derby and Oxford, with Robert of Artois as his "chief of staff",[1] all four of whom had shown their military talents in the Flanders campaigns.

On August 14, 1342, a fleet of 260 sail transported Northampton's army, about 3,000 strong, to Brest, where it arrived four days later. Charles de Blois, who had now overrun nearly all the provinces, was besieging the port, so the English army had to land on the open shore near by. But only light resistance was offered and Northampton entered the town amid scenes of rejoicing. Charles immediately raised the siege and fell right back to Guingamp, 40 miles to the east, leaving the country open to the invaders. Western Brittany was strongly pro-Montfort, and some Bretons may be presumed to have joined the English army. Advancing without impediment, Northampton arrived within sight of Morlaix on September 3, and at once attempted to take it by storm. The attempt lasted all day, but failed, and Northampton sat down to besiege it methodically. This did not seem likely to be successful as the town was strongly fortified and amply supplied.

Meanwhile de Blois, at Guingamp, was vigorously strength-

---

[1] Robert of Artois had impressed the king with his military ability, and Edward had brought him back to England and kept him at Court. As to the relative share in the operations of the forthcoming campaign, historians are at variance. But Northampton was with the army, and as the king's representative had to bear the responsibility and must therefore be regarded as the commander in chief.

ening his army and enlisting local levies, until it attained prodigious numbers for those days. The careful French historian of Brittany, A. de la Borderie, estimates these numbers at 30,000, which seems quite impossible. If they did not pass 15,000, however, they still outnumbered the little English army by more than four to one, a proportion that seems well substantiated. With this large and probably rather unwieldy army, Charles de Blois began an approach march for the relief of Morlaix. His route lay *via* Lanmeur, a large village seven miles north-east of Morlaix. On Michaelmas Day the earl of Northampton received news of this advance. Its purpose was obvious; it would never do to allow his own army to be caught between the two forces, the town on one side and the relieving army on the other. Northampton immediately broke up the siege and that night marched out towards Lanmeur.[1]

By dawn a suitable position was reached. This position strides the road, and is just on the beginning of a gentle slope into a dip about 300 yards in front. The road then ascends an equally gentle slope and disappears some 500 yards from the position. Immediately in rear is a wood. The spire of (the new) Lanmeur church can be seen over the horizon. If this is in truth the position occupied by the English army, the wood that I have mentioned is the veritable wood that figures so prominently in the battle that took place that day.

### THE BATTLE OF MORLAIX (SEPTEMBER 30, 1342)

The English army took up position just in front of this wood, in a line astride the road, and perhaps 600 yards in length. The selection of a position with a wood in rear was popular with English troops in those days, because it could not be effectively

---

[1] No attempt has ever been made, so far as I can ascertain, to establish the site of the battle that ensued. It is usually called vaguely Morlaix, or the battle near Morlaix. The battle itself, in spite of its great military significance, has passed almost unnoticed by English historians, with the sole exception of Professor Tout, who touched on it in an article in the *English Historical Review* for 1906. The obscurity in which the battle has been allowed to remain is no doubt in large measure due to this fact that the site is unknown. The one given here is of course conjectural, but I give my reasons for this site in the appendix to this chapter.

attacked in flank by cavalry, and formed a useful baggage park.[1] Some hundred yards in front of it, on a line now marked approximately by a hedge and a cottage, they dug a trench, and covered it with grass and other herbage as a "booby-trap" for the horsemen of the enemy. It was only 30 years since the battle of Bannockburn and the English troops had not forgotten the lesson taught by the "pots" of the Scots.

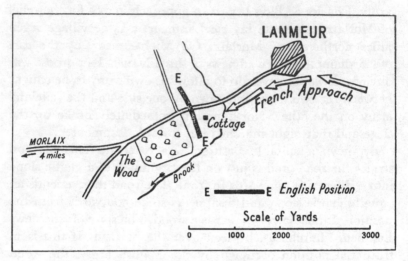

3. BATTLE OF MORLAIX

The dismounted men-at-arms occupied the centre of the line, the archers were stationed on the flanks. During that morning the French army was apparently stationary a league away, which would seem to indicate billets in the village of Lanmeur –at least for the mounted troops–and we may suppose that the footmen arrived on the scene next morning. This would account for the fact that the French did not attack till three o'clock in the afternoon. In the battle that ensued there were at least four points of resemblance with the battle that was to take place at Poitiers 13 years later. It is not too fanciful to

[1] It should be noted that Northampton had a responsible command at Crecy four years later, and some features common to both battles may be due to his influence.

suppose that the Black Prince was mindful of this battle when making his dispositions at Poitiers.

The count of Blois drew up his army in three huge columns, one behind the other, with an appreciable space between each. The leading column consisted of irregulars, presumably local levies. These were all dismounted troops. On the order being given they advanced straight to their front, descending the hill into the slight dip and up the other side. When they got within effective range the English archers drew bow, and a hail of arrows dispersed the column before it had got into close contact with the men-at-arms. The contest was short; the Bretons went reeling down the hill.

Charles was disconcerted by this sudden disaster and took counsel with his chief captains regarding the next step. Eventually it was decided to launch the second column, the men-at-arms, in a mounted attack. This was, of course, exactly what Northampton wished and had prepared for. His stratagem worked admirably. The French horsemen, who had not been warned of the concealed trench by the irregulars for the simple reason that they had not reached it, rode forward impetuously and unsuspectingly. Men and horses plunged into the concealed trench; the archers plied them with arrows to add to their confusion, and the attack practically came to a standstill. A few horsemen, 200 in all, did manage to negotiate the trench and, indeed, to penetrate the line. But local reserves came up and they were cut off and captured, including their commander, Geoffrey de Charni.

The second attack had ended as disastrously as the first, and again there was a considerable pause while the attackers licked their wounds and consulted on what to do next.

Northampton waited to see if there were any signs of a general retreat. But there was none. Though two columns, each greater in number than his own tiny army, had been worsted, the third column, also bigger than his own, remained drawn up on the opposite ridge. His archers were by this time short of ammunition, each man carrying 36 arrows at most. Had time allowed, the archers would doubtless have run forward to recover their arrows (as did their successors at Poitiers). But the hostile column was now on the move, and at the sight of the huge mass of fresh troops approaching, the English showed signs of discouragement. The trench was by this time battered in or filled with corpses; it was no longer a defence. Moreover there are indications that the third French column extended beyond the flanks of the position and thus threatened the flanks. Seeing and weighing all this, the earl (with or without the advice of Robert d'Artois, of whom we hear nothing in the battle) decided on a novel manoeuvre. If he did not retreat he could not prevent the enemy surrounding him if they had the will. He decided to adopt a course of action in battle that is almost unprecedented in that era: he would fall back into the wood less than a hundred yards in rear, and form what we now call a "hedgehog", a defensive line along the edge of the wood and facing in all directions. No doubt he had this eventuality in mind when he selected a position immediately in front of a wood. So into the wood his victorious troops fell back in good order, taking with them their prisoners, and a new position, facing all ways, was taken up.

The details of what followed are scanty and rather puzzling. What seems clear is that the English reserved their "fire", preserving their scanty ammunition, and that the French came on and engaged, but everywhere failed to penetrate the wood. Some of them swung round the flanks, till the occupants were practically, if not quite, surrounded.

A fresh pause now ensued. We are reminded of the *Ballad of the Revenge:*

> "The Spanish fleet, with broken sides, lay round us all in a ring,
>   But they dared not touch us again, for they feared that we still could sting."

Charles was at his wits' end. Many of his troops had fled the field, including his Genoese crossbowmen; the English position was still intact and unbroken, and there seemed to be no means

of getting at it. Night was coming on, and Charles decided
to abandon the contest, to give up his intention of relieving
Morlaix, and to beat a retreat. Orders were issued accordingly
and gradually the troops still left on the battlefield drew back
and retreated to Lanmeur.

Northampton had been doing some thinking too. Food had
run out, and his troops were, according to one chronicler,
famished. The French had been fought to a standstill, and their
advance on Morlaix had been frustrated. Darkness was falling;
his immediate task was accomplished; he would return to the
siege of Morlaix. So, collecting his little band, he charged out
of the wood in a body, cutting his way through the still en-
circling enemy, and returned with his prisoners to the siege
lines of Morlaix. This decision was reached approximately
simultaneously with that of his opponent. The curious spectacle
was thus witnessed of both armies falling away from one
another, as if by mutual consent.

The two armies disengaged, but whereas the English army
had achieved its purpose, although outnumbered by four or
five to one, its opponent had failed in his purpose, and had
retreated the way he had come. He is next heard of in the
south, resuming the siege of Hennebout.

\*     \*     \*

The battle of Morlaix was the first pitched battle on land
of the Hundred Years War, and it made a deep impression
at the time. Le Baker, writing some 18 years later, declared
that such desperate fighting was not seen at Halidon Hill,
Crecy or "Petters".[1] Regarded from the point of view of the
art of war, the battle has great interest. The tactics pursued
by the English were evidently founded on the lessons of
Bannockburn and Halidon Hill. The men-at-arms were used
dismounted; the trench took the place of the marsh as an
obstacle in front; a defensive position on a ridge was selected;

[1] Phonetic spelling of course: the Black Prince spelt it Peyters. These two
examples are an indication to the pronunciation of the day—far removed from the
modern French pronunciation, Poitiers.

the fire power of the archers was a feature in both battles, and lastly the two arms cooperated skilfully in defeating the mounted attack. It is not surprising that Edward's first great victory should form the prototype for Morlaix and for all the other great battles of the Hundred Years War–except the last.

## APPENDIX

### SITE OF THE BATTLE OF MORLAIX

At first sight the paucity of information concerning the site of the battle might well deter us from further investigation. Yet I think something can be made of it. The only positive and unimpeachable information is provided in a letter written only two days after the battle by Carlo de Grimaldi, a captain of the Genoese crossbowmen (who, he clearly implies, ran away at the end of the day). He states definitely that the battle took place between Lanmeur and Morlaix. This is only what we should expect. Lanmeur is on the road from Guingamp to Morlaix. It is seven miles from Morlaix. Northampton would hardly wish to march further from Morlaix than the seven miles to Lanmeur if he wished, as he did, to resume the siege after repulsing the approaching army–even if Charles de Blois allowed him the requisite time to advance beyond Lanmeur. On the other hand, he would hardly select a position close to Morlaix, the garrison of which might sally out and attack him when his back was turned. One would expect a position at least three miles away. Now the Genoese captain also states that in the evening the French army retreated to Lanmeur, so the battlefield must be appreciably short of that village, say over a mile. Thus we should expect to find the field somewhere between the third and fifth milestone from Morlaix.

Next, we must consider the type of position favoured by English armies of the period. Almost invariably they would seek for a ridge or hill or commanding ground which would allow of a position on the forward slope with a long view to the front, so as to get as much warning as possible of the hostile approach and of any attempt to turn the flanks. This position, being defensive, should stride the road by which the enemy was expected to approach. Examining the map, we find that the ground slopes upward gradually from Morlaix more than half-way to Lanmeur, thus offering commanding positions facing Morlaix, but not in the opposite direction. At about four miles from Morlaix the ground becomes flat, the top of the table-land, and so continues for about one mile. It then–nearly two miles short of Lanmeur–begins very gradually to fall, to rise again one mile short of Lanmeur, thus forming the dip we have mentioned. *A priori* one would expect the battle to be fought near here.

There is a further consideration. There was a largish wood in rear. Now ancient records show that the table-land was wooded–as it still is–in medieval times. It was only after I had hit upon this site that I noticed the passage in Knighton's *Chronicon*, which states that the English army occupied the whole night (*tota obscura nocte*) in advancing to the position. This must imply a march of several miles, indicating that it could not be far short of Lanmeur. Everything therefore points to the position being near where I have indicated. There is today a bus service from Morlaix to Lanmeur, with a bus-stop at a small café, three kilometres short of Lanmeur. By alighting here, one finds oneself almost surrounded by woods, and on walking forward 1,000 yards, the position I have described, just in front of the wood, is reached. If my elucidation is sound we have here the identical wood that played so large a part in the battle. The English position would be, say, 50 yards in front of it, the trench 100 yards further forward, along a tall hedge.

SOURCES

There is no need to list sources, since they are practically the same as for the preceding chapter. But the following comparatively modern works are essential for a close study of the campaign: *Mémoires pour servir de preuves à l'histoire . . . de*

*Bretagne*, edited by Dom. P. H. Morice, in 1749; this work, as its title implies, contains many additional sources for the battles of the campaign; *Histoire de Bretagne*, by G. A. Lobineau (1707); and *Histoire de Bretagne*, Vol. III, by A. de la Borderie (1898). I can trace practically no modern work written from the English side (apart from the standard histories) except two papers by Professor T. F. Tout: an account of Mauron in *E.H.R.* for 1905, and an account of Morlaix in his *Collected Papers* (1932).

CHAPTER IV

# BRITTANY, 1342–47

LONG before sending out the Northampton expedition, Edward had decided to undertake a campaign in Brittany in person; the earl's army was merely an advanced guard, which should establish a foothold, as it were, and fight the first battles.[1] He accordingly instructed Northampton, as soon as he was established on shore, to send back the ships for the second "lift", *i.e.*, for the main army under the king. They were to return to Sandwich, and there the king collected his army. As the day approached when he calculated the fleet should appear, Edward went down to Sandwich, after appointing his son Edward, then aged 12, as Governor of the kingdom in his absence.

He arrived at Sandwich on October 4, but there was neither sign nor news of the expected fleet. After waiting by the sea for a fortnight with as much patience as he could muster, the king changed his plans and marched his army along the coast to Portsmouth. Here he chartered the bare minimum of ships, placed his troops on board, and on October 23 set sail for Brest. According to Adam Murimuth, who was alive at the time, the king collected no less than 400 ships, into which he embarked 6,000 men-at-arms and 12,000 archers. These figures are evidently "round numbers", and almost certainly exaggerated, but by how much it is impossible to say. Certainly 400 vessels should suffice to transport that number of troops, but it is doubtful if the king could have collected at Portsmouth at short notice anything like that number of ships.

The army landed safely at Brest on October 27, to find that much fighting had gone on since the battle of Morlaix three

[1] In just the same way in 1799 General Abercrombie was sent with an advanced guard army to capture the Helder, where he fought the opening battle, being joined later by the main army under the duke of York.

weeks before. The second siege of Hennebout by Charles de Blois proved as unsuccessful as the first, although de Blois brought up 18 large "engines" against it; the walls had been strengthened since the first siege and his "artillery" was not powerful enough to breach them. After only ten days Charles had had enough of it and departed for Nantes, where he proposed settling into winter quarters.

Such was the medieval custom, but the English leaders had unorthodox ideas. They had come over to Brittany to fight, not to languish in winter quarters. The siege of Morlaix was therefore resumed, and with assistance from inside, it fell shortly afterward. Robert of Artois then conceived the bold plan of laying siege to Nantes, the largest city of Brittany, and the count de Blois's capital. Embarking a little army, less than 5,000 strong, he sailed round the coast, intending to land opposite Nantes. But he was forestalled by the French fleet, attacked, and obliged to sheer off. Not disconcerted by this, he landed opposite Vannes—then the second city of Brittany—and besieged that place. In the course of the Hundred Years War there were literally hundreds of cases of fortified places being besieged, but the siege of Vannes by Robert d'Artois and his little band of English men-at-arms and archers is different from them all.

The city of Vannes was small, confined to a peninsula of elevated land jutting out to the south like a sort of appendix. It had three main gates. They all remain to the present day, as also does much of the wall. It is thus easy to picture the course of events. After spending the first few days in making preparations for the assault, d'Artois delivered it early one morning. The opening move had a modern flavour. The archers—the artillery of the period—put down what we should now call a standing barrage on to the battlements. So fierce and accurate was it that, according to Froissart, the battlements were soon cleared and not an enemy dared show his head. Covered by this fire the men-at-arms advanced to the assault. The attack met with a strenuous resistance and was everywhere repulsed. Not discouraged by the first failure, d'Artois put in attack after attack throughout the day, but when dusk fell the defences were still intact. Silence descended with night and the inhabitants went to bed; hoping for a respite at least till dawn. But they had reckoned without d'Artois's resource.

Suddenly in the middle of the night there arose a great din: trumpets sounded, drums beat, a heavy fire was poured upon two of the gates, where the attackers could be seen to be massing. Amid the cries and hubbub two fires burst alight opposite the gates, lighting the sky. All available troops were rushed to the threatened points, where they then awaited the attack. But no attack came−from without. Instead the watchers suddenly found themselves assailed from within−by English soldiers. What had happened was that when the walls had been denuded of defenders except near the threatened gates, a party if English men-at-arms had crept up to the walls at a spot as far removed as possible from the two gates, armed with scaling ladders. Silently putting these against the walls they as silently mounted them and attained the battlements without a blow being struck. Then, penetrating into the town, they rushed forward to the two gates, attacked the defenders from behind and dispersed them, and then opened the gates to their waiting comrades without. Robert's brilliant stratagem had won the powerful city of Vannes at practically no cost. The French garrison, including Olivier de Clisson, the city's governor, fled toward Nantes. The triumph of Robert d'Artois was complete and the countess de Montfort came over from Hennebout to congratulate the victors.

But Robert d'Artois and his English band had not long to enjoy their triumph. Olivier de Clisson gradually rallied his troops, de Blois sent reinforcements, and in less than a fortnight after the fall of Vannes he reappeared with an army that vastly exceeded that of d'Artois. De Clisson was intent on revenge, but his opponent again did the unexpected. Instead of shutting himself up in the city and sending for help to Hennebout, d'Artois left a small garrison in the town and

boldly advanced with the remainder to face his enemy in
the open. The clash took place some distance outside the city,
but the odds were too great for Robert and his little band.
He was obliged to fall back upon Vannes, closely followed by
de Clisson. But to his consternation he found the gates shut
in his face, and no sign of his garrison within. In his absence
the inhabitants of the town, strongly pro-Blois, taking advantage
of the absence of the main body, had risen against the depleted
garrison and driven them out of the city. Thus caught between
two enemies and vastly outnumbered, the plight of the English
force was desperate.   D'Artois did the only thing possible: he
fought a rearguard action all the way back to Hennebout,
25 miles away. He got them there fairly intact, but he was faint
from the loss of blood, caused by wounds. A few days later in
the last days of October, this gallant Frenchman in the service
of England breathed his last—one of the most remarkable of
the many remarkable soldiers produced by the Hundred Years
War. Thus, when on October 30, 1342, Edward III set foot on
land at Brest, it was to learn that though a great part of
Brittany had been won back for the Montforts, one of the chief
instruments in that achievement, and one of his right-hand
men, had fallen.

The beginning of November is a curious time of year in any
age to undertake a campaign, and it was especially so in
medieval days. Charles had done the conventional thing in
going into winter quarters, but the English king was not a
conventional soldier. Like Northampton and d'Artois before
him, he had not risked the passage to Brittany to find a pleasant
spot in which to winter. He made a plan of campaign, a plan
that has been described by a French historian as "simple and
sound". Only a limited number of troops can play an effective
part in the siege of a town. When, as frequently happened, a
large army concentrated to besiege a fortified place (as did
Edward at Tournai or Cambrai), the principle of "economy
of force" is broken. The English king did not repeat this
mistake. The three most important towns in Brittany were still

in the hands of the enemy. Edward decided to attack all three simultaneously. But before he could do so he must make good the intervening territory. Most of the south of Brittany except Hennebout held Bloisian garrisons. These must first be dealt with and the speediest way of doing it would be by advancing on a broad front. This is what Edward did. Setting out from Brest about November 8 he marched with concentrated forces as far as Carhaix, 50 miles to the east, which he quickly captured and made his base of operations. Here he split his army into two; the northern column, under Northampton, was to advance in an easterly direction towards Rennes, which it was to capture, while the southern column, commanded by the king, would strike south to the coast and then work east to Vannes which it would attack, at the same time sending a detachment forward to besiege Nantes. It was certainly an ambitious plan, but its very audacity favoured its prospects.

On November 11 the two columns set off. The northern one marched by Pontivy, Ploermel, and Redon, capturing all places en route with ease, whilst the southern column marched by Hennebout to Vannes, which it promptly besieged. In accordance with his plan the king now sent a small force under the earls of Norfolk and Warwick to besiege Nantes, which they did, Charles de Blois fleeing the city before their arrival. It is noteworthy that Edward found time en route to write home formal instructions that the body of his good friend and servant, Robert d'Artois, which he was sending to England, should have a ceremonious burial in the Black Friars in London.

As the English troops swept through the country, only feebly opposed, the king imposed on them a strict discipline, forbidding all pillage and burning; it was a friendly country— indeed in his eyes his own—and the inhabitants were to be treated as friends. This sensible policy probably conduced to the ease and rapidity of the operations.

Vannes was besieged about November 25 and Nantes at the end of the month; Rennes not till a week later, for North-ampton had been taken out of his direct route by going by

Redon. The reason for this apparent detour was doubtless to keep the two columns within mutual reach of one another as long as possible. Thus they were never more than 30 miles apart–a nice example of the principle of advancing in parallel columns.

After setting siege to Rennes, Northampton sent flying columns in various directions, including one under the earl of Warwick to Dinant. This town was strongly held, so Warwick contented himself with burning its suburbs and he then returned to Rennes.

Charles de Blois was naturally surprised and perturbed by the rapid advance of the English army at such an unusual season of the year, yet he dared not oppose it, although his available troops were probably numerically superior. Instead he fell back from Nantes and appealed for help to his suzerain and uncle. Philip VI responded, and not only assembled a large army at Angers, 50 miles north-east of Nantes, but came there to command it in person. Thus, after a lapse of two years, the kings of France and England seemed likely to confront each other face to face once more.

The French army, when augmented by Bloisian contingents, was big, though we can dismiss the figure of 50,000 given by the chroniclers (and accepted by la Borderie). It was however greatly superior to the English army. Edward did the only possible thing; he called off the sieges of Nantes and Rennes, and concentrated his army in strong lines of circumvallation and contravallation before Vannes. He had no intention of abandoning the siege of this town–if only out of respect for the memory of Robert d'Artois, who had received his lethal wound outside its walls. The siege was therefore carried on with energy and with all the means and processes available at that period–catapults, battering rams, snaps and mines.

Meanwhile the great Franco-Breton array was on the move. But instead of advancing straight toward Vannes–that is, due west–the duke of Normandy marched north-west on Rennes, where he arrived on or about Christmas Day. Thence he turned south-west towards Vannes, but halted midway at Ploermel, where his army was joined by the French king. This curious halt can only be explained by the assumption that it was done under the orders of the king. The situation had suddenly become exciting. The English were between the garrison of Vannes on the one side and the combined Franco-Breton army on the other. It was the Morlaix situation again. But Edward's solution differed from Northampton's. He did not throw up the siege, but prepared to fight it out in his own lines if attacked, as he had every reason to suppose he would be. It was an anxious time, and the king sent repeated and urgent messages to England for reinforcements.

But the unexpected happened, as it so often did in this extraordinary war. The French army at Ploermel was 25 miles away, but apart from sending out patrols which bickered with the English patrols, Philip sat still for over a fortnight. At the end of that time, just as the English army was about to assault the town, two cardinals, sent by Pope Clement VI, descended on the scene of operations and in a remarkably short time had arranged a truce, the Truce of Malestroit, between the two parties. By this truce, which was to last for three years (unless peace was declared in the meanwhile), both sides were to hold what they had, with the exception that the Franco-Bretons were to depart from Vannes, which was to be "neutral" for the duration. Accordingly the French king departed with his army, and shortly afterward the bulk of the English army sailed for home. Edward remained on the spot in camp opposite Vannes for some weeks, suspecting that Philip might suddenly reopen hostilities. Thus abruptly and unexpectedly the first English campaign in Brittany came to an end.

On the surface it appears something of a fiasco, like the two Flanders campaigns, but in reality the English intervention had saved the Montfort party at a time when their position seemed desperate. Half the country was now in their hands, the south and west, and though the north and east remained under Bloisian control, many of the nobility who had thrown in their lot with de Blois began to waver and some came over to the Montfort party, notably the influential Olivier de Clisson.

It is possible that the truce saved the English army, though de la Borderie believes that if the French had attacked, it would have been *"une première édition de la journée de Crecy"*. As for Philip VI, any remnants of military reputation left over from his two abortive Flanders campaigns had now vanished. Thrice had he come face to face with an inferior English army when by a single stroke he might have ended the struggle for the French throne, and thrice had he shirked the challenge. The conclusion is inescapable; whatever bellicose intention he may have had when he collected an army and marched to war, his resolution failed him when he found himself confronted by the redoubtable English king and his formidable troops.

On February 22, 1343, king Edward set sail for home, accompanied by the indomitable countess Joan of Flanders, and after a terrible storm which blew his ship almost to the coast of Spain, he landed at Weymouth ten days later and went straight to London, while the countess went to Exeter. To Edward the storm was the work of Philip's necromancers, and it was frustrated by the direct intervention of the Almighty, and to show his thankfulness he went on pilgrimage to Waltham Abbey, Canterbury, and Gloucester.

\* \* \*

SIR THOMAS DAGWORTH

The following two years were distinguished by great tournaments at home, in most of which the king took a prominent part. It was the zenith of the age of chivalry, signalized by the revival of the Knights of the Round Table and the building of the Round Tower at Windsor to accommodate them. But while junketings were the order of the day in England, war again threatened in Brittany because of repeated breaches of the truce by Philip VI. He unlawfully seized and put to death some of the Breton nobility, and the English retaliated by occupying Vannes. In May, 1345, the unfortunate John de

Montfort escaped from France to England, where he did homage to Edward, recognizing him as the lawful king of France. Next month de Montfort and the indispensable earl of Northampton took ship for Brittany. This time Northampton's right-hand man was another notable soldier, Sir Thomas Dagworth. They landed with a powerful army at Brest about June 10.

Sir Thomas Dagworth immediately set out with a flying column through the centre of Upper Brittany. In seven days he covered over 100 miles. Just short of Ploermel he met and put to flight a French army at the village of Cadoret. Following up his success he almost reached Rennes, capturing many places in its vicinity. The strategical object of this operation in Upper Brittany had been to relieve the pressure on the Montfort region of the south, where the count de Blois had made incursions and had captured Quimper. John de Montfort attempted its recapture, but the siege lasted so long that Blois had time to come to its relief. This he effected, and John count de Montfort and earl of Richmond, to give him his full title, died shortly afterward. The countess Joan had gone mad and their son, the young John, was in England and only six years of age. The affairs of Brittany appeared to have reached their nadir. But the king of England was not easily discouraged, as we have seen, and he now took the war completely into his own hands. It thus became more than ever a contest between France and England, fought out on Breton soil. Operations were to continue, though winter was at hand.

The next move was made by Northampton himself. Setting out from Carhaix on November 29 in the dead of night, he marched with such rapidity that by dawn of November 30 he had covered the 25 miles to Guingamp, which he summoned to surrender. It closed its gates against him, and Northampton, having no siege engines with him, and having a further target in view, pushed on another 20 miles to the north and before nightfall arrived opposite Roche-Derrien. Thus he made the remarkable march of 45 miles or more in under 24 hours, and

in winter too. It is evident that the whole of his force must
have been mounted. Roche-Derrien surrendered after a three-
day siege, and Treguier, five miles further north, fell without
resistance. Thus the English had obtained a footing in a region
that had been Bloisian throughout the war. Moreover Treguier
possessed a harbour, which might prove of the greatest value
to the English. Lannion, 12 miles further west and also connected with the sea, fell early next year (1346). This considerable success de Blois seemed incapable of averting or avenging,
and the English offensive was continued. Dagworth was sent
out with a flying column which mopped up a number of towns
in the north and centre, including Ploermel. De Blois at last
brought up his army to deal with this enterprising and elusive
Englishman and on June 9, 1346, managed to come up with
him, at St. Pol de Léon, N.W. of Morlaix.

The French army was, as usual, greatly superior in numbers.
Its first attack was repulsed, but, as at Morlaix, the second line
came on, and overlapping the diminutive English force on
each flank, put in a simultaneous attack from three sides. An
astonishing thing then happened. The English army, standing
its ground and taking steady aim, poured in such a stream of
arrows that "a veritable massacre" ensued. The French were
crushingly defeated and put to flight. Thus again was exhibited
the power of the English longbow: Dagworth's victory was
just in time to add to the morale and prestige of the English
archers at Crecy. It is unfortunate that we have not full details
of this remarkable action. At Morlaix the archers are not
specifically referred to in the accounts, and Dagworth's great
victory of St. Pol de Léon was thus the first field battle in
Brittany where the work of our archers was specifically
mentioned. Dagworth's surprising victory made a big impression at the time and a chivalrous Frenchman, writing of
him a hundred years ago, described him as: "The English
Achilles who covered himself with glory in resisting with a
handful of men the whole army of Charles de Blois."

It was only one of many victories in this *Annus Mirabilis*, or

Year of Victories (strictly speaking two years) in four different
and distant but simultaneous campaigns, extending from the
south of France to the north of England.

King Edward had finished with tournaments, for the time
being at least. By 1345 the defeat of France had become the
predominant object of his life, and Northampton's expedition
to Brittany was only a part of the king's wider plan for the
conquest of France. Simultaneously with sending one expedition to Brittany he had sent another, under the earl of Derby,
to Gascony, while he himself crossed to Flanders, to cement
the alliance and concoct plans with the faithful Artevelde.

The king had conceived the tremendous scheme of an attack
on France on exterior lines—from Flanders in the north-east,
from Brittany in the north-west, and from Gascony in the
south-west. The first of these was still-born, for on the very day
of his interview with Artevelde the latter was murdered. With
the Gascony attack we will deal in the next chapter. In Brittany
Dagworth's operations had already played their part in attract-
ing French troops away from the vital spot—Normandy.

*               *               *

The count of Blois took several months to recover from his
severe defeat at the hands of Sir Thomas Dagworth. Meanwhile the English victors looked upon the Penthièvre territory
as a foreign country, and "made the war pay for itself" by stern
exactions from the inhabitants. They did not resort to the
senseless burnings that had disfigured the campaigns in
Flanders (albeit the chief offenders there were not English
troops but Hainaulters). But the inhabitants were antagonized
still more, and may be presumed to have appealed to Charles
to drive out their unwelcome guests. Charles was burning to
avenge his humiliating defeat, but it was not till the following
spring (1347) that he could get together an army sufficiently
strong, in his opinion, to meet the English in the open field.
Hence he had not dared to attempt the recapture of Roche-
Derrien in the meantime. Crecy had saved it.

By May, 1347, his preparations were complete and on May 20 he appeared before the walls of the doomed Roche-Derrien, plentifully equipped with all that was requisite for a full-scale siege.

## THE BATTLE OF ROCHE-DERRIEN (JUNE 20, 1347)

The little town of Roche-Derrien stands picturesquely on a rocky foundation (as its name implies). The west side falls almost precipitously to the river Jaudi, here about 30 feet wide. To north and east the ground slopes down gently, but to the south it slopes up towards a wooded plateau. In other words it forms a sort of appendix from the high ground, jutting out to the north.

Though small in area it was a walled town, complete with a castle that commanded the bridge over the river below. The Bloisian army had been recruited from Bretons, French, Normans, and other nationalities. Charles set about the siege systematically. He first constructed an extensive camp, entrenched it, and cleared the ground around it of trees in order to provide a good "field of fire". The camp was laid out like a town complete with streets and houses, and even markets were held. This camp—it is quite clear from the terrain—was on the south side of the town. In addition, de Blois stationed a detached force in an old earthwork, called the Black Castle (see appendix), 500 yards to the west of the bridge over the river. Its special mission was to guard against the inevitable attack by Dagworth, which it was reckoned was likely to come from that side. The garrison of the Black Castle had strict instructions that they were on no account to quit their post without express orders from the count.

The siege now commenced. It took the usual form: siege "engines" were brought up and the walls were bombarded in order to make a breach. Charles had nine of them, all of considerable size, but one so huge that it discharged stones of up to 300 lb. in weight. One of these landed on a house where the governor, Richard Totsham, and his wife were

sitting, and half the house was destroyed. The good lady then
pleaded for the town to be surrendered, as did others whose
nerves were shaken. But Totsham held on resolutely, though

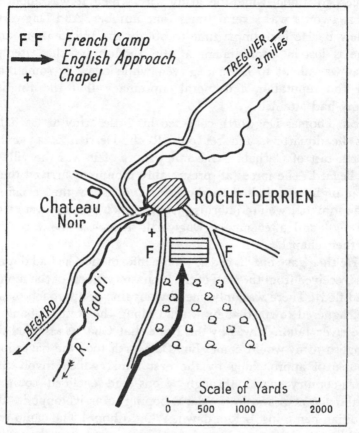

4. ROCHE-DERRIEN

three weeks elapsed without a sign of any approach by the
relieving army.

Why Sir Thomas Dagworth delayed so long in going to the
relief of the sorely stricken town is a mystery. The reason
cannot have been that he required time in which to assemble
a large army, for the one with which he eventually set out was

astonishingly small. It consisted of but 700 combatants, 300 men-at-arms and 400 archers. Even if we add a few armed attendants on the knights, the total number cannot have exceeded 1,000, while the army with which it was about to cross swords was several times that number. And Dagworth knew it. He had ample time to obtain the information, and one is lost in astonishment at the audacity of the attempt that was about to be made, even while allowing something for the reputation and moral supremacy that the English army had attained.

Sir Thomas Dagworth collected his little army at Carhaix, his headquarters, and set out. Roche-Derrien is 45 miles north-east of Carhaix. Nine miles short of it was the village of Begard. The force (all presumably mounted) arrived there that night and halted in the large monastery that evening. The inmates, we are informed from French sources, were well treated, and after supper Dagworth attended divine service in their chapel.

He then gave out his orders on the information he had doubtless received from the staff of the monastery (most of the monks had fled). There was only one obvious line of approach to the beleaguered town, that by a road along the western bank of the river Jaudi. It was by this route that Charles assumed the English army would come. But Dagworth took the hazardous course of approaching by the east bank, which involved a cross-country march through woods and enclosed country, without a map and in the dark, hoping to arrive opposite the Bloisian camp just before dawn. What a hope! The camp was to be rushed by surprise; after which a mêlée was bound to take place in the darkness. The far-seeing Dagworth allowed for the inevitable confusion that would characterize it and resolved to profit by it. The mêlée usually sorted itself out into duels. In the dark neither side would be quite sure who was friend and who was foe. Sir Thomas Dagworth therefore gave out a secret signal, or password. When two men met in the mêlée and were not sure of each other's nationality, one was

to ask for the signal, and the man challenged was to give it in a
low voice; if he gave it in a loud voice he was to be despatched
by his comrade.[1] The reason for this is obvious: if it were given
out loud the French would soon learn it and use it themselves
to deceive their opponents.

The army then moved off. It was about midnight. By some
extraordinary means (Froissart says there were three guides,
which is quite likely), the column found its way without
mistake or mishap and arrived "at the right place at the right
time", that is, opposite the Bloisian camp "a quarter before
dawn". The French had no sentries out, and no password had
been circulated. The English emerged from the woods, charged
across the open space and entered the camp. The surprise was
complete. Most of the defenders were asleep, and the knights
were of course not clad in their armour. To struggle into it in
the dark, with the enemy running amok and hacking down the
tents and pavilions, was a difficult task, as may be imagined.
The scene would baffle description even if we knew all the
details, which no one at the time did, and no one ever will.
Suffice it to say that the attackers carried all before them in
their first impetuous rush. But then the temptation to indulge in
destruction proved too strong for most of the elated troops.
According to Froissart's Amiens version, they began cutting
down the tents, as mentioned above. The delay thus caused
gave a breathing space to those defenders who occupied the
outlying parts of the camp, and presently a counter-attack was
thrown in. It was repelled. A second met with the same fate.
It was still dark, but some Frenchmen had made and lit some
torches with which they were enabled to take stock of the
situation and to concert plans. Eventually, while it was still
dark, a third attack, stronger and better organized than the
preceding ones, was made. The band of Englishmen was in a
sea of enemies, still outnumbered in spite of its initial success.
The tide began to turn against them.

[1] Somewhat similar orders were given by the duke of Monmouth for the march
to Sedgmoor fight.

In one mêlée Dagworth was wounded and captured. A prompt counter-attack was then launched by the English and their beloved leader was rescued. But ever fresh enemies were coming up, and as daylight gradually appeared, the slender numbers of the attackers became evident and their plight began to look serious. But with daylight came help. The struggle was taking place on the plateau some 500 yards from the town. During the night the garrison heard a great clamour, but the men did not dare leave their posts till the situation clarified with the dawn. Then they took in the situation; the relievers were evidently in a bad way; help must be sent them at once. Leaving a skeleton force to hold the walls in case of a sudden attack from across the river, Totsham made a spirited sortie with the remainder into the backs of the French. Only a few hundred men were available for this attack, but it proved enough. Dagworth's men cooperated and everywhere the French gave way, till eventually there was a general flight from the field.

Meanwhile the besiegers on the far bank of the river remained inactive. Some historians, anxious to find a scapegoat, have blamed them for this inactivity. But they were not only obeying orders, but doing the only sensible thing during the hours of darkness. Their camp was about a mile from the scene of action and separated from it by the river. Though they could hear the clamour they could not know or even guess that the defenders were being put to rout. For all they knew it was a feint attack designed to draw them over the river, after which the real attack, led by Dagworth in person, might come on their own front. By the time it got light enough to establish the situation, it was too late to help. The bridge over the river led into the town. They would have to go some way up stream, ford the river, and then climb a steep bluff. It was too late.

An army had defeated another army several times its own strength, largely because of the inherent advantage the attacker possesses of being able to concentrate his strength against a single point, whereas the defender has to try to defend everywhere and fritter his strength accordingly all along the line.

Large numbers of the French were killed and many captured. The rest fled. And what of the French commander? Charles de Blois had fought the fight of his life. Surprised in his tent (according to Froissart) he managed to get out, but evidently not to don his armour. For, fighting heroically, he received wound after wound, yet continued to fight. Eventually, covered with blood, he was overpowered late in the fight and captured. He was taken to various castles in Brittany while he made a slow recovery, after which he was taken to England. On the voyage he was serenaded by eight guitar players, presumably in order to ward off sea-sickness. On arrival in London he was placed in the Tower, alongside the king of Scotland, who had recently been captured in the battle of Neville's Cross.

The results of this shattering victory were considerable. The tables were now turned: a short time before, the Montfort party had lost its leader; now a like fate had met the de Blois party, while their rivals had found a fresh leader in their new suzerain, king Edward III of England. One thrust of the English king's triple attack on France was going well.

EPILOGUE

This victory had a grim sequel. After his signal triumph Dagworth crossed to England and the defeated side took advantage of his absence to appeal for help to the French king. Philip complied and sent an army to retake the town. Its attack came as a surprise, and after three days' siege and some good sapping by Genoese soldiers, a breach was made, an entry forced, and all the inhabitants, men, women and children, slaughtered. The English garrison, 250 strong, had withdrawn to the castle, but they surrendered on condition that they were given a safe conduct to friendly territory. They were therefore escorted unarmed out of the town by two French knights, but on reaching Chateauneuf they were set upon by the butchers and carpenters of the town, in spite of the efforts of their French escort, and massacred to a man. The story sounds almost incredible, but we have a French source for it.

# APPENDIX

### BATTLEFIELD OF ROCHE-DERRIEN

There can be little doubt about the site of Charles's camp. The one obvious place is on the wide, gently-sloping plain, on the high ground overlooking the town from the south. This area seems made for a camp, and we get partial corroboration from a statement by the *Grandes Chroniques* that it was the opposite side of the town from the Black Castle, which it approximately is. I estimate the northern edge of the camp at 300 yards from the town. A wayside shrine or chapel to Notre Dame de Pitié runs through this line. The upper or southern edge would be a few hundred yards south. Beyond that the country was wooded and it is easy to picture the English troops charging down the slope to that astonishing battle.

The Black Castle is popularly supposed to have been constructed by the earl of Northampton when besieging the town in the previous year. That is impossible. That siege only lasted a few days; it would have taken Northampton's troops over six months to construct the great earthwork which still exists. Compare it, for example, with the earthwork that Jean Bureau made opposite Castillon in four days before besieging that town. It is still visible, but a mere scratch in the ground. The Black Castle on the other hand has a circumference of about 500 yards, and a height of vallum up to 18 feet. It is no doubt much older than the fourteenth century, though de la Borderie cannot be right in thinking it Roman.

### NUMBERS

There seems no reason to doubt Dagworth's statement about his numbers, astonishingly small though they be, "about 300 men-at-arms and 400 archers". He gave this figure in an official dispatch soon after the battle. It would be published in England and Brest, and if it was badly wrong his veracity would soon be impugned. De la Borderie gives no reason for his estimate that the English numbers were 2,000 to 2,500.

It is a quite different matter with the French. Dagworth would have no exact knowledge of the French strength when he wrote, or at any other time. Indeed, even de Blois was probably ignorant of the exact number of his army. Throughout the war we find this vagueness about French numbers. For what it may be worth, here are Dagworth's figures: 1,800 men-at-arms, 600 archers, 2,000 crossbowmen, and an unknown number of "commune" (probably Breton infantry). Knighton gives the French 25,000; Froissart makes the number 1,600 men-at-arms and 12,000 footmen, a figure accepted by Laconteau in his *Histoire de Bretagne*. No doubt this is exaggerated, but it seems clear that the army was exceptionally large. Charles had spent a long time in amassing it, and the *Grandes Chroniques* assert that it consisted of "a great quantity of people, both French and Bretons and other nationalities". However much we scale down these figures we are left with an army many times the strength of its opponents.

### SIR THOMAS DAGWORTH AND COUNT CHARLES DE BLOIS

De la Borderie retails a story to the effect that "Dagworth, after his victory, coming to regale himself with the sight of the generous, defeated Charles de Blois, and finding him drenched in blood dripping from his seventeen wounds, lying on a feather bed, supported by charitable hands, had the infamy to snatch this bed from him and cast him brutally on to the straw."

He asserts that this tale is "perfectly true" and speaks of "the dastardly and odious blackguardism of this Dagworth" (*le goujaterie odieuse et lâche de ce Dagworth*).

Considering how much at variance with Dagworth's chivalrous character this story is, I had the curiosity to examine de la Borderie's evidence. It is printed in *Mémoires pour servir de preuves à l'histoire . . . de Bretagne*. It is contained in the deposition made at the inquiry regarding the canonization of

Charles de Blois by Georges de Lesnen. It is in Latin, and I translate the salient passage thus: "On his bed there was a feather mattress. Dagworth . . . had this mattress drawn from under him (*ipsam calcitram* [sic] *sustrati de subtas ipsum*) in order to insult him, as it appeared, and thus remained the lord Charles on the straw, only one linen cloth remaining on the straw."

Notice first how de la Borderie has embellished the story, more in the manner of Froissart than of a serious historian whose history is accepted as standard.

Now let us examine the credentials of this witness. Lesnen had been Charles's doctor for 20 years. He does not claim to have been captured with him in battle, which he would scarcely have omitted when giving evidence if it were true. Thus his evidence, at best, must be hearsay. His deposition is one long unadulterated paean of praise for his hero. Such testimony by a friend should be treated with the same caution that one treats the evidence of witnesses at the Rehabilitation of Joan of Arc. Moreover, this witness had been guilty of prevarication in another case. In short, his testimony must be regarded as suspect unless corroborated by another witness or unless it is inherently probable in itself.

In this case it is inherently improbable. Dagworth had been brought up in the Edwardian school of chivalry. Knights might treat lower orders with harshness and cruelty, but once the battle was over, they observed a strict rule of chivalry and courtesy among themselves. Dagworth's comrade-in-arms, the earl of Derby, had recently set the fashion in Gascony by inviting to sup with him his defeated opponent, a fashion that the Black Prince followed on the night of Poitiers. Dagworth's later conduct also gives the lie to this story, for he allowed the defeated count to have with him his own friends during his convalescence, and to allow his wife to visit him.

The serious historian must regard this story as, at the most, "non proven". If there is any basis for it the culprit was probably some subordinate, whose name Lesnen would not be likely to know, and in order to add verisimilitude to the story he inserted the only English name he did know.

In most respects de la Borderie is careful in his facts (if rather credulous regarding numbers), but in this case national bias seems to have got the better of his cool judgment.

# CHAPTER V

# THE WAR IN GASCONY,
### 1345–47

THOUGH the first act of aggression that precipitated the outbreak of the war occurred in Gascony[1]–it was the seizure of Penne on the Lot, 30 miles north-east of Aiguillon–little of moment happened in that province for the first seven years. The French commander, the count de l'Isle, contented himself with a leisurely advance against inappreciable resistance (from Penne), down the rivers Lot and Garonne as far as St. Macaire (ten miles below La Réole) and thence down the Dordogne as far as Libourne, where he halted. Libourne is 25 miles from Bordeaux, the capital of Gascony, and St. Macaire is about twice that distance. Practically all that was left of the old English dominion in the south of France was a strip of territory bordering on the sea between Bordeaux and Bayonne, 100 miles further south. But the exact boundary between the contending forces at any time during the war was vague and ill-defined, and very indented. It amounted to this: the country was studded with castles and *bastides* (roughly corresponding to the peel castles on the Scottish border). These castles changed hands frequently, and the domain of the castle-owner at any time could be considered the territory of whichever king the castle-owner acknowledged. Thus the war assumed the pattern of a struggle for castles, and as these castles were chiefly grouped along the two great rivers, the Garonne and the Dordogne, the war became in practice a struggle for the possession of these two rivers.

Although the French carried all before them in the early

---

[1] Most of the fighting took place in Guyenne, which is to the north of Gascony, but the two words are almost synonymous in the Chronicles and, as the inhabitants are indiscriminately described as Gascons, it seems more convenient to keep to the word Gascony. It is also taken to include the whole of Aquitaine.

stages of the war, a large number of the Gascon barons remained faithful to the English connexion. They instinctively looked to England for help, and when an appeal of this nature reached Edward III in 1344, he took heed of it, and all the more readily because it fitted in with his grand triple design of attack on France which we have noticed in the previous chapter. An army was therefore fitted out and a commander appointed – the earl of Derby, who had been so prominent in the Flanders campaigns. It is time to say something about this remarkable man, who may be described as one of England's "forgotten worthies". Henry of Lancaster, or of Grosmont, as he was sometimes called after the place of his birth, was the son of the first earl of Lancaster. From the days of his early manhood until his death 40 years later, Henry was almost continually engaged in war or diplomacy, and for the latter third of that time he was the right-hand man of his sovereign in both those callings. His name became almost legendary during his lifetime all over Europe, for he had fought on the Continent and in the Mediterranean, in crusades as well as in "home wars" in Scotland, Flanders, Brittany, Gascony, and on the sea. That his name is not now better known is partly due to Froissart, who was inclined to ascribe the credit for his achievements to his subordinate, Sir Walter Manny, as a fellow Hainaulter who was Froissart's especial *protégé*. As an example of Derby's fame in his own time, when in 1352 he led a deputation to visit the Pope in Avignon, the road leading into the town was so thronged with the populace that he found it almost impossible to get over the bridge into the city.

This was the man to whom the king of England entrusted the command of the southern arm of his grand offensive against France. He was now 46 years of age – that of Wellington and Napoleon at Waterloo – and at the height of his powers. The army he took with him consisted of only about 500 men-at-arms and 2,000 archers. But it required ships and sailors as well, and the fact that Edward could send from these shores two expeditions simultaneously – one to Brittany and one to Gascony –

illustrates the expansion in warlike resources that the war had brought about at home. The principal officers in the army were the earls of Oxford and Pembroke, Lord Stafford, and the indispensable Sir Walter Manny.

The expedition was ready in the spring, but adverse winds prevented it setting sail from Southampton till late May. It landed at Bayonne on June 6 and Derby very sensibly remained there seven days in order to refresh the men, and particularly the horses, after their long sea voyage. Then he marched straight to Bordeaux where great crowds came out of the city to give him a rapturous welcome. The earl of Derby (as we will continue to call him during this campaign, for though his father died in the course of it he continued to be known generally as Derby for some time) had been given a free hand; he was to act as he saw fit in the military sphere, while in the civil sphere he became "the king's representative", and shortly after his arrival he was nominated "the king's lieutenant". Thus his hands were full, and the 14 days that he spent at Bordeaux must have been among the busiest of his life.

Meanwhile the count de l'Isle, still in command of the French forces, heard of the earl's arrival and summoned a council of war to decide on a plan of campaign. The conclusion arrived at was to make a stand at Bergerac on the Dordogne, 70 miles east of Bordeaux, and thither reinforcements were hastened from all sides. The earl of Derby learned of this concentration and decided to attack the town before the enemy had time to make it impregnable. For this purpose he assembled his army at Libourne, which the French had not managed to capture. Accompanied by a fleet of small boats, he pushed on up the river, through the little town of Castillon— later to become famous—thence along the south bank to Bergerac. This town lies on the north bank of the river, connected by a bridge with a suburb on the south bank. This suburb the enemy were holding, so that it became necessary first to eject them from the suburb and then to capture the

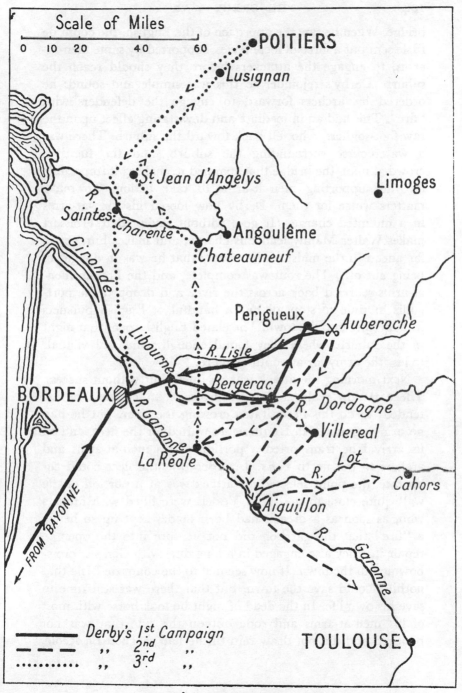

**Scale of Miles**

0   10   20        40        60

**POITIERS**

Lusignan

St Jean d'Angelys

Limoges

R. Charente

Saintes

Gironde

Angoulême

Chateauneuf

Perigueux

Auberoche

Libourne

R. Lisle

BORDEAUX

R. Garonne

Bergerac

R. Dordogne

Villereal

La Réole

R. Lot

Cahors

Aiguillon

R. Garonne

FROM BAYONNE

Derby's 1st Campaign

 ,,    2nd   ,,

 ,,    3rd   ,,

TOULOUSE

5. DERBY'S CAMPAIGNS IN GASCONY

bridge. When he saw the approach of the English, the count de l'Isle sent out a force of local levies, supported by some men-at-arms, to engage the attackers before they should reach the suburb. Derby's rejoinder to this was simple and sound: he ordered his archers forward to engage the defenders with "fire". This had an immediate and devastating effect upon the raw foot-soldiers, who fell back toward the suburb. There was a watercourse surrounding the suburb, and the fugitives crowded upon the bridge that spanned it, making it impossible for the supporting men-at-arms to take action. To make matters worse for them, Derby now loosed his men-at-arms in a mounted charge. (It goes without saying that Froissart makes Walter Manny lead this charge, and makes him get so far ahead in the midst of the enemy that he was in danger of being cut off.) The rout was complete, and the French men-at-arms scurried back across the river and dropped the portcullis in time to stop all but a handful of English pursuers from getting into the town. The elated English spent that night in the suburb, where they found enough wine and victuals to last the army for a month or more.

Next morning the attack was resumed, but without success. The earl now realized that the front of attack must be extended; to do this necessitated crossing the river, but he had no bridging material. He therefore waited for the fleet, and on its arrival he transported a portion of his men-at-arms and archers to the north bank. In order that the fleet could cooperate, the point selected for attack was at a portion of the wall quite close to the river. Vessels were filled with archers who, as soon as a breach had been made, kept up so heavy a "fire" that the garrison did not venture into the open to repair it. They also engaged in a long duel with Genoese crossbowmen in the town. It now seemed to the count de l'Isle that nothing could save the town, but that there was still time to save his own life. In the dead of night he took horse with most of his men-at-arms and rode out on the side that was not besieged and did not draw rein till he had reached La Réole,

40 miles to the south. Next morning the inhabitants awoke to find their French leaders fled, and they at once entered into negotiations for the surrender of the town. These were carried out by the earls of Oxford and Pembroke and, as a result, on August 26 the gates were opened and the English army entered the town.

This was an encouraging start, for Bergerac was a considerable town, in a strong position, and a great road centre–even in those days. Thus it effectually blocked progress along the river valley by whichever side did not hold it.

After halting for a few days at Bergerac the earl of Derby resumed his advance, first upstream 12 miles to Lalinde in a northerly direction, capturing a number of small places, till he arrived before Périgueux, the capital of Périgord. But when he saw how strongly fortified this old Roman city was, he left it alone and marched nine miles eastwards to the castle and hamlet of Auberoche. Here he made serious preparations for assault, but when they saw this the garrison surrendered at discretion. It was now autumn and, the presence of the king's lieutenant in Bordeaux being desirable, a garrison was left in Auberoche and the remainder of the army returned with its prisoners and booty to Bordeaux. The earl of Derby's first campaign had gone almost without a hitch, and much of Agenais and Périgord had been recovered.

## DERBY'S SECOND CAMPAIGN

While the victorious English army returned to Bordeaux, the defeated French army was being reconstituted at La Réole by the count de l'Isle. As soon as his preparations were complete and siege engines constructed, this enterprising commander sallied forth from La Réole, marched rapidly to Auberoche, and laid siege to it. Froissart retails a fantastic story (repeated gravely by the historians) that a messenger sent out by Sir Frank Halle, the governor of the castle, with an appeal for help, was captured by the besiegers, placed alive in a great "engine" and catapulted back into the castle where he landed more dead than alive. The fact is, Halle did manage to get word to Bordeaux and Derby responded at once. Hastily he collected a small army at Libourne, consisting of 400 men-at-arms and 800 archers, and ordered the earl of Pembroke, who had a force at some unspecified spot, to join him at once. Pembroke failed to keep the appointment so, after waiting for 24 hours, the earl of Derby marched off toward Auberoche, hoping that the other earl would join him en route. At Bergerac there was still no sign of the missing Pembroke, so Derby went a stage further, marching swiftly and under cover of the woods. He was thus able to reach a concealed position in the woods only two miles from Auberoche without the enemy having any suspicion of his presence.

The castle of Auberoche is picturesquely situated on a rocky prominence overlooking the little river Auvezere, some nine miles east of Périgueux in one of the most secluded and little-known valleys of Gascony. Its situation in many respects resembles that of Chateau Gaillard. Each is a "promontory fort", one side precipitous, the other nearly so; each overlooks a river which it completely commands and each is on slightly lower ground than the *massif* to which it is joined. The valley is narrow at this point and the castle dominates and blocks it as effectually as a cork blocks a bottle. Its strategic importance is thus obvious.

The surroundings have, in all probability, changed but little during the 600 years that have elapsed since the battle. The little valley was, and is, meadow-lined; the slopes on each side were, and are, heavily wooded; as sketch-map 2 shows, the meadow to the west of the river is about 220 yards wide. In this valley de l'Isle placed his main camp, with a smaller one in the still narrower valley on the north side of the castle. The little hamlet of Auberoche lies at the foot of the castle at the junction of the two valleys. As sketch-map 2 shows, the river Auvezere hereabouts makes a series of hairpin bends and the English line of approach from the south-west involved crossing at least two of them.

## THE BATTLE OF AUBEROCHE (OCTOBER 21, 1345)

On the evening of October 20, 1345, the tiny English army settled down silently into its bivouacs, hoping to be joined at any time by Pembroke, to whom a message had been sent indicating the position of the new rendezvous. Dawn broke on October 21, but still there was no sign of Pembroke. Strict

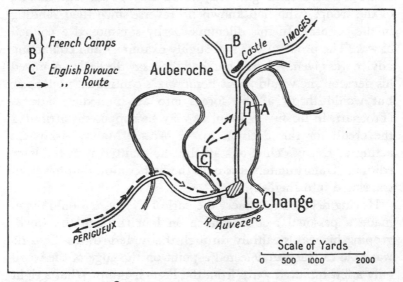

6. BATTLE OF AUBEROCHE: I

orders had been issued for the preservation of secrecy and so far the presence of the English army had not been discovered. Foraging was forbidden, though the horses were grazed near the bivouac. All food for the men had purposely been brought on pack-horses, and from this supply a morning meal was served.

As the morning wore on and still there was no sign of the reinforcements, anxiety began to reign in the camp. The English knew they were hopelessly outnumbered; they could only muster 1,200 whereas the French were reported to be 9,000 to 10,000 strong. Though the real figure was only 7,000 the proportions were six to one, formidable odds indeed. It was impracticable to remain indefinitely awaiting the reinforcements that might never arrive; the food brought with them was practically exhausted, and to forage for more would probably involve detection and the loss of surprise. To give up the venture and retreat, apart from playing false with Frank Halle and his English garrison, would damage the high morale of the troops, who had known no reverse since their landing in the country. In this dilemma Derby summoned a council of war. The problem was thoroughly examined and conflicting advice was given. After all had had their say the earl announced his decision: he would await Pembroke's contingent no longer, but would throw all his forces into an immediate attack. (Froissart, in his first edition, as may be supposed, attributed the credit for this decision to Sir Walter Manny, who was acting as Derby's chief of staff, but he omitted it in the later editions. Unfortunately it is only the first edition that has been translated into English).

Having decided to attack, the earl of Derby, it would seem, made a personal reconnaissance on foot through the wood, groping his way stealthily through the undergrowth. Thus he was able to reach undetected a point on the edge of the wood only a few hundred yards from the French camp. What a sight met his gaze! In the open space between wood and river he could see the French tents and pavilions in serried lines. All was quiet, the afternoon was well advanced and coils of smoke were rising above the tent tops: the enemy was cooking his evening meal.

The question was, how to take advantage of this unexpectedly favourable situation. A mounted charge from the wood seemed indicated, but the ground sloped down so steeply through the wood opposite the camp that this was out of the question. About 300 yards south of the camp, however, there was a fairly level approach, practicable for horsemen. Moreover there is, and probably was then, a track through the woods leading out into the meadow at that point. If this point could be attained without detection, the camp could be charged from the rear. At the same time, the archers, dismounted, could creep through the undergrowth to the edge of the wood dead opposite the camp and from there give supporting "fire" to the charging cavalry—a good example of "fire and movement". For, thus situated, the archers could keep up their "fire" till the cavalry had reached the camp, and by switching it continuously to the left they could continue to provide covering "fire" even after the arrival of the horsemen in the camp.

Derby went back and gave his orders. A ticklish operation with very nice timing was involved, so orders must be precise and detailed and discipline perfect. Froissart specifically states that they were thorough. When all understood their orders and the final preparations had been made, the attackers cautiously advanced and silently took up their respective positions. The signal for the attack was to be given by the earl himself; on receipt of it the archers were to utter their battle cry: "Derby! Guyenne!" at the same time unfurling their banners. At the sound of the battle-cry the cavalry were to emerge from the wood and charge. It must have been an exciting moment when all were in position awaiting the signal from their leader, while the smoke continued to rise lazily above the French tents, so close that the smell of the repast may even have been wafted into the wood; and still there was no movement in the hostile lines.

"Derby! Guyenne!" The signal is given, the archers wave their banners and discharge their arrows; the cavalry utter their war-cry, gallop out of the wood, form some sort of ragged line and charge straight forward over the 200 or 300 yards of intervening meadow into the outer line of French tents. The surprise was as complete as that of their comrades at Roche-Derrien was to be (indeed, the one may have inspired the other). A scene of utter confusion ensued in the French camp, that may be likened to that which arises when a stone is raised from on top of an ants' nest. The French chief officers,

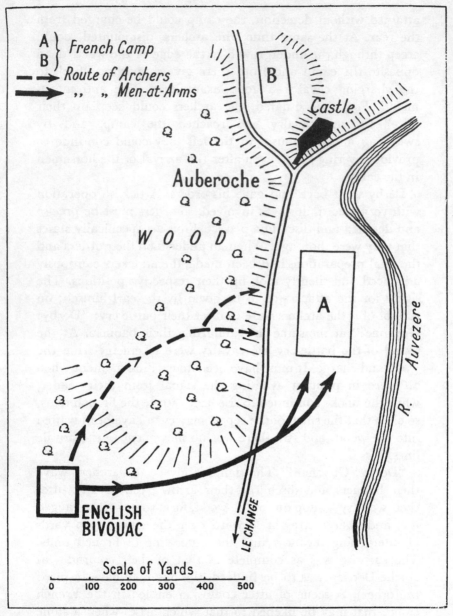

A } French Camp
B }
– – – → Route of Archers
"       "  Men-at-Arms

B

Castle

Auberoche

W O O D

A

R. Auvezere

ENGLISH
BIVOUAC

LE CHANGE

Scale of Yards

0    100   200   300   400   500

7. BATTLE OF AUBEROCHE: 2

out of their armour and mostly supping in their tents, rushed out and tried frantically to don their armour, while all the time a hail of arrows was striking them from one direction and the mounted charge was coming from another. The casualties caused by the first flights of arrows into those crowded lines were immense: Murimuth estimates them as over a thousand, though this is of course a pure guess and no doubt exaggerated. As the horsemen penetrated further into the centre of the camp and became invisible to the archers, the latter were obliged for the time to cease their "fire". A few French officers managed to struggle into their armour and to unfurl their banners on the outskirts of the camp, as a rallying point for their own men. But as they thus began to form clumps, a fresh target was provided for the English archers, who opened on them once more.

How long this extraordinary contest lasted no man knows. Contestants lose all sense of time under such circumstances. But before it was over a fresh assailant came into the field of action. Not only were the French men-at-arms hastily donning their armour. High up in the castle the same thing was happening. For Sir Frank Halle, from his eyrie, had the whole scene laid out before him. His course was clear; he would join in the battle with every available horseman. The French detachment blocking the exit from the gateway had its attention attracted to the exciting events directly in its rear, whither their gaze was riveted, so the garrison's mounted troops found no difficulty in bursting out and charging into the French camp from their side. Even before this the archers in the castle joined in the attack with their "fire",[1] though it must have been at extreme range and could only have reached the near edge of the French camp. Be that as it may, the sudden irruption of Halle's little band of horsemen proved "the last straw". The last semblance of resistance crumpled, every man who could fled the field, and the English were left in possession of it. The French to the north of the castle took no effective part in the battle, and by

[1] According to a local tradition, told me on the spot.

their hasty flight only added to the immense booty. (This inaction is discussed in the appendix.)

The victory was complete and staggering. Though no two accounts agree about the casualties, there is no doubt that the flower of the chivalry of the south of France was accounted for that day in killed, wounded, and captured. Many of the French leaders were prisoners, including the count de l'Isle himself.

That evening the great-hearted Lord Derby, anticipating the Black Prince 11 years later,[1] entertained at dinner in the castle his captive generals. During the meal, who should appear but the dilatory earl of Pembroke. While approaching the rendezvous, he explained, he was met by fugitives from the field who told him that a battle was proceeding. He had hurried forward at his best pace, but had arrived to find all was over. Derby was in a jovial mood and welcomed his brother earl with mock delight. "You have arrived just in time—to help us finish off the venison!" he exclaimed.

The results of the battle of Auberoche were considerable, indeed astonishing, considering the small number which took part. The French immediately abandoned the sieges of three towns that they had hoped to take, a campaign that was being prepared by the duke of Normandy was delayed by six months, while his communications with the duke of Bourbon in the south were abandoned. For the capture of Auberoche by count de l'Isle had been intended as the prelude to a general campaign for the recovery of the territory recently lost to the earl of Derby. The latter's sudden attack against vastly superior forces was almost breath-taking in its audacity and dazzling in its brilliance. A French historian of our time has described it as *un choc terrible*.[2]

In the psychological domain the results were equally important; though judged by the numbers engaged Auberoche was one of the lesser battles of the war, it established in Gascony

---

[1] I suspect that the Black Prince followed the example of his second cousin the earl of Derby in this and in other ways.

[2] BERTRANDY, HENRI, in *Études sur les Chroniques de Froissart*.

the moral supremacy that Morlaix had established in Brittany, and that Crecy was nine months later to establish in Picardy. Henceforth till almost the end of the war 100 years later no French army engaged an English army in the field if it could honourably avoid doing so.

The earl of Derby only allowed two days' rest at Auberoche— a short breathing space—for there was much to be done. His troops required a rest, the wounded required tending, arrangements had to be made for the prisoners to be escorted to Bordeaux, the army had to be reorganized with Pembroke's contingent incorporated in it, and plans had to be made for the future after this surprisingly complete victory. Should Derby return to Bordeaux with his captives? As Governor-General—as we should now call him—he would find plenty of work awaiting him. Moreover he had left the capital at short notice with much business half completed. Froissart guessed that the earl did return to Bordeaux and he couched his guess in a positive statement. But the chronicler guessed wrong. Far from returning, Derby resolved to "strike while the iron was hot", and while the enemy was still reeling under his blow. In which direction should he strike? The dukes of Bourbon and Normandy were keeping prudently out of his reach. The duke of Normandy had been on his way south from Limoges when he heard of the disaster at Auberoche. Though only a few leagues from that place, this ineffective commander, instead of hurrying forward to avenge the defeat, fell back to Limoges— fell back before a tiny band of Englishmen.

So Derby resorted to the recovery of more territory and castles. But in which direction? Of the two main approaches to Bordeaux—the valleys of the Garonne and the Dordogne—the latter was now effectually blocked. There remained the Garonne valley. Here there were two strong and important fortified towns still in French possession, La Réole, recently the French headquarters, 65 miles to the south-west of Auberoche, and Aiguillon, the same distance almost due south. Derby seems to have divided his forces, sending one body under Pembroke and

Lord Stafford against Aiguillon, while he led the other against La Réole.[1]

Pembroke and Stafford attacked and captured Monségur, a few miles north of Aiguillon, and then besieged Aiguillon itself. Meanwhile Derby had marched direct to La Réole, to which he laid siege about October 26. This town had a more remarkable history during the period of English dominance in Gascony than any other town except the capital. It has a striking situation, perched on an outcrop of rock overlooking the river Garonne. The walls were strong, and the castle, situated at the south-west angle, was considered almost impregnable because of the thickness of its fortifications and the fact that it was founded on rock and so could not be mined.

The earl of Derby was doubtless aware of its strength, for it had been a favourite abode of English kings and princes, and though it had changed hands with almost bewildering frequency this had been due to starvation or treachery rather than to direct assault. The English commander therefore went about his task methodically. This was no Bergerac, where he could break in at the first attempt without the assistance of siege engines. These had first to be constructed. Catapults were of comparatively simple construction, but they were not by themselves sufficient for the work; Derby also had built two enormous *beffrois*–to use the technical French term–*i.e.* movable towers, so high that they overtopped the town walls. Such towers were manhandled right up to the wall to be breached and archers stationed on the summit discharged their arrows on to the garrison manning the parapet walk below them. By this means the battlements were soon cleared of defenders. The next stage was for pioneers to advance into the ditch and up to the foot of the wall to be breached, which they would then hack away or mine beneath with their picks.

While these two *beffrois* were being made, the ditch at the points selected for their attack was filled in till it was level

---

[1] Here I accept the suggestion first made by Simeon Luce in his edition of Froissart, vol. III, xx Note.

with the surrounding ground, and beaten down firm. Then the *beffrois* were hauled right up to the walls, at points some hundred yards apart, and, the garrison having been driven from the walls by the archers, the pioneers began their breach in the section between the *beffrois* comparatively unmolested. When the inhabitants saw this they surrendered at discretion—indeed with relief and gladness for the most part. It should be noted that the French had only been in occupation for 21 years, and the sympathies of the Gascons were more favourably inclined toward the English than the French.

The commander of the garrison, Agout des Baux, was not however a Gascon. He and his troops hailed from distant Provence, and he refused to surrender. Instead he withdrew into the castle when the town was seen to be lost. Here he sustained a siege of anything up to ten weeks. All we know for certain is that it fell very early in the New Year (1346). According to Froissart, its fall came about in the following way. The English opened proceedings by bombarding the walls and two towers with their catapults, but the stones they threw made little or no impression on the massive walls. (One of the towers was so strongly built that it is still occupied as a private domicile.) They then had recourse to mining, but this also proved almost insuperably difficult, for the castle, as we have said, was founded on the solid rock and before the era of gunpowder the work of hacking out the naked rock was extremely slow. Nevertheless it was persisted in for so long that the garrison became alarmed, and a deputation to the commander suggested that honour was now satisfied and that the place should be yielded up before it was destroyed and taken by storm, in which case all their lives would be forfeit. Agout yielded to their representations and descended from the top of the tower to the lowest floor, where (following Froissart) he put his head out of the window and asked the besiegers if he might parley with Lord Derby. The earl appeared, in company with Sir Walter Manny, opposite the foot of the tower on horseback, and the following remarkable conversation ensued:

AGOUT: "Gentlemen, you know the King of France has sent me to this town and castle to defend them to the best of my ability. You know in what manner I have acquitted myself, and also that I should wish to continue it: but one cannot always remain in the place that pleases one best. I should therefore like to depart from hence with my companions, if it be agreeable to you."

EARL OF DERBY: "Sir Agout, Sir Agout, you will not get off so. We know that you are very much distressed, and that we can take your place whenever we please, for your castle now only stands upon props" (referring to the mining). "You must surrender yourselves unconditionally, and so shall you be received."

Sir Agout went on pleading in a wheedling tone till Derby withdrew for a short distance and discussed the matter with Manny. Then he came forward again and addressed the French commander as follows:—

"Sir Agout, we shall be happy always to treat every stranger knight as a brother at arms and if, fair sir, you and yours wish to leave the castle you must carry nothing with you but your arms and horses."

Sir Agout joyfully agreed, and the last view we get is that of the French marching out with their six remaining horses, and bartering with the English soldiers for fresh ones. The English, we are told, charged heavy prices for them. Thus, by a magnificent piece of bluff, Derby secured the strongest castle on the Garonne without having to assault it.

*       *       *

The siege of Aiguillon was shorter. Though the exact date of its surrender is not known it must have taken place before December 10 and there are indications that it may have been the work of what we should now call "fifth columnists" inside the place. However that may be, Lord Derby had now secured the two bastions, as it were, that barred the approach to Bordeaux of a hostile army, or, conversely, the two gateways that opened the way to further advances into Agenais and Quercy.[1]

[1] In these respects his action may be compared with that of Wellington in capturing the twin bastions of Badajos and Ciudad Rodrigo before embarking on his invasion of Spain.

The earl of Derby was quick to take advantage of the open-ing. It would seem that he retained his army in two columns, one of which advanced up the Lot and the other up the Garonne, capturing or receiving the submission of all the towns in succession right up to the frontier of Quercy.

\*       \*       \*

Derby's first two campaigns had been brilliant in the extreme. He had regained a large area of territory, he had routed the best army that the French could put into the field against him, and he had established the moral superiority of the English army. And all this had been accomplished with a tiny force and at inconsiderable cost in lives.

Neither Froissart nor any of the other chroniclers report details of the latter campaign, but the evidence for it rests upon incontestable local documents which have been collected by Bertrandy, while the broad results are attested to by three English chroniclers who state that about 50 towns and castles fell into English hands. (Curiously enough, however, Agen, the next town up the Garonne and only 15 miles from Aiguillon, seems to have remained in French hands.)

The actions and intentions of John duke of Normandy during these first campaigns of Derby are extremely obscure.[1] The *Grandes Chroniques* alleges that in the course of them he returned to Paris in despair, where he was roundly taken to task by his father the king and sent south again. This French source would hardly have invented such a story (though it is often discredited by historians), but it is a fact that Philip, in spite of his dissatisfaction with his son, left him in command of the huge army that he now set about amassing for the reconquest of the lost province.

This army was drawn from all over France and it took several months to collect. The duke of Burgundy brought a contingent and the duke of Bourbon, who was the king's

[1] Bertrandy has with great ingenuity traced the main movements of the duke of Normandy during this period, but they throw little light on his intentions ud plans.

lieutenant at Agen, accompanied it. Jean le Bel gave its strength at the round figure of 100,000. Froissart blindly repeated this preposterous figure in his first *rédaction*, but later reduced it to 60,000. (Here again this correction has been over-looked by historians, who continue to repeat the figure 100,000). The sober and careful Robert of Avesbury gives 12,000 men-at-arms and a grand total of, say, 40,000 and this figure is cor-roborated by a French source, which includes large numbers of Genoese crossbowmen and many siege engines. Everything points to the fact that this army was exceptionally large for the period and it must have approached 20,000 in numbers. There is also good evidence that 24 cannon were constructed at Cahors for the siege of Aiguillon, at least five of which were taken to that siege by the army.[1]

The chroniclers are at variance about the rendezvous of the French army. By one account it was at Orleans, whence it advanced south toward Aiguillon, capturing en route various places including Angoulême, said to have been taken by Derby. It seems, however, that the rendezvous was Toulouse, 80 miles south-east of Aiguillon, and that the army advanced thence without opposition to Agen, which it reached on April 5, 1346. Here the duke tried to enlist some local levies, but was outwitted by the governor. A few days later the army moved forward to Aiguillon, apparently approaching it from the south.

Aiguillon is a small town with a dwindling population, prettily situated in the angle formed by the confluence of the Garonne and the Lot, both considerable rivers at this point. The castle is on an eminence commanding the Lot, and not far from the Garonne. The duke of Normandy rightly recognized its strategic importance, and accordingly selected it for his main objective. It was held by an English garrison under Lord Stafford, assisted by Walter Manny, and, according to some accounts, by the earl of Pembroke. Stafford had the foresight, on the approach of the enemy, to lay in a good store of pro-

[1] See LACABANE, LEON, *De la Poudre à Canon* (1845).

visions and warlike stores. He was thus well prepared for the siege that ensued. The French on the other hand experienced great difficulty in providing enough food for their immense host, the very size of which proved an embarrassment. The country round was soon swept bare of food and the lack of food may partly explain the large number of deserters from the invading army.

The siege was one of the most famous of that age and Froissart gives a spirited description of it. The French army took up its station in the first instance along the south bank of the Garonne, that is, on the far side to the town and castle. Here I follow Froissart, though it is hard to understand why the French did not approach along the north bank. No bridge was available, so the first task was to construct one, and this the French proceeded to do. Twice the English made a sortie and destroyed it, but eventually it was completed and the French crossed to the north side and the siege proper began. The duke of Normandy had such enormous forces that he was able to divide them into four parties or "shifts", one of which was always at work bombarding, attacking, and threatening the beleaguered town. The English, however, repelled every attack, and made constant sorties, in some of which it would seem they managed to replenish their supplies. In one audacious sortie they destroyed two barges full of supplies from Toulouse. John's next step was to get eight large catapults from Toulouse, together with four vessels specially constructed or adapted to convey them as close as possible to the walls. In a subsequent age they would be called bomb vessels, and in a still later age, monitors. The garrison received them with such a heavy "fire" from four large catapults of their own, that when one of the attacking machines had been damaged the attempt was abandoned. This was only one of many examples of what we should now call "counter-battery work" between the two "artilleries". Nothing could quench the spirit and resolution of the garrison, and John decided to sit down and reduce the castle by starvation, a course in which Philip VI at first concurred. To effect this he placed a blockading force down-stream, cutting off completely communication with La Réole.

All this time Edward III was preparing a great expedition for the relief of Aiguillon – as it was supposed. On July 11 the expedition set sail from the Isle of Wight, but instead of steering for Bordeaux it touched land in Normandy and soon overran that province. The situation was thus suddenly altered; Philip's best and biggest array was far away in the south, conducting a never-ending siege; it must be recalled at once. Messengers conveying orders to this effect were sent off hot-foot. As soon as he heard of the landing in France of Edward III, John sued for a truce. But Derby had also received the news and he contemptuously rejected it. There was nothing left but to raise the siege and depart for the north. On August 20, just six days before the battle of Crecy was fought, the great army of the duke of Normandy hastily broke up the siege and marched away to the north, leaving tents standing and an enormous quantity of supplies. The English army was left in undisputed possession of all its conquests.

During the siege the earl of Derby had taken up his head-quarters at La Réole. Here he collected supplies of troops and food, and on one occasion at least, June 16, he succeeded in running the blockade and throwing reinforcements of men and food into the beleaguered place. When, later in the siege, the blockade was tightened, this became impossible.

A week before the end of the siege Derby moved north to Bergerac, where he received and rejected the truce overtures to which we have already referred. Immediately following this he received the news that the French had abandoned the siege of Aiguillon.

The successful outcome of the siege of Aiguillon had an effect only slightly less striking than that of the victory of Auberoche. It was known throughout France that the king was making a supreme effort and concentrating overwhelming forces to drive the English into the sea. But the gallant defenders of Aiguillon, Gascon inhabitants and English soldiers, took on themselves the full brunt of the blow, and parried it. The duke of Normandy, who conducted more abortive operations against the English than any other general of his time, showed a pitiful lack of enterprise in this campaign. With his vast army it should have been possible both to ensure a more effective blockade of Aiguillon and at the same time to take the offensive elsewhere with a portion of his troops. As it was, "a handful of troops"–in the generous words of a French historian–"braved the united efforts of a complete *grande armée*, while another French historian declared that "the defence of Aiguillon covered with glory Sir Walter Manny and the earl of Pembroke".

When news of the abandonment of the siege of Aiguillon reached the earl of Derby he was at Bergerac with a small force. Immediately he set off for Aiguillon, which was 40 miles due south. He did not, however, take the direct road, but marched south-east to Villereal, 25 miles distant, which he captured. It is likely that his intention was to cut off any stragglers from the French army in its march to the north; but of this we have no particulars. He reached Villereal on August 27, seven days after the departure of the duke of Normandy, and next day pushed on to Aiguillon, where it is easy to imagine the scenes of rejoicing and congratulations when he met the victorious garrison. Here Derby remained for five days. There was much to be done: the place had to be "re-established", revictualled, sick and wounded removed, defences repaired and detachments sent out to keep touch with the retreating French and to restore English rule in the towns that had temporarily fallen to duke John.

### DERBY'S THIRD CAMPAIGN

But Henry of Lancaster, as he was beginning to be called, had no intention of letting the grass grow under his feet: the campaign of the English army in the north of France was in full swing, and diversions must be made in the south to detain as many enemy troops there as possible. Offensive operations must therefore be carried out in all possible directions, even though his numbers were pitiably small. The earl envisaged three campaigns; two based on Aiguillon were to recover and extend the English conquests in Agenais and Bazardois, while the third, under his own command, should operate in Saintonge and Poitou. To this end he reorganized his forces in three armies, and it is highly significant that he gave the command of the two southern armies not to English but to Gascon captains, for they were operating in the old English dominion of Aquitaine, and were themselves liege subjects of the king of England. Their task was to recover and hold, by friendly action rather than by force, those parts that had been lost. The army left available for the expedition into Poitou was a very small one, only 1,000 men-at-arms, according to Derby's own statement. It seems incredible that there should be no archers included, and he may have meant "lances" rather than "men-at-arms", and that one or possibly two mounted archers were attached to each man-at-arms. Froissart gives the numbers as 1,200 men-at-arms and 2,000 archers, and here the chronicler may for once not be so very far from the mark. He also mentions 3,000 infantry, and as Derby himself mentions posting some infantry in St. Jean d'Angelys later in his campaign, it may be that some infantry followed up the expedition on foot, catching up at towns where halts were made. Froissart's Rome edition also mentions the use of archers at the capture of Poitiers.

Derby spent eight days at La Réole, September 4 to 12, making these preparations, and on the 12th he set out on his third and last campaign. At the same time the other two armies set off in opposite directions. It has been suggested that by this dispersion of force the earl transgressed the principle of concentration of force. It would be truer to say that he fitted the means to the end. His French opponent had indeed kept his whole force concentrated in front of Aiguillon and to what end? The principle of economy of force implies a nice appreciation of the minimum number of troops required for a given task, and such a distribution of forces that the maximum effect can be produced. Judging by results, this right distribution was attained by Derby. Though the chroniclers are disappointingly silent as to the operations in the south and east, it is established that all went well and that English troops penetrated far into Quercy, and almost to the walls of Toulouse. The consternation aroused extended to the shores of the Mediterranean.

Henry's own campaign can be followed in more detail and without having recourse to the unreliable and imaginative Froissart, for fortunately we possess the dispatch that Derby wrote toward the end of his campaign, the accuracy of which cannot be impugned.[1]

Poitou, whose capital was Poitiers, had not been in English hands since Henry III lost it, but parts of Saintonge, which lies immediately to the north of the Gironde, had had a more chequered history and might be expected to return willingly to the English allegiance. Derby's little army therefore set out full of hope on September 12, and spent that night at Sauveterre, nine miles to the north. For the next eight days they marched on the most direct route to Chateauneuf on the Charente, a distance of 75 miles, and arrived on September 20. The inhabitants closed their gates and as the town was on the north side of the river, which was unfordable, and the only bridge was broken down, they might well feel secure. But Derby set about repairing the bridge, and with such vigour did his men work that next day it was passable and the army marched over it to the attack of the town. Then some totally unexpected news arrived, to explain which we must hark back a little way.

On the relief of Aiguillon, Sir Walter Manny had pleaded to be allowed to join his old master the king in his Normandy campaign. The ways of medieval chivalry never cease to surprise us, and incredible as it may seem, this redoubtable

---

[1] This remarkable document is in medieval French, and is given with an English translation in the Rolls Series edition of Robert of Avesbury's chronicle.

knight, who had so often been a thorn in the side of the French, was by them granted a safe-conduct, not only for himself but for his own retinue, across France. They promptly set off, and no more was heard of them. But now, just as Derby was about to assault the town of Chateauneuf, the startling news arrived that Sir Walter Manny and his companions had been seized, in spite of their safe-conduct, and imprisoned in the castle at St. Jean d'Angelys. Manny and two others had "with great trouble" escaped, but the remainder were still incarcerated. Had Froissart heard of this adventure of his hero, what a story he would have made of his "great trouble"! St. Jean is 40 miles north-west of Chateauneuf, and the army was about to assault that town; but the good faith of an English knight had been violated, and Henry of Lancaster blazed with anger. His mind was made up at once; everything else must give place to the rescue of Sir Walter Manny's comrades in distress. The attack was called off, and the whole army marched that very day post haste to St. Jean. They arrived by the following day at the latest and promptly assailed and stormed the town. "We marched on towards the said town and assailed it and it was won by force, thank God, and the men brought forth from prison", wrote the earl in simple soldierly language.

It might be supposed that Derby would wreak his vengeance on the town for this shocking breach of faith, but he evidently realized that it was the fault of an individual, not of the whole town, and his treatment of it was lenient and statesmanlike. To quote his own words again: "And we stayed there eight days and established the town, and they of the town took oath and became English, and were bound at their own cost during the war to find 200 men-at-arms and 600 foot soldiers as garrison of the said town. . . ."

The comment of the French historian Henri Bertrandy is worth recording:—

"This conduct seems to me most honourable to the memory of Derby and also of Walter Manny. I do not descry anything more beautiful in the Guyenne war. The efficacy of the protection of

England could not show itself in a fashion more striking, more just or more happy. The act of Derby was at once the act of an honourable man, a courageous soldier and a skilful diplomat."

Henry of Lancaster spent nine days at St. Jean d'Angelys, occupying himself less as a soldier than as a diplomat, a role in which he had already had ample experience. The fruits of his activities will be seen presently. On the last day of September he departed, setting his face for Poitiers. The capital of Poitou lay 70 miles to the north-east, and, with little to impede the army, good progress was made. Three days later they came to Lusignan, described by Derby as "a strong town", but they took it by assault in the minimum of time. Continuing their advance early next morning, October 4, they reached Poitiers, after a march of 15 miles, early enough in the morning to deliver an attack that day, after summoning it to surrender in vain. The first assault failed, so the earl made more elaborate preparations for the next attempt.

The historic city of Poitiers, which gave its name to three famous battles, occupies a striking position on a crescent-shaped knoll, with a great bend of the river Clan sweeping round its eastern face. Thus the easiest approach is from the opposite side–the west–and the English probably approached from that side. (If they approached from the south-east, they must have crossed the swelling upland on which almost exactly ten years later another English army was to repeat the glories of Crecy.)

Derby seems to have acted with amazing speed. His troops had already marched 15 miles that day and had failed in an attack on a strong walled city. One might have supposed that the commander would spend the remaining hours of daylight in reconnaissance and preparations for another attack on the morrow. But that was not the way of Henry of Lancaster. Reconnaissance, plan, preparations and execution were all squeezed into what remained of that same day. Reconnaissance showed what appeared to be three weak spots in the defences. Derby decided to assault these three simultaneously. Dividing his slender army into three (it is unlikely that his dismounted troops had yet come up) he posted them opposite the three indicated points. Then at a signal the concentric assault was delivered under the usual covering fire from the archers, and was crowned with success. The French leaders managed to escape (probably swimming the river), but most of the garrison were rounded up inside. By the custom of the time, a town which, after being summoned, refused to surrender, could expect no quarter, and Derby in his dispatch writes: "All those in the city were taken or slain." Froissart avers that "the earl's people put everyone to the sword, men, women and little children". French historians have accepted and repeated Froissart's statement. But it is not true. Such conduct was foreign to Derby's nature and previous conduct. He had won golden opinions from the inhabitants of those parts since his arrival in the country; nor had the city offended in the way that St. Jean d'Angelys had in his eyes. Moreover, Froissart himself states that the earl prohibited any burning of churches or houses "under pain of death". Wholesale looting there was, and no doubt indiscriminate killing in hot blood by the excited assailants in the moment of victory, as there usually was in such circumstances until quite recent times. (For further examination of Froissart's statement see the appendix to this chapter.) But there is documentary proof that Derby undoubtedly showed greater sternness with the capital of Poitou, which he regarded as practically a foreign country as it had been outside the English dominion for so long, whereas St. Jean d'Angelys was situated in Saintonge, which had more recently accepted the king of England as its lord. More than that we cannot say.

On October 13 the army marched out of Poitiers on its return journey. The main body returned to St. Jean d'Angelys and detachments were dispatched throughout Saintonge during the next fortnight seizing or accepting the submission of most of its towns. It is almost certain that the towns which Froissart reports Derby as taking in the course of his advance to Poitiers were in reality taken during this fortnight. Meanwhile Henry established his headquarters at St. Jean, for which town he had acquired a liking. His diplomacy and moderation had procured a rich dividend. In Saintonge he came to be regarded as a popular hero. He was in excellent spirits and he entertained royally, by no means forgetting the ladies of the neighbourhood, who came flocking to his banquets. He was naturally pleased with what he called a *belle chevauchée*–inadequately translated "raid" by historians: it was more than a mere raid–it was an expedition.

On October 30 the earl re-entered Bordeaux amid the plaudits of an enthusiastic populace. After a short stay he handed over the duties of King's Lieutenant and sailed for England. On New Year's Day, 1347, he landed in the home country. On January 14 he arrived in London and the very same day he visited David king of Scotland, who had been captured at the battle of Neville's Cross and incarcerated in the Tower. Henry of Lancaster was not the man to let the grass grow under his feet.

*    *    *

In just 14 months the diminutive English army which had landed in Bayonne in June, 1345, had fought three campaigns and, under the inspiring leadership of Henry of Lancaster, had not only driven the French out of most of the old dominions of our Angevin kings, but had spread the dread of the English arms far and wide, even to the shores of the Mediterranean. The first campaign, on the Dordogne, had removed the threat to Bordeaux from the direction of Paris, and recovered a large part of Périgord; the second, on the Garonne, had safeguarded the capital from the direction of Toulouse, had regained most of Agenais and Quercy and had penetrated into Languedoc almost as far as Toulouse itself; the third campaign, with a minimum of fighting, had recovered Saintonge and subdued most of Poitou. For the moment there was no fight left in the French. The land had peace: for the moment.

Before leaving the war in Gascony, a final word must be said about the illustrious Englishman who, with a mere handful of troops, had so signally reversed the fortunes of his country in south-western France. For though Comte d'Erbi, as the French called him, lived to do important work, both military and diplomatic, and indeed became the king's right-hand man, his "maid of all work" . . . his most notable campaign was that in Gascony. In spite of the regrettable paucity of records, such as do exist point unerringly in one direction: Henry of Grosmont, Derby and Lancaster, was a *chevalier sans peur et sans reproche*. There were giants in the land in those days and Derby was one of the greatest of them. But an assessment made by a compatriot may be biased and suspect. Let us hear then what a dispassionate French historian, one who has made a deeper study of Derby's campaigns than anyone, has to say. I refer, of course, to Henri Bertrandy. He has sensed the grandeur of this redoubtable opponent of his country, so that he is able to write on the last page and in the last paragraph of his *Études:*

"These campaigns have imprinted upon the memory of Derby an indestructible glory. This illustrious Englishman displayed all the qualities which in their entirety form the appanage of the truly great."

A soldier is not without honour – save in his own country.

## APPENDIX

### THE BATTLEFIELD OF AUBEROCHE

This battle, though the most important of the whole war in Gascony until the final contest at Castillon, is so little known that a rather extended note on the subject seems justified. Its very site had been forgotten, and even Sir James Ramsay, whose reputation for accuracy is great, located it wrongly. The correct site was suggested by a French monk in 1742 and was established definitely in 1865 by the French historian, M. Bertrandy, Director of the Archives at Bordeaux, but his researches

in this field have never been translated into the English
language. They are tucked away in a series of *Études* on
Froissart's *Chroniques*, and thus have been too easily overlooked. Further reference to Bertrandy and his *Études* will be
found later.

## THE SOURCES FOR AUBEROCHE

There are, so far as I can discover, eight sources for the battle.
Four of these give only bald facts, such as numbers and names
of participants. From the remaining four sources, the story of
the actual battle must be reconstructed. The first of these is
Adam Murimuth's *Chronicle*, written within two years of the
battle. The second is the *Continuatio chronicarum*, written a few
years later. The third is *Istoria Fiorentini* by Giovanni Villani.
(It has never been translated into English.) The fourth is
Froissart's *Chronicles*. His original edition dates from 1369–72;
the Amiens edition about 1376, the Rome edition about 1400,
and the *Abrégées* (or abridged version) a few years later. The
first two sources are naturally the most reliable, but they differ
on the important question of the relative damage inflicted
by the archers and men-at-arms. Villani's account, though
useful for numbers, gives few details. We thus have to rely
almost entirely on Froissart for details of the actual fighting. A
further cautionary word must therefore be said about the reliability of the famous chronicler. Where he could, he followed
Jean le Bel, whose bald story he shamelessly embellished with
figments of his own imagination. But among these fanciful
passages he frequently inserted stories that he had heard from
the lips of participants or at second or third hand from them.
This is particularly the case where Gascony is concerned, for
he twice visited the country and picked up many of his
details on or near the spot. We must therefore look for circumstantial details which seem to ring true. Where they seem to
do this there is no *a priori* reason to reject them entirely,
though embellishment had become so ingrained in Froissart's
work that even here it may be present. M. Henri Bertrandy,

9

probably the most profound Froissart scholar for the period, sums up the Chronicler as "une autorité des plus suspectes".[1]

In judging the reliability of any of his stories where they are not corroborated by other sources, one is therefore reduced to the test of inherent military probability. If his account of a battle can be shown to fit in with the terrain about which he can have had no personal knowledge, it follows that he probably received it from an eye-witness. In the case of Auberoche, that is precisely what it does. To prove this I must record my own experiences when visiting the battlefield. From his description I formed in my mind a picture of the terrain and scene, indeed a clear-cut one. When I approached the field and, turning a corner in the road, came into full view of it, I felt almost as if I had seen it before, so exactly did it agree with the picture in my mind's eye. This, I felt, justified me in accepting all the essentials of Froissart's account of the battle.

LOCATION OF THE BATTLEFIELD

It is no easy matter to ascertain the approximate location of the field, and then to get to it. In 1865, M. Bertrandy visited Auberoche and described it. Probably very few Englishmen have visited the place since then, or indeed since the end of the Hundred Years War. As to the location, there are several places with the name Auberoche in Gascony. In 1863 the French historian of Gascony, Henri Ribadieu, identified it with Caudrot on the river Garonne.[2] Five years later he was refuted by M. Bertrandy who established the location as Auberoche-en-Périgord, and his location holds the field. If anyone doubted it he would obtain instant corroboration by visiting this place and noting how exactly it tallies with Froissart's description.

This Auberoche must be one of the hardest to find and most inaccessible places in southern France. The region lies in a backwater; it is sparsely inhabited, and there are few roads and

---

[1] *Études sur les Chroniques de Froissart* (1865), p. 84.
[2] In *Les Campagnes du Comte de Derby* (1863).

railways though a good road traverses the battlefield. It is practically impossible to obtain a large-scale map of it, and I found the only practicable method of reaching it was by taxi from Périgueux. This involved a nine-mile journey, and even the taxi driver was doubtful of its location.

The castle occupies a striking situation, dominating two straight stretches of the valley. A few houses cluster round the foot of the rock on which the castle is perched. Of the castle itself nothing remains above ground except the chapel and owing to thick undergrowth it is difficult to trace out the lines in places. But the natural strength of the place is obvious at a glance, and the anxiety of the Comte de l'Isle to recapture it is understandable.

## LA RÉOLE

No town in Gascony was more closely connected with the English occupation than La Réole. Six English kings, one after another, made their mark on it. Henry II on succeeding to it demolished the main tower known as *Des Soeirs*: Richard Coeur de Lion often resided there; he restored the walls—some of his handiwork remains to this day—as also does the house in which tradition declares he stayed; he is also reputed to have made it the rendezvous for the contingents that accompanied him on his famous crusade, though this is disputed. John granted it commercial rights; Simon de Montfort was once its governor, so was Richard of Cornwall, king of the Romans; Henry III besieged it twice and took it once. Prince Edward (afterward Edward I) came here to receive the fealty of his barons; his son, the earl of Kent, occupied it, but eventually lost it to Charles le Bel, king of France. In the course of 300 years I calculate that it changed hands between English and French, sometimes peacefully but more often by violence, no fewer than 16 times. All the above is eloquent testimony to the value placed upon it by succeeding generations of kings and soldiers, this being mainly because of its strong strategic situation, blocking or protecting the line of approach to Bordeaux from the south-east. The river does not now lap the foot of the castle but no doubt it did so originally. The walls, still immensely strong, remain for a large part of the perimeter.

## FROISSART'S ACCOUNT OF THE SIEGE OF LA RÉOLE

I have so frequently had occasion to warn readers against statements by the old chronicler, that readers may be surprised at the amount of credence I have placed upon his accounts of La Réole, but it is almost certain that he visited the scene during either or both of his sojourns in Gascony. No doubt he over-dramatized the story, but if we allow for such embroideries there still remains a solid core of fact. Froissart, in his account of the war in Gascony, is weakest in his chronology. This was first thoroughly probed by Henri Bertrandy, who in 1870 exposed the errors that had been accepted by Henri Ribadieu in his *Les Campagnes du Comte de Derby*–the only attempt at a detailed account of these campaigns that has been written. Unfortunately it is very difficult to obtain a copy of this book. It is printed in a rare French publication entitled *Actes de l'Académie des beaux arts . . . de Bordeaux*, Vol. XXV for 1863. The author subsequently admitted that he had been mistaken in his chronology, which he had accepted unquestioningly from Froissart, and it is significant that he skated very lightly over all Derby's campaigns in his subsequent *La Conquête de la Guyenne*. But for the student, a study of his "Campagnes" is indispensable.

## FROISSART AND POITIERS

In the text we have discussed the inherent improbability of Froissart's assertion that all the women and children were put to the sword. The following note examines in greater detail the passage in question.

(1) There is documentary proof that Froissart exaggerated, to say the least, for the names of certain Frenchmen who were ransomed are known.

(2) The words "every man, woman and child" tripped too easily off the irresponsible tongue of the chronicler. He made the same accusation (though with more imaginative detail) against the Black Prince at the sack of Limoges, and its falsity has since been proved up to the hilt[1] Froissart was more an artist than an historian, and he required ample light and shade for his picture.

(3) The only local and contemporary French account that I can trace does not mention killings at all; its indignation is centred on the pillaging of ecclesiastical property. It is contained in the little-known *Cronique de Maillezais* and the Latin may be translated as follows:

"In the year 1346 on October 4 was captured the city of Poitiers and the castle of Lusignan on the previous day, by Henry count of Lancaster, lieutenant of the king of England. For nine days with all his army he devastated much and seized the goods of the said city and took away with him ornaments from the churches."

But the most revealing proof that Froissart was in error comes from Froissart himself. In both the *Rome* and *Abrégées* editions he quietly omitted the offending passage that all women and children were put to the sword; in the *Rome* edition he substituted the statement that there was much killing ("grand ocision") and in the *Abrégées* he borrowed from le Bel the statement that many women were violated. Le Bel adds that the earl of Derby was much distressed thereby, but could do nothing about it. That is likely enough. But the trouble is that both our English translations were made before the discovery of the *Amiens, Rome* or *Abrégées* editions, none of which has been translated into English. It is as if, for example, only the original edition of Oman's *Art of War in the Middle Ages* had been published, the second edition being left in manuscript.

BIBLIOGRAPHICAL NOTE ON DERBY'S CAMPAIGNS

The earl of Derby's campaigns in Gascony have been studied by English historians less than almost any other

---

[1] By A. Leroux, *Le Sac de la Cité de Limoges* (1906). See also *The Sack of Limoges*, by A. H. Burne (*The Fighting Forces*, Feb. 1949.)

campaign in the Hundred Years War: indeed it would not be far from the truth to say that they have not been really studied at all. It may therefore be of help to the student of the war if I devote some space to the literature on the subject.

The sources, as will have been apparent from the preceding pages, are scanty. That erudite scholar Henri Bertrandy, after burrowing into the deepest recesses in his efforts to arrive at the truth, wrote despairingly of the "dense and distant darknesses" (épaisses et lointaines ténèbres) that cloud the path of the researcher. The French chronicles of the period pass it by almost in silence. The *Grandes Chroniques* for example allot but a single page, and the *Chronique de Richard Lescot, Chronique Normande* and *Chronographia* are equally brief. The English chronicles provide a good deal more, particularly *Robert of Avesbury* (Bertrandy alludes aptly to "the bald but accurate laconicisms of Robert of Avesbury"). Also useful, but in a lesser degree, are *Knighton, Murimuth* and *Walsingham*. The above must be supplemented by contemporary documents – mostly local – which have been collected by two Benedictine monks, Vaisseté and Duvic,[1] in their *Histoire de Languedoc* and published in 1742. On the above sources a framework of the war in Gascony can be built up. But detail is almost completely absent. For this we have to depend upon Jean Froissart (who in turn based his Chronicles on another Jean, the Liégois Jean le Bel).

Fortunately, in the case of the war in Gascony, we have an admirable guide in Henri Bertrandy, to whom we have frequently referred in the foregoing chapter. The closer one examines his work the deeper becomes one's admiration for this erudite and fair-minded scholar. His book is a curious one. It was published in 1870 under the misleading title "*Etudes sur les chroniques de Froissart*". It takes the form of six letters addressed to Leon Lacabane "Mon cher Oncle et très excellent Maître". These letters are primarily directed to an examination of Henri Ribadieu's *Les Campagnes du Comte de Derby*, and by deft and penetrating criticism he demolished the claims of

[1] Cited as Vic in Ramsay's *Genesis of Lancaster*.

the book to be genuine history. This, though we must accept it, is regrettable, for Ribadieu's book is the only single work on the war in Gascony that exists. M. Ribadieu sets out to prove that Froissart did not deserve the criticism and suspicion heaped upon him, but that his chronicle of the War in Gascony was accurate in chronology, indeed more so than even Derby's dispatch. The book, however, contains some useful notes and identifications of places.

Yet another invaluable book hides its nature in an unexpected title: *La Désolation des Églises . . . en France pendant la Guerre de Cent Ans* by Father Henri Deniflé, published in 1899. It is factual, accurate and precise, and can be used conveniently to establish the chronological and topographical framework for the war and is admirably documented. (This applies to the whole war, not only to the campaigns in Gascony.)

The above exhausts the list of essential books. It will be noted that it is not only short, but contains not a single work written by an Englishman, or even translated into English. The best edition of Froissart is that of Simeon Luce, and it is invaluable for its notes. Incidentally, it makes full use and acknowledgment of Bertrandy's work, so that it to some extent replaces that work if it cannot be procured (though there is a copy in the British Museum Library).

# CHAPTER VI

# THE CRECY CAMPAIGN, 1346

ALL through the winter of 1345 and spring of 1346 Edward was preparing for the invasion of northern France. His plan of campaign was what we should now describe as a strategical combination on exterior lines: in other words three armies, operating from three widely distant points, were to face inward toward the centre, from the north, the north-west, and the south-west respectively. This must not be understood too literally: there was no question of the three armies advancing on three radii, as it were, all directed on Paris, the centre; but there was *the threat* of such an operation, and it was calculated to upset the mental equilibrium of the French king. The fact that, in reality, one army might not get very far in the direction of Paris mattered little if it drew away hostile forces from the other two, thus making their progress the easier.

But Edward's plan went further than this: a fourth army was involved, that of the Anglo-Flemings. This army, small in numbers, was to advance south-westward through Artois simultaneously with that of the king, whose landing was to be somewhere on the north coast of France. These two armies while approaching the enemy's capital would be approaching each other, and before the main French army was engaged they looked forward to uniting their forces.

It was an ambitious plan in any period of warfare, but particularly so for a medieval army whose communications were slow and, when dependent on the sea, very precarious. Even as late as Napoleonic times this form of strategy was looked upon askance until it succeeded signally against the Corsican himself in the Leipzig campaign of 1813. How far Edward planned ahead and what measure of success he expected to reap from it is a fascinating question, but one that will never be answered, for the English king was secretive in his words and writings where military operations were concerned. Just before his Flanders campaign of 1340 he had ordered all foreigners trying to leave the country to be detained till after he had sailed. In the present case he gave out that his objective was Gascony: he was going to the help of the earl of Derby in general and to the relief of Aiguillon in particular. He may indeed at one time have had the intention to act in the South, and if so it is again a fascinating but insoluble speculation about when and why he changed his mind. On April 6, 1346, he had ordered certain troops to collect at Portsmouth "for service wherever he might lead them", but on May 6 he informed the church authorities in London that he was going to Gascony. This was evidently dust in their eyes, being intended to reach the enemy, for prayers were to be said for the success of the expedition. We have related the part played in this plan by Brittany and Gascony. Let us now follow the king's army.

For months preceding the actual invasion, desultory negotiations were going on with France through the Pope, for a renewal of the truce. Edward can hardly have been serious in these negotiations, and at times his conduct appears to us as uncomfortably reminiscent of that of Adolf Hitler. But it would seem that if the king of England was not serious and was utilizing the time gained to increase his armed forces, the king of France was doing the same. Apart from the large army that Philip had sent to Gascony under his eldest son, he was taking various measures to strengthen his forces in the north, and in particular to collect a formidable fleet in the English Channel. Whether this was for offensive or defensive purposes was never made really clear. Probably the French king had both eventualities in mind. As for the morality of preparing for a possible war under the cloak of pacific utterances, this has been an almost normal procedure throughout recorded history. An aggressor will obviously do all he can to prevent his potential opponent strengthening his forces *pari passu* with his own. This may sound like casuistry, but it at least shows that Edward was not any worse than the normal commander of an army about to invade another country.

By early April Edward had concentrated at Portsmouth and Southampton an army of about 15,000 combatants, over twice as large as had ever previously crossed the Channel. Only 2,000 were men-at-arms. They were, as far as possible, picked troops. Froissart's *Abrégées* is careful to point out that the king called for "the best" archers. (For details see the appendix.) To transport this army a fleet of upward of 700 vessels had been brought round the coast to Spithead and Portsmouth harbour. The flat expanse of Southsea Common was a mass of tents and pavilions: but it could be hidden from prying French eyes more effectually than if the base had been Dover or Margate.

All through May and June foul winds blowing up from the south-west prevented the fleet from setting sail. At length, on July 5, all seemed favourable and the leading vessels of the great armada set off. But again adverse gales forced them to turn back. The whole fleet then anchored off St. Helen's and prayed for a favouring wind. For nearly a week they were obliged to wait and it would be surprising if the morale of the wretched troops, cooped up for long days in their cockle-shells, did not suffer; for "hope deferred maketh the heart sick".

On July 11 Edward again gave orders for the whole fleet to weigh anchor and follow him out to sea, under sealed orders. When out of sight of land these orders were announced, and to nearly everyone's surprise the destination was found to be, not Gascony, but Normandy. The landing was to be made on the Cotentin peninsula, at St. Vaast la Hogue, 18 miles east of Cherbourg. It is natural to inquire the reasons why Edward selected this point. The answer usually given is that the king was merely following the advice of Godfrey de Harcourt, a French baron who had been banished from his ancestral estate

of St. Sauveur le Vicomte. Harcourt was thirsting for revenge
and did not hesitate to go over to his king's enemies and offer
to serve under the English banner in Normandy. This may
appear treasonable conduct to us, but we must remember
that the instinct of nationalism was not fully developed in
those days, that Edward was by many regarded as the lawful
king of France, and that Normandy had been throughout the
twelfth century an English possession. Harcourt knew the
country all over the Cotentin and should thus prove a valuable
guide, if nothing more. Moreover, quite a number of the
Cotentin nobility favoured the English cause. Furthermore, the
Cotentin was the nearest land to the Isle of Wight, and a short
sea crossing provided obvious attractions in those days of sail,
and especially in that summer of storms.[1] But Edward may
have had other and deeper strategical reasons for selecting
the Cotentin. Cherbourg and Ghent are equidistant from Paris.
Now Ghent was the base from which the "Three Towns"–
Ghent, Bruges and Ypres–were to operate in the combined
operation. The two lines–Cherbourg-Paris and Ghent-Paris–
enclose a right angle. Thus, if Paris was the common objective
Philip VI would be confronted with two widely separated but
equidistant opponents. In approaching each other they would
be approaching his capital, and he would find it difficult to
know how to distribute his forces in order to oppose each enemy
successfully.

As for the French, Philip had just achieved a notable diplomatic success: he had drawn the shifty duke of Brabant partially,
and John of Hainault wholly, to his side; indeed John fought
under his banner at Crecy. Hence Philip was not very concerned about the upshot of the fighting in Flanders; he decided
to concentrate the bulk of his army against the English attack.
As his land troops were slow in gathering he depended for
immediate protection on his fleet. This he collected in the
English Channel; but he made the mistake of scattering it
all along the coast in such a manner that it was weak every-

[1] Probably as bad as the summer of 1944.

where, for, as has been pointed out by Frederick the Great, Napoleon, and Sir Winston Churchill, "if you try to defend everywhere you will be weak everywhere". The French fleet was weak everywhere and was quite ineffective in preventing the English from landing.[1] Meanwhile the French army was concentrating in the neighbourhood of Paris, but the records are distressingly scanty on the subject.

### THE OPENING MOVES

The voyage of the English expeditionary force across the Channel was a speedy and uneventful one, the French ships keeping at a prudent distance, and on the morrow, July 12, the expedition made land at St. Vaast. The first thing the king did on setting foot on land was to knight his son, the Prince of Wales, and several of his companions. There was a practical reason for this, as the Prince was to be the titular commander of the advanced guard. He was now 16 years old, quite a usual age for a prince in medieval times to be given a military command. Besides the royal prince, the other leaders of the army were the earls of Warwick (the Marshal) and Northampton (the Constable) and Sir Richard Talbot; but most of the baronage of England who were of military age and not employed in other theatres of the war were also with the army.

Edward decided to direct his march slightly to the south of Rouen in the first stage. This was the shortest route to Flanders, as Rouen was the lowest point on the river Seine that was bridged. Moreover, this route would not be far distant from the sea in its early stages, and the fleet would thus provide a sort of movable base. Finally, it was almost the direct route to Paris.

The headquarters of the army moved inland three and a half miles to Morselines on July 13, while the troops and stores were being disembarked. Allowing five days more for organization—a short enough period—the army set off on its great

---

[1] Almost exactly 600 years later Rommell made the same mistake on the same coast.

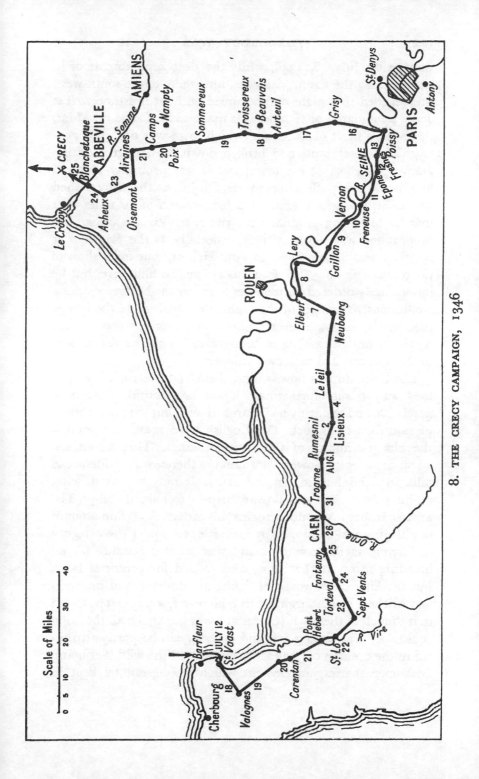

8. THE CRECY CAMPAIGN, 1346

venture on July 18, 1346, while the fleet kept abreast of it,
sailing along the coast. Valognes, nine miles to the south-west,
was reached that night and occupied without resistance. Next
day a long march of 16 miles was made to St. Come-du-Mont,
three miles short of Carentan, which town was occupied next
day. The inhabitants had broken down the bridge over the
Douve just short of the town, but it was promptly repaired
by Edward's very efficient pioneers. On July 21 the army pushed
on for St. Lô, which entailed a long march of 16 miles over
marshy low-lying ground, with the river Vire to cross. The
programme was too ambitious, especially as the bridge over
the river was broken down at Pont Hebert, four miles short of
the town. The king therefore was obliged to halt here, but he
immediately ordered his pioneers to repair the bridge. Working
continuously throughout the night, they had made the bridge
passable by dawn. It seems likely that special stores for the
repair of bridges had been brought out with the expedition.
St. Lô was reached next day, July 22.

The Cotentin was now behind them and the road lay open
for Caen, 26 miles further east. Up to date resistance had been
negligible and the army had marched well, but the same cannot
be said for its conduct. The English were marching through
the old patrimony of the Norman kings. Throughout the
advance across Lower Normandy there was widespread
pillaging and burning by the army. It may be asked, what
military advantage did Edward expect to gain thereby? The
answer is that it was done against his orders. A certain amount
of pillaging was condoned by him: it came under the category
of "living on the country" and was usual procedure for an
invading army at that time, and indeed for centuries later.
But the king disapproved of deliberate damage and burnings
and Michael Northburgh, writing home a few days later, stated
that "much of the town (Carentan) was burnt, for all the King
could do." The lawless acts and excesses can be partly attributed in the opinion of James Mackinnon to "the wild Welsh and
Irish mercenaries, an element which would not be kept in

control by the canons of chivalry". But there was probably a further explanation of the widespread and apparently senseless burnings. A considerable number of the English army came from the south coast, where there had been many recent burnings by French sailors; Portsmouth and Southampton were sufferers in this respect. To such people it was a mere act of revenge. Also the fact that the army advanced on a wide front made effective control by the senior officers impossible. There were however times when the king did resort to burnings for a military object. For example, he wrote complacently to the archbishop of York that his fleet had ravaged and burnt the whole coast-line including every ship they could find. This seems to have been both an act of revenge and one of security. If the French had no ships they could not repeat their raids on the Hampshire coast.

We need not therefore be too exercised by the incessant accusations by the old chroniclers of burning and pillaging—*ardant et gastant*—the words come tripping off their pens with almost mechanical reiteration. At the same time it must be admitted that a vast amount of damage was done, and that the peasants fled in terror before the advancing army—an act that made the pillaging all the worse, for soldiers will pillage an abandoned domicile when they will respect one still lived in.

After passing St. Lô the army opened out, marching on a front of several kilometres. The king marched in the centre with the main body, the right wing had with it Godfrey de Harcourt, while the left wing was under the earl of Warwick. On July 23 the main body reached Sept Vents, one mile south-west of Caumont, 14 miles east by south of St. Lô, the left wing taking the more direct Caen road—that is, due east—to Comolain. The next day only five and a half miles were covered, to Torteval. On July 25, still making straight for Caen, the army reached Fontenay, an eight and a half miles march. The reason for the shortness of these two last marches is not apparent. Possibly the fleet was lagging behind, or possibly Edward suspected the near approach of the French king and army. If so, he was mistaken: Philip was far away. At Fontenay the army was only ten miles from Caen, and Edward that evening sent a cleric as envoy to the city with a message to the burgesses that their lives and property would be respected if they would submit peaceably. The message was contemptuously rejected by the bishop of Bayeux, who was the leading spirit in the threatened city. Indeed, so spirited was he that he ostentatiously tore up the message and threw the unfortunate cleric into prison. The glove of defiance having been thrown, the militant bishop withdrew into the castle with 100 men-at-arms and 200 Genoese archers, leaving the constable, count Eu, and the chamberlain, count Tancarville, to defend the town as best they could.

Receiving no reply to his peace overtures, next morning, July 26, Edward resumed his advance, his army now narrowed into a single column—advanced guard, main body (with the baggage), and rearguard.

## CAPTURE OF CAEN

The historic old town of Caen, the stone of which enriches so many great English buildings and the story of which is so intimately connected with William the Conqueror, was—and is—curiously situated. At the point where the river Odon runs into the Orne, the latter river divides into two branches, thus forming an island. The northern branch of the river divided the town into two parts; the old town to the north, and the new town, on the island to the south, known from its church as the Île de St. Jean. The castle is on a slight eminence on the northern edge of the old town. Neither old nor new town was fortified, but the latter, being on an island, possessed a natural line of water defences; moreover its three bridges—those of St. Pierre and the Boucherie on the north, and the Millet on the south—were protected by fortified gateways. The castle, largely the work of William I and Henry I, with its forbidding moat on two sides, constituted a formidable obstacle to an army that did not possess engines for siege warfare. Situated a

few hundred yards west and east of that old town lie respectively the famous Abbayes aux Hommes and aux Dames. The
weakest sector was the old town which, apart from what protection the castle could give it on the north and the river on the

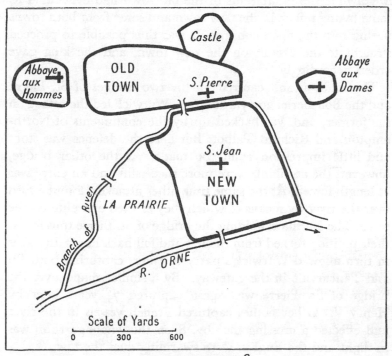

9. CAEN IN 1346

south, was quite defenceless. Edward rightly resolved to
concentrate his first attack against the old town, leaving the
castle for the time being unmolested. The advanced guard was
therefore ordered to march round the north side of the castle
and take possession of the Abbaye aux Dames as a first step to
a general assault. The remainder of the army followed in three
columns, and formed up facing the northern and western sides
of the old town. When the whole army was thus deployed for
action the king ordered the troops to be rested after their ten

10

mile march and for food to be served out. The advantage of
having the baggage in the middle of the long column was now
apparent, for no long delay was required before it should
appear. By the time all had fed it was about nine o'clock.
Meanwhile the inhabitants of the old town had evacuated it,
some taking refuge in the new town and some from both towns
fleeing into the open country. It was thus possible to proceed
straight to the assault on the new town, and the king gave
orders accordingly.

The main assault centred on the two bridges of St. Pierre
and the Boucherie, 200 yards apart. Warwick led the attack on
the former, and was backed up by the contingents of Northampton and Richard Talbot. But here the defence was stout
and little impression could be made. At the other bridge,
however, the assailants were more successful and an entry was
at length forced. At the same time other attackers found a ford
over the river by means of which they crossed and entered the
town. The Normans holding the bridge of St. Pierre thus found
their position turned from the left and fell back hurriedly. This
in turn allowed Warwick's party to enter, capturing both Eu
and Tancarville in the gateway. (By a similar manoeuvre the
bridge of St. Pierre was again captured 74 years later by
Henry V.) Other bodies captured French vessels in the river
and effected a crossing thereby. Soon the whole garrison was
in flight and the English were swarming over the town.

While this attack was going on under the very eyes of the
garrison of the castle, scarcely 300 yards away, not a single
attempt was made to assist the hard-pressed townsmen, or
even to make a demonstration on their behalf. The castle
defenders were ideally situated for this purpose, and we can
only suppose that Edward, anticipating some such action, had
taken counter-measures of which no record has survived.

The navy also played its part in the capture of Caen. Whilst
the army had, as related above, been marching eastward
towards the town, the fleet had kept abreast of it, sailing along
the coast of Normandy and ravaging and burning various ports

on the way. Reaching the estuary of the Orne at Ouistrehan it had sailed up the river and arrived opposite the town at approximately the same time as the army. It is possible that the simultaneous arrival was deliberately planned, but such synchronization of land and sea forces was extremely difficult to effect, as King John had discovered to his cost when attempting to relieve Chateau Gaillard 150 years before. Whether fortuitous or not, the arrival of the fleet was a happy one, for 30 French vessels were afloat in the port or in the river, and the army and fleet between them speedily accounted for every one of them. The arrival of the fleet was happy in another respect: prisoners had been taken, also spoil; there were sick soldiers to be sent home, including the earl of Huntingdon. All these returned to England, accompanied by part of the fleet. The prisoners were, of course, those who were fortunate enough to be able to offer a ransom; the remainder met with no quarter, for by the custom of the time the defenders of a town which had been duly summoned and had refused to surrender had no right to quarter once the town had been stormed. Looting also was widespread, again a custom of the time, especially in the case of a town from which the bulk of the inhabitants had fled. The number of Frenchmen who perished that day is put by our best authority at 2,500.

The army halted for five days at Caen. This halt is not as easy to explain or justify as the halt at St. Vaast. There was, of course, much to do; reorganization, dispatch of the sick, wounded, prisoners and spoil, the latter including an incriminating letter written by Philip VI to the burgesses of the city in 1338, enjoining them to prepare for an invasion of England. The troops also required some rest, having marched 82 miles in nine days, shortly after being cooped up for days on board ship. During the halt Bayeux, which had been by-passed, surrendered to the English army.[1]

[1] A portion of the fleet sailed for home without orders and this has led to the untenable suggestion that Edward had intended to abandon the expedition and sail home by it, but that its departure obliged him to carry on with the campaign.

THE ADVANCE TO PARIS

By July 31 all was in order and the advance was resumed. Marching at a steady pace due east, the army made eight miles that day to Troarne, ten miles on August 1 to Rumesnil, and nine on August 2 to Lisieux. If the army continued on the same line it would strike the river Seine midway between Rouen and Paris. Its future movements were likely to depend on the counter-moves of the French king and on the supporting moves of the Flemish allies. It is time therefore to glance at both these armies.

Though Philip had, of course, been aware that an invasion was to be expected he had no inkling of where it would take place. Prudently therefore he retained his main army centrally situated at Paris. News of the invasion reached him at his chateau at Becoiseau. He repaired instantly to the capital, arriving at Vincennes on July 19, the second day of the English advance. Three days later he went to St. Denys to obtain the sacred Oriflamme, with which to lead his army against the invader. The next move was obvious–to Rouen, the capital of Normandy–and thither he marched at a rapid pace. He and his army, of which we have no indications as to the strength, arrived at Rouen on August 2, the day on which the rival army reached Lisieux. The two opponents were now 40 miles apart, and the French held a commanding strategic position in a straight line between their two opponents, and in possession of the main crossing of the river Seine, here about 300 yards wide. Up to date it is difficult to criticize Philip's strategy. He had correctly gauged the route taken by Edward, and had acted accordingly.

And now, what of the Flemish army? To answer this it will be necessary to go back to June 24. On that date a meeting at Ghent of the Three Towns–Ghent, Bruges and Ypres–had agreed to cooperate with the king of England in the forthcoming campaign, and to go wherever he should desire them. Taking advantage of this satisfactory development, Edward had fitted out a small expedition, consisting of some men-at-

arms and 600 archers, under the command of Sir Hugh
Hastings, John Molyneux and John Maltravers. On July 16 this
force sailed for Flanders in 20 vessels and joined the Flemish
army at Ghent. The whole allied army was put under the
command of count Henry of Flanders. On August 2, as
Edward was marching into Lisieux, the Anglo-Flemish army
set out, probably from Ypres, to cooperate with the English
army that was advancing to meet it. Edward's plan of campaign
was, it will be remembered, to unite these two armies before
committing his own forces to a close engagement with the
probably superior French army. But Ypres was distant 190
miles from Lisieux, and there were at least two formidable
rivers in the way, the Seine and the Somme. The shortest line
of approach for the Flemish army would take them via Arras
and Amiens, where, if both armies advanced at the same pace,
they should join forces. The combined allied grand army could
then turn with some assurance of success against the main
French army. Such was the plan, and despite its ambitious
nature, it was one to be commended. Communication between
the two armies was, of course, the main difficulty and, though
we are told that each army was informed of the other's progress,
it must have been only at wide and uncertain intervals, as
communications had to go by sea.

The English army, as we have said, reached Lisieux on
August 2. It halted for one day at Lisieux, while two cardinals,
sent by the Pope, put out fruitless pleas for peace, and news
or rumours of the French king's movements probably reached it
at the same time. But Edward pursued his march next day,
August 4, on the old line, reaching Le Teil Nollent that night, a
long march of 16 miles. Next day, still continuing eastward, the
march was even longer and 19 miles were covered. The route
was via Brienne, and Neubourg was reached that night.

On Sunday August 6, the main body halted while a reconnaissance under Godfrey de Harcourt was thrown out toward
Rouen, which now lay 23 miles to the north-east. The French
king had put in charge of the defences of Rouen the count de

Harcourt, elder brother of the traitor Godfrey. The count dug trenches on the southern outskirts of the city and sent forward a small body which had a skirmish with Godfrey's party. The latter, having obtained the required information, fell back to the main body and reported. If Edward had ever hoped to cross the Seine at Rouen (which is unlikely) he now realized that it was impossible. Only one course remained open—to attempt a crossing higher upstream between Rouen and Paris. His previous advance had had this possibility in view. Instead, however, of continuing on the same line and meeting the river at about Gaillon, Edward turned sharp to his left on August 7 and after marching 11 miles touched the river at Elbeuf. This rather surprising move brought him within a dozen miles of the main French army, but Edward no doubt banked on securing the river crossing by this sudden unexpected move. In this, however, he was disappointed; the bridge was destroyed and on August 8 he was obliged to push on upstream, looking for a further crossing. Pont de l'Arche was the first place bridged, but he hardly expected to obtain this crossing for the town lies to the south of the bridge and was walled and strongly fortified (as Henry V discovered 70 years later). The river Eure joins the Seine just east of Pont de l'Arche and the army pushed up it to Lery, a march of nine miles. While passing Pont de l'Arche, according to the *Grandes Chroniques*, Edward received from Philip a challenge to single combat. To this he sent answer that he would fight his rival in front of Paris. What did either king mean by these exchanges? It is hard to say, but probably Philip's reason was a psychological one: he had declined Edward's challenge to single encounter seven years before, and his conscience was no doubt a trifle uneasy on the subject. He may have overheard some caustic comments in his Court and may have decided to "wipe out the stain". If this be so, Edward no doubt saw through it. He possessed a continental reputation in the lists, and Philip would have received short shrift had it come to a duel. It would not come to that: both kings were convinced on that point. Edward's reply—that he would fight at Paris – may have been a case of deceptive bluff: he had no intention of going as far as Paris if he could manage to cross the Seine short of that place. If his answer induced Philip to hurry back to Paris so much the better.

On August 9, the English army made a long 18-mile march to the suburbs of Vernon, skirting Louviers (which they sacked), and past Gaillon (the castle of which they took), and along the river, looking vainly for a crossing-place. All bridges had been either broken down or were adequately defended; moreover the French army, which had had ample warning of the movement of its opponents, who were clearly visible from the line of lime cliffs on the north bank of the river, was marching abreast of them. For several miles the English army followed the road by which King John's troops had gone to the relief of Chateau Gaillard 150 years before; but no attempt seems to have been made to cross at Les Andelys. Vernon was too strongly held to justify an attempt to storm it: both time and English lives were too valuable. The army accordingly bivouacked outside the town, a short distance to the south. August 10 was a repetition of the day before, except that the march was only half as long. That night was spent at Freneuse, well inside the Moisson bend of the river. It looks as if they were heading for that town, but next day, August 11, they quitted the bend, marching the 13 miles *via* Mantes to Epone. The army was now inside another bend of the Seine and Warwick and Northampton took a strongish force to attempt the crossing at Meulan, in the middle of the bend. Unsuccessful here also, the army continued on its way to Equevilly, a march of only five and a half miles. The shortness of this march was probably due to the delay caused by the Meulan operation: till the issue was decided there the rest of the army could hardly push on beyond that possible crossing-place.

On August 13 a six and a half miles march brought the army to Poissy, where the bridge, though broken down, was only weakly guarded. Philip, with his main army, had gone right past to Paris. Had Edward's bluff succeeded? The English king was quick to take advantage of this situation. Strong parties crossed the river on boats and drove off the guard on the bridge. Then the carpenters and pioneers started repair work on the bridge, working desperately day and night, for they realized their lives depended upon it. Not content with this bridge alone, Edward is said to have started the construction of other bridges in the vicinity (though the *Acta Bellicosa*, which is very detailed at this point, is silent as to this). The inactivity of the French is hard to understand. It is true that on August 14 a considerable force did come up to the bridge and for a time there was a fierce contest, but they were driven back by Northampton, who crossed by a single beam 60 ft. long and 1 ft. wide spanning two piers, and killed 500 of the enemy.

It took nearly three days to repair the bridge, and meanwhile two things happened. The English king sent Prince Edward to demonstrate opposite the south-western suburbs of Paris, burning nearby villages including St. Cloud in full view of Paris, in order to complete the deception. This had the desired effect of keeping the French king in a painful state of indecision. He kept shifting about from one side of his capital to the other, St. Germain des Prés to the west, St. Denys to the north, and Antony to the south, being all in turn occupied —anywhere except the right place, which was Poissy. The second event was that during this period Philip sent a further letter to the English king, this time suggesting a set battle between the two armies, on some mutually agreeable ground. But was Philip serious? Edward, remembering what had happened after a similar challenge in Flanders, might well doubt it. He seems to have taken the measure of his opponent, and to have treated the suggestion with contempt. For the moment, however, he gave no formal answer but went on bridge-building. The Parisians became incensed by the lack of activity and enterprise exhibited by the French army which, grossly superior in numbers, made no attempt to come to grips with the invaders, but which rested supinely in its quarters while the suburbs of the city were aflame. It was probably the inflamed state of public opinion that induced Philip to send that second letter to Edward; it was in fact a "face-saver".

Meanwhile what progress was being made by the Flemish allied army? It had set out, as mentioned earlier, on August 2, under the command of Henry count of Flanders, probably from Ypres (though Li Muisis, the chronicler, does not say so specifically). From there it advanced through the Bailleul area—so familiar to our troops in the 1914–1918 war—to the river Lys. After engagements along the course of this river at Estaires, Merville and St. Venant (where the French hanged an Englishman by the heels and the town was stormed and burnt as reprisal by the allies), they reached Bethune on August 14, and laid siege to it, while the English army was halted at Poissy. It is doubtful if Edward had up-to-date information of the movements of the Flemish army, but he must have been aware of its general line of advance. Bethune is 125 map miles from Poissy. If both armies approached one another continuously at a speed of ten map miles a day, they should meet within a week. Amiens is in a direct line and midway between these two places, and the junction, if all went well, might be expected to take place near that town. But it was far more likely that the English army would move the faster and have to cross the Somme before meeting the Flemings. To make straight for Amiens would entail delay, for it might be presumed to be strongly held by the French. The same applied to Abbeville, 28 map miles to its north-west. Edward therefore decided to direct his march midway between these two towns towards an area where there were at least three bridges over the unfordable river Somme.

### THE ADVANCE TO THE SOMME

August 15 was the Feast of the Assumption of the Virgin Mary and Edward ordered no burnings or military activity to take place that day, but next day the English army crossed the now completed bridge, Prince Edward's division having presumably been called in on the previous evening. The army marched due north, fast and straight–uncannily straight. For no less than 68 miles its halting-places did not diverge as much as one and a half miles from a dead straight line, a straightness of march unparalleled in military history, so far as my knowledge goes. How Edward managed to steer so straight a course in the absence of maps–if he had none–must always remain a mystery, for Harcourt can have been of no assistance as a guide once the army was north of the Seine. Edward had not only marched fast, he had given his enemy the slip, for he had not answered Philip's challenge to battle till the end of the first day's march, at Grisy, 16 miles north of Poissy and the same distance from St. Denys. Edward's letter was couched in sarcastic, almost jocular terms. It was, in fact, barely polite. The *Grandes Chroniques* stigmatizes the English king's conduct in all this as deceitful; and deceitful it was. One of the maxims of war is to deceive your opponent, but the good cleric of the abbey of St. Denys would not be conversant with such maxims. Edward had deceived Philip and gained at least one day's march on him in the race to the Somme. But his success was even greater than he had a right to expect, for Philip did not immediately pursue. When he received Edward's letter, presumably early on August 17, he was at Antony to the south of Paris with his main army, daily expecting an attack in that quarter. He moved from there through Paris to St. Denys that night and only set out on his pursuit to the Somme on August 18.

Thus Edward had completely outwitted Philip. He had two days' start, and marched rapidly into the bargain, averaging 14½ miles for the first five days. We hear little of pillage and burning on this march: no doubt its speed did not allow much time for such things and the troops were getting sated with their excesses. His route took him two miles to the west of Beauvais, which the prince of Wales wished to assault, but his father forbade it. Thence the only town traversed was Poix, on August 20, where his exuberant troops stormed the town with scaling ladders against his orders, for speed—not fighting—was for the moment his aim. Later two advanced-guard actions were successfully fought against the king of Bohemia's contingent. This king, whose crest was a plume of feathers, was a fine soldier and was frequently instrumental in opposing the English advance. Edward slowed the rate of march on August 21 to six miles, for he was by all calculations well ahead of his enemy, and no doubt he heaved a sigh of relief on arriving safely at Airaines on August 21. Here he was ideally placed for his purpose, which was to find and utilize a crossing-place over the Somme, for Airaines is midway between Amiens and Abbeville, five miles north of the river, while roads branch off to Picquigny, Longpré, Long and Pont Remy, all of which had bridges over the river. The precision of his march direct to this point from Poissy, 67 miles distant, is quite remarkable. King Edward must have been well pleased with the situation in which he found himself.

But King Philip with his army was that night on the Somme at Amiens! How had he managed it? Historians, both French and English, have slurred over this truly remarkable performance on the part of the French king, the finest military feat of this somewhat unmilitary monarch. The bald facts speak for themselves. He left St. Denys on August 18 and was reported in Amiens on August 20. The distance is 73 miles, *i.e.*, 24 miles a day. Amiens was undoubtedly the right place to make for, and the king had sent orders in advance for the levies north of the Somme to meet him in that town. His route also was nearly as direct as that of his rival; it took him through Clermont, which he is reported as reaching on August 18, a 35-mile march. How are we to account for this phenomenal speed? In three possible ways. First, though he himself did not set out till August 18 he may have dispatched the dismounted portion of his army on the previous day. Second, though he himself arrived at Amiens on August 20, the bulk of his army may not have arrived till later. Third, he did not in fact reach Amiens on August 20, but Nampty, which is described as "near" the

city. In point of fact it is a good nine miles to the south-west.
If we plot out on the map the respective itineraries of the two
armies in this exciting race, we shall find that, when the French
were at Clermont, the English were four miles north of Beauvais, 18 miles to the north-west; when the French reached
Nampty the English were at Camps, only ten miles west-north-
west; the two armies were now each distant eight miles from
the Somme. But next day the French entered Amiens, across
the river, while the English army stopped five miles short of it
at Airaines. Clearly the moral victory went to the French. Could
they exploit it?

The strategical situation was becoming exciting. The gap
between the English and Flemish armies had narrowed to
55 map miles; in only two days they might join hands, but the
formidable obstacle of the river Somme, with its broad
marshy valley and numerous channels strongly defended by
French troops, blocked the way. Edward's immediate object
was to force this line. With that object in view he sent out on
the morning of August 22 a strong reconnaissance force under
the earl of Warwick, to discover the most favourable place for
the attempt. Warwick's party made straight for the river at
Longpré. The bridge there was strongly guarded. He turned
left and found the same thing at the neighbouring bridge of
Long. He pushed on another four miles to Pont Remy where
a considerable engagement took place between his party and
the detachment of the king of Bohemia. Warwick was obliged
to return and report that no impression could be made on any
of the crossing-places. A similar report came from the crossing
at Picquigny, midway between Longpré and Amiens. The
situation of the English army had suddenly become critical.
Boots were worn out, bread was scarce, the army was reduced
to eating the fruit–ripe and unripe–on the wayside (just as did
its descendants over ground not far distant in the same month
of August, 1914, during the retreat from Mons). They had lost
heavily in horses, and many of the knights were reduced to
riding rough country horses captured during the advance. The

army was out of touch with the fleet and out of up-to-date information regarding the Flemings. Reinforcements had flocked to the French army at Amiens and it was now of overwhelming numerical superiority. The half-despised Philip had, to all appearances, out-manoeuvred his rival. Froissart describes Edward III as almost distracted with anxiety. Doubtless this was only a guess on his part, and Northburgh gives the impression that the English king was not in the least put out–at the same time he dared not risk a battle here except in the last extremity. Like Admiral Jellicoe in 1916, he was in a position to lose the war in an afternoon, for in the event of defeat there was little chance of his army ever seeing England again.

Edward that night, after careful thought, came to the conclusion that to force a crossing between Amiens and Abbeville was now out of the question. This was reasonable enough. But the action he decided on taking was surprising. Next morning, August 23, he marched his whole army eight miles due west–away from the river–and carried by storm the town of Oisemont. The rearguard was about to move off from the old billets at Airaines at 10 a.m. when news came of the approach of the French army from the Amiens direction–Philip had recrossed the river! Quartermasters bustled about their business, but there was not time to pack up and remove everything, and when the French arrived in the town two hours later they saw evident signs of a hasty departure.

But why had Edward marched in such a curious direction and why did he waste time in attacking Oisemont? It reminds one of a hunted fox stopping in the course of its flight to rob a hen roost. The clue to his motive is found in his next movement: making almost a right-angled turn to the right he marched straight to Acheux, eight miles north-north-west, where he halted for the night. His object must have been two-fold: to mislead the French king–in his "deceitful" way–by appearing to abandon the attempt to cross the river, and to reduce the danger of being seen by the Abbeville garrison as he would have been if he took the direct road to Acheux.

Whether he succeeded in his stratagem or not, his position still remained anxious and precarious. His new intention was to cross the river between Abbeville and the sea if it proved practicable, but he was utterly ignorant of the condition of the lower reaches of the river, which in any case widened out a few miles below Abbeville into an estuary nearly two miles broad. The faithful Harcourt was now of no service, being out of his home country. The king therefore did the only possible thing. That night he summoned to his headquarters all prisoners who had been captured that day and offered handsome rewards to any who could give him reliable information about the possible crossing-places below Abbeville. Tempted by this bribe, one Gobin Agache (whose name still stinks in French nostrils) averred that he knew of a practicable ford at Blanche-taque–The White Spot–where at low tide a man could cross with the water only knee-high. It ran from Saigneville on the south bank to a point nearly one mile north-west of Port on the north bank, its length being exactly 2,000 yards. Edward decided to trust the man, and gave orders for departure before dawn next day. Meanwhile, Philip had halted his main body for the night at Airaines, sending a division to Abbeville.

### BLANCHETAQUE

Before dawn on August 24, the English army set out on its desperate venture. It marched in a single column. Warwick led the advanced guard with a force of archers, followed by his men-at-arms. Then came the baggage, while the rear was brought up by the king's own division. When the French king heard of the move he set off in pursuit, but had much leeway to make up. Acheux was 14 miles distant and Blanchetaque nearly 18 by the shortest road. Philip had however posted a force of 500 men-at-arms and at least 3,000 infantry, including Genoese crossbowmen under Godemar du Fay, on the north bank guarding the ford, and they could, if necessary, be reinforced from Abbeville, five miles away. Thus he had little fear that the bottle was not firmly corked.

The English army had a six-mile march in the half-light of
a summer dawn. They made good progress and their leading
units are reported to have reached the ford at dawn, which
seems scarcely credible. In any case, there was no great cause
for haste as the tide was only just starting to ebb at dawn and
at least four hours' wait was involved before the ford would
be practicable. During this long and anxious wait the rear of
the column closed up till the whole army was concentrated
on the south bank, immediately opposite the ford. It was
about 10 a.m. before the first man stepped into the water of
the ebbing tide. Hugh Despenser seems to have led the vanguard of archers. Progress along the causeway—one and a half
miles in length—was uneventful and unopposed till the leading
files came within a few hundred yards of the shore. Here they
were greeted with a discharge from the Genoese, to which they
could not for the moment effectively reply, and considerable
casualties resulted. But the English archers marched on
doggedly and silently till they came within effective range,
when they opened on the Genoese and a duel took place
between the two "artilleries". The causeway was sufficiently
broad for about 11 men to stand abreast; the remainder must
have shot over the heads of the front file. But the English
"fire" was effective: the Genoese fire began to slacken. This
was the signal to launch the men-at-arms of Warwick's advanced guard to the attack. The archers edged to the sides of
the causeway to make room for the passage of the horsemen
and the latter splashed and plunged past them slowly towards
the bank. Some French cavalry pushed forward into the water
to dispute the passage and a strange contest took place, with
much confused splashing and shouting—a type of mounted
mêlée for which neither men nor horses had been trained.

This contest was of short duration (and has entirely missed
the attention of most chroniclers). The French fell back to dry
ground and Hugh Despenser led his fellow knights up the bank
and out of the water, while the archers covered their advance
with a steady "barrage" of arrows.

Godemar du Fay's troops had had enough; they took to flight, making for the safety of Abbeville. Northampton and Reginald Cobham, bringing forward the main body of the leading division, took up the pursuit, following closely and giving the fugitives a rough handling, till the latter gained the refuge of Abbeville.

It was a brilliant and inspiriting piece of work and according to one account—probably exaggerated—no less than 2,000 Frenchmen fell. So precipitate was their flight that Godemar du Fay was later accused of treachery, though without any real foundation.

While Northampton swung to the right towards Abbeville, Hugh Despenser swung to the left, charging through Noyelle two and a half miles down the estuary, and on as far as Crotoy, another five miles. Here he quickly seized the town and with it a large number of ships which he burnt, and returned in triumph to the main army.

To return to Blanchetaque; just as the last vehicles were entering the water, which was now becoming uncomfortably deep, the vanguard of the French army, under the king of Bohemia, came in sight. There was a short sharp engagement and a few wagons and men fell into French hands, but the bulk of the wagons with their precious load of arrows, under which lay some strange-looking iron tubes, escaped. While this was happening the remainder of the rearguard, already in the water, pushed on as rapidly as possible, so that when the engagement was over the tide was too far up to allow of any pursuit. At any rate, Philip, perhaps mindful of the fate of Pharaoh's army in the crossing of the Red Sea, did not make the attempt. In any case, a mere vanguard of French troops were not in a position to do more than capture a few stragglers; an attempted pursuit over the ford would have been hazardous in the extreme. Philip therefore called off his forward troops and turned his army into Abbeville for the night. His prey had escaped him.

\* \* \*

The English had gained an improbable—indeed a near-impossible—success. All the factors conspired against them. Let us for a moment consider them. The English were devoid of surprise, cover or protection; they were hampered by the still-flowing waist-deep tide, they were massed into a narrow target for the powerful crossbows of the Genoese; they wielded their own bows awkwardly, some with wet bow-strings; the cavalry stumbled in the churned-up water, frequently slipping off the causeway into deep water, and eventually emerging in no sort of order, to face the strong infantry force lining the bank. Three Anglo-Saxons had sufficed to hold up a whole Danish army at Maldon; three thousand Frenchmen did not suffice at Blanchetaque. Richard Wynkeley, who made the crossing, wrote home "It was marvellous in the eyes of all who knew the place". Taken all in all, there have been few feats of arms so astonishingly successful against odds in the whole of our proud military history.

*          *          *

It was August 24: the English army was safe across the Somme, no big natural obstacle now separated them from the Flemish army. But where was that army? By a sour coincidence, at the very moment when Edward's troops were ploughing their way successfully through the waters of the Somme the troops of Henry of Flanders were in the act of breaking up the siege of Bethune and falling back on Merville.

How had this come about? Details are scarce, but the outline of events is as follows. On August 14, as related above, Henry of Flanders had laid siege to Bethune. The town was energetically defended by Godfrey d'Annequin. On August 22 he learnt that the Flemings who were also besieging Lillers, ten miles to the north-west, had suffered heavily, and hearing also that there was considerable dissension in Bruges between the war and peace parties, he decided to make a sortie. This he effected with striking success, burning a number of tents of the besiegers and getting back into the town practically unscathed.

This achievement so disheartened the Flemings, who cannot have been aware of the rapid advance of the English army toward them, that on August 24 they incontinently broke up their camp and retreated to the line of the Lys.

Edward, of course, did not know of this untoward turn of events, but three new factors decided him to offer battle to his old opponent. In the first place, he now had a fair chance of escape should he be worsted in the battle; for friendly Flanders now lay behind him and so long as he did not allow Philip to outmarch him, his line of retreat was secure. Secondly, he was now in Ponthieu, his grandmother's patrimony, on soil that he considered his own; he would not give up this possession without a struggle. Thirdly, the success of his army in crossing the Somme in the very face of the foe appeared, in that age of faith, to be a miracle; the God of battles was evidently on his side, his cause was a just one in the eyes of the Almighty, who would not allow them to be defeated. The morale of the troops rose with a bound, their trust in their leader was now absolute; he could "go anywhere and do anything" with such troops; if Philip wanted a fight, he should have one.

*          *          *

The English army encamped that night at some undefined spot in the forest of Crecy, which covered a wide strip of land north of the Somme. The French army had had a long march that day, and it bivouacked near the ford, chagrined and disheartened. Next day, August 25, it doubled back to Abbeville where it spent that night. The same day the English marched to the edge of the forest, nine miles north-east of Blanchetaque, looking for a suitable battlefield, and halted, still in the forest, on the banks of the little river Maye. Beyond the river lay a village called Crecy-en-Ponthieu.[1]

[1] There are several towns named Crecy in France, just as there are several places named Mons. Gobin Agache came from Mons-en-Vimeu.

# APPENDIX

THE SOURCES

So deep is the interest in the Crecy campaign and so wide the literature on the subject that I will devote more space to the subject than I have done in the preceding chapters. It can conveniently be divided into three sections:

I. The evidence of eye witnesses;
II. The contemporary or near-contemporary chroniclers;
III. Modern writings.

I. We have accounts by at least four eye-witnesses: King Edward, Bartholomew Burghersh, Michael Northburgh, and Richard Wynkeley. The king wrote four or five letters during the campaign, the longest and most important being that to Sir Thomas Lucy, written from before Calais on September 3 and covering the whole campaign. He also wrote to "his subjects in England", to the archbishop of Canterbury and the archbishop of York.

Burghersh's letter is contained in Adam Murimuth's chronicle, as are those of Michael Northburgh and Richard Wynkeley. The last two were priests in the army, Northburgh being Clerk of the Privy Council and Wynkeley being the king's confessor. Theirs are the most valuable of the letters. (The letters are also given in Robert of Avesbury's chronicle.)

II. Of the original chronicles the best is, curiously, the least well-known, not having been used by Sir James Ramsay, General Köhler, nor any of the biographers of Edward III except the first, Joshua Barnes, who wrote in 1688. It is contained in MS No. 370 of Corpus Christi College, Cambridge. It is variously cited as *Chronique Anonyme*, Corpus Christi Fragment, *Acta Bellicosa* (from its opening words) or *Moisant*, the name of the transcriber. I favour the title *Acta Bellicosa*. It appears in Moisant's *Le Prince Noir en Aquitaine*–an unlikely place in which to find such a transcription. The document has never been edited, but it must have been written by someone present, for on one (and only one) occasion he qualifies a statement by the words "as I later heard". Delbrück describes it as of the highest value, and I agree with him. It starts with the landing in France, evidently intending to cover the whole campaign, but unfortunately it ends abruptly on August 18, in the middle of a sentence.

The chief English chroniclers are the above-mentioned Murimuth and Avesbury, Geoffrey le Baker and Henry Knighton. There are also two documents useful, indeed essential, for the itinerary of the army. They are the *Journal of the King's Kitchen* and the *B.M. Additional MS 25461, f.11*.

The French chroniclers of this campaign are very weak, and only the *Grandes Chroniques de St. Denys*, the Continuation to Guillaume de Nangis' Chronicle, the *Chronographia* (called *Berne Chronicle* by Lettenhove) and the *Chronique Normande du XIVe Siècle* need be mentioned here.

Of what may be called neutral sources, we have two from the Low Countries, those of Jean le Bel of Liége, and of Gilles li Muisis the Fleming, whose chronicle–a weighty one–is contained in the *Chronique de Flandres*. The third is Giovanni Villani, an Italian who based his account largely on the stories of Genoese crossbowmen returning from the war. His account is absolutely contemporary for he died two years after the battle of Crecy.

III. Lastly come modern books. There are three substantial biographies of Edward III, those of Barnes cited above, Longman (1864) and Mackinnon (1900). They all tend to slur over the campaign prior to the actual battle of Crecy. The same applies to Sir James Ramsay's *Genesis of Lancaster* (1913) and T. F. Tout's volume in the Political History of England (1906). Finally, E. Maunde Thompson has some useful notes in his edition of le Baker (1889). It is not an impressive list of English contributions to this world-famous campaign.

The French, on the other hand, have produced some very helpful works dealing with the campaign. The massive edition of Froissart's *Chronicles* edited by Simeon Luce contains valuable notes. *La Désolation des Églises*, by P. H. Deniflé (1899), contains a short but extremely useful account, because it is so thoroughly documented. The same applies to *La Prise de Caen* by Henri Prentout (1903), which is the standard work on the subject. But far and away the best work on the campaign in any language is *La Campagne de Juillet et Août 1346* by Jules Viard (1926), whose notes in his edition of le Bel are also useful.

Of neutral writers only two need be mentioned. The first is Belgian, Baron Kervyn de Lettenhove, whose massive edition of Froissart contains some useful documents and references and gives in full the little-read *Chroniques Abrégées*, or shortened edition of Froissart. The second is the German, General Gustav Köhler, whose *Die Entwickelung des Kriegswesens* appeared in 1886–1890. This distinguished author was not, however, fully acquainted with the English sources, nor with modern researches by Ramsay and Tout.

I have omitted Jean Froissart because this list is confined to sources and writers who I consider have something of original value to offer, and I do not think that Froissart can be said to provide that to any material degree. So far as he copies le Bel he may be considered fairly reliable, but not original; where he is original he is not reliable–no, not for a single statement–without corroboration from another source. When, however, we come to Crecy we shall be able to use him.

ITINERARY OF THE ENGLISH ARMY

Some readers may feel surprise at the precision with which Edward's itinerary has been established. But the material has always been available. It was Maunde Thompson who first "married" the different accounts into one whole. Geoffrey le Baker's chronicle, written only a few years after the event, formed the basis, but the most detailed and precise evidence was obtained by him from two other sources. The first is the

King's Kitchen Journal. This was evidently compiled by some unlearned member of his household who jotted down *as he heard them* the names of the places where the royal kitchen spent the night. His spelling was arbitrary and sometimes rather humorous in our eyes, but by comparing it with the second source, the Cotton MS *Cleopatra* D. vii. f. 170 and the Corpus Christi MS (which Maunde Thompson did not use), certainty and exactitude as to the king's own movements is attained.

Subsequent historians seem to have accepted the distances given for these marches by Maunde Thompson on trust. As a matter of fact they do not quite tally with my own measurements: in nearly all cases they appear to be too long if map miles are indicated, and too short if march miles are indicated. I fancy the latter was intended. It is, of course, impossible to assess with any degree of exactitude such mensuration, but marches always tend to be longer than would appear from a study of the map. Be this as it may, I have in the preceding pages made the marches on an average nearly two miles longer than Maunde Thompson.

The only modern historian, so far as I know, who does not accept Maunde Thompson's itinerary completely is Hilaire Belloc, who cuts out the two-day halt at Airaines, and makes the army halt from August 21 to 23 at Acheux. This is quite contrary to inherent military probability, for the king wished to cross the Somme between Amiens and Abbeville, so he would not be likely to march right past this sector of the river before making his attempt at a crossing. Moreover, both the Cotinian MS and le Baker agree in making the two-day halt at Airaines and it is confirmed by the *Chronographia* on the French side.

NUMBERS OF THE ENGLISH ARMY

It would be pointless to record the varying figures given by the chroniclers: the modern method is to discount them and to trust only to written contemporary rolls and lists such as the exchequer pay rolls. Wynkeley, writing only a few days after the battle of Crecy, gave the number present at that battle as 17,000, which, allowing for wastage, would mean slightly under 19,000 at the landing.

General Wrottesley, writing in 1898, after careful research computed a total of 19,428, which agrees remarkably with Wynkeley's, but this figure was subjected to damaging criticism by, among others, J. E. Morris, Sir James Ramsay and General Köhler. They show that Wrottesley's figure for the Welsh troops must be cut by 3,500 which, without allowing for other slight deductions made by them, brings the figure down to 16,000. Ramsay bases his computation of 10,100 on two sets of figures: the number of those for whom there is written record of having been called up for the campaign, and the total number on the pay roll during the siege of Calais. The first figure reached by him is 10,123, and the latter 31,294. He maintains that this figure refers to all who had been on the pay roll *at any time since the landing*, from which he reasons that only about one-third of these were actually at Crecy. But A. E. Prince[1] has shown that Ramsay has no grounds for this assumption. Nor is the evidence of the pay rolls sufficient. J. E. Morris has shown that some soldiers did not appear on the exchequer rolls, and instances an error on the part of Wrottesley caused thereby, where a category given by him as 600 should be 1800. This seems to put the whole computation into the melting pot, but Morris himself seems to favour 4,000 cavalry and 10,000 infantry, total 14,000.

Retaining in mind these figures and Wrottesley's (corrected) figure of 16,500, let us make a cross check from the number of ships required to transport the army. The number varies considerably, and it will be safest to take the lowest figure given, which is about 700 ships. Allowing for non-combatants, horses and war stores, we can hardly allow an average of more than 20 to 25 combatants per ship. If 20 per ship, the total would come to 14,000, and if 25 per ship, it would come to 17,000—the two figures arrived at by the two above-named

[1] In the *English Historical Review*.

authorities. I am content to leave it at that, suggesting the round figure of 15,000, which is not far short of the figure given by Wynkeley (for Crecy), our most reliable contemporary source.

### CONDUCT OF THE ENGLISH ARMY

The following passage from the *Acta Bellicosa* (Corpus Christi MS No. 270), as translated for me by a friend, seems to have been overlooked by recent biographers who are severely critical of Edward III. The order in question was issued while the king was at Valognes. It reads:

"The most mild king of the English, having mercy in many ways on the miserable population of that country issued an order throughout the army, that nobody should set on fire towns or manors, nor rob churches or holy places, do harm to the aged, the children or women, of his realm of France, nor do harm to any other person if they did not follow, by punishment to life and limb. Further he commanded that anyone who brought to the King anyone caught guilty of the same should obtain 40 solidos reward."

# CHAPTER VII

# THE BATTLE OF CRECY

WHEN the English king decided on August 26, 1346, to take up a defensive position on the Crecy ridge, he can have had no assurance that the French king would accept the challenge and attack him. Indeed he might well have had grave doubts in the matter. Philip VI had so often in the past exhibited hesitation–to put it no stronger–when confronted by his old opponent that he might well be expected to show it again. Edward III in his "haughty and ironical letter" of July 16 had made pointed, indeed scornful, reference to the fact that Philip had had ample opportunity to attack him during the three days he halted at Poissy, but so far from doing so, had broken the bridge and taken up a defensive position behind the Seine. This suspicion might have been strengthened in Edward's mind by the passivity of his opponent on August 25th. Instead of pursuing the English army, the French king had, ostensibly in order to observe the feast of St. Denys, remained halted at Abbeville. Whether this was the true reason or whether it was an excuse to allow time for laggard contingents to join him, as suggested by one chronicler, is not evident. He did, however, make use of the day to strengthen the bridges across the river. Why then should Edward appear so confidently to expect attack next day! The explanation probably is that by some unknown channel of communication he had received certain information, of which we know nothing, pointing to the probability of an immediate pursuit. This may be so, for his intelligence service, considering the fact that it was acting in a foreign country, was good. But it remains an interesting speculation as to how long he would have remained at Crecy had he not been attacked on August 26. August 25 was evidently spent by Edward in reconnaissance, while his army remained hidden in the forest of Crecy, enjoying a well-earned rest, for they had covered 335 miles in 32 marching days: that is, just over ten miles per day. A nice position was found on the ridge immediately to the north-east of Crecy. This ridge is formed by a little valley (known as La Vallée aux Clercs) which is scooped out of the prevailing high ground on the east side of the valley of the little river Maye. This river runs through the lower end of Crecy, from the south-east, and the Vallée aux Clercs joins it one mile from the centre of that village. The Vallée aux Clercs is only 2,000 yards long, its left or upper end merging into the plateau just in front of the village of Wadicourt. The ridge thus formed between Crecy and Wadicourt was about 2,000 yards long, exclusive of both villages. The depth of the Vallée ranges from nothing on the left to nearly 100 ft. on the right.

Edward decided to make this ridge his position. On the highest point of the ridge, only 700 yards from the centre of Crecy, stood a windmill. A few hundred yards behind the centre of the ridge was a small wood, the Bois de Crecy-Grange. The slope in front of the right flank of the position was about one in twelve, and on the left of the position it was almost imperceptible. The right flank was protected against cavalry attack by the village and river (which was wider than it now is) whereas the left had merely the small village of Wadicourt as protection, with open country beyond: it was thus much the weaker flank of the two.

THE ENGLISH POSITION

The strength of the English army, allowing ten per cent. for wastage since the landing, was between 12,000 and 13,000. A front of 2,000 yards was distinctly extensive for an army of such a size, but it is probable that there were slight gaps between the two flanks and the two villages, thus reducing the frontage to about 1,700 yards. Even this may appear rather wide for a medieval army, but there is a feature of the terrain that tends to remove this objection. There are, on the forward slope, three terraces or *raidillons* as the inhabitants call them, 350 yards in length and forming in all probability ancient cultivation strips. No reference is made to these terraces in the chronicles, which may seem surprising because they must have been in existence at the time of the battle, but it must be remembered that we have no eye-witness account of the actual fighting. These terraces would prove an effective obstacle to the French horsemen and thus could be very weakly held; by this means a longer frontage could be held than would otherwise be the case. The terraces no doubt formed a convenient boundary between the two divisions that held the front line.

The division on the right was, in accordance with normal custom, the vanguard of the army—the division of the Black Prince.[1] His chief executive officers were the earls of Warwick and Oxford, and the king put his trusted Godfrey Harcourt to act as his escort and " tutor", as we might say, his chief duty being to see that the boy came to no harm. He placed his troops well down the slope, almost, if not quite, within 300 yards of the valley bottom, the right half standing on a smaller terrace than that mentioned above. (It is not marked in the sketch map, p. 179, which should be consulted here.) The rear-guard held the left of the position under the experienced leadership of the earl of Northampton, who selected a line slightly higher up the slope than the first division. The third division, that of the king, was kept in reserve a short way behind the centre of the line. The baggage was parked in a " leaguer " abutting on the Bois de Crecy-Grange. The sides were made of the wagons and carts, one entrance only being made, for greater security. The interior was occupied by the horses, for the king intended to fight the battle dismounted, no doubt advised thereto by Northampton who had so successfully adopted that course at Morlaix a few years before. It had also been adopted at Falkirk, Halidon Hill and Dupplin

---

[1] It is convenient to use this title, although its first appearance in writing did not take place until 1569 (Grafton).

Moor. The king selected as his post of command the windmill which, though not centrally situated, allowed an uninterrupted view of the whole position and of the French advance.

The reconnaissance being completed, the divisions took up their appointed positions–carefully and methodically. Of the exact nature of the dispositions there has been much controversy. It centres round the meaning to be attached to the word "herce", the formation in which Froissart states that the archers were drawn up. Herce means a harrow, and there have been two interpretations given to the word in this connection. One school maintains that it means that each archer represented the prong of a harrow, the prongs being placed chequerwise, an interval of perhaps four to eight feet separating the archers. Each archer could thus shoot unimpeded and over the head of the archer immediately in his front. The other school maintains that the word means "wedge" and that the archers were drawn up in a series of hollow or solid wedges along the line, each wedge projecting slightly in front of the line of men-at-arms like a bastion flanking the curtain-wall of a castle. This would provide a double advantage: attacking horsemen tend to shoulder away from hostile fire as they advance, and the fire from these wedges would thus tend to "herd" the enemy cavalry charge towards those portions of the line held by the men-at-arms; when the cavalry got close up to the line they would be enfiladed by fire from both flanks whilst at the same time engaged by the men-at-arms in their front.

I unhesitatingly favour this latter school on grounds of inherent military probability. A wedge formation for infantry against cavalry was adopted by the Saxons against King Arthur's Britons at Mount Badon: we get a semblance of the same idea in Wellington's measure to frustrate the French cavalry charges at Waterloo, namely by forming squares between which the French horsemen surged, being raked from both flanks as they did so.

The only point that remains in doubt is how many of these

*herces* were formed, and were they solid or hollow? I think it is fairly clear that each division had a wedge on each flank, *i.e.* that there were four *herces* altogether;[1] and that they were solid, each *herce* being in the harrow formation favoured by the first school. The gap between the two divisions filled by the terraces would be covered by the fire from the inner flank wedges. Some Welsh spearmen may have lined the terraces.

Each man in the army was allotted his exact position and he took it up as for a review. The archers dug small holes in front of themselves and planted a plentiful supply of arrows in the ground, recourse being had to the ammunition wagons for this purpose; for a longbowman could shoot off his own supply of 24 or 48 arrows in a very few minutes.

When all was in order the "review" took place. It was one of the most momentous inspections in our history, for on it might depend whether the reviewing officer would continue to wear a crown on his head next day. The king rode on a white palfrey slowly along the line, unarmed but carrying a short white staff in his hand. With his experienced eye he peered intently at every man, occasionally halting to utter a few words of encouragement and good cheer to each unit in turn. (Battle orders would have been issued previously by the marshals.)

It was perhaps midday before the review was over and still there was no sign of the enemy. Meanwhile the cooks had been busy in the wagon leaguer; a meal was prepared and the king now gave orders that each man should fall out, relax and feed. At the sound of the trumpet everyone was instantly to resume his place. Each archer laid his bow alongside his arrows to mark his position, while each man-at-arms removed his helm.

The meal was served, nature satisfied, and the men stood about in little groups discussing whether that Philip would dare show his face, and many a bet was made.[2]

Still the hours passed; vespers (4 p.m.) approached but no

---

[1] This seems to be in accordance with le Baker, a good authority on military points.

[2] At Agincourt the archers had a sort of sweepstake on the number of Frenchmen each would account for: much the same may have happened here.

French army. The heavens became black with clouds, and at the threat of rain there was a sudden rush by the archers to protect their precious bowstrings; each man unstrung his bow, coiled up the bowstring and placed it inside his cap. The storm, when it came, was of short duration and it passed off before any appearance of the French.[1]

## THE FRENCH ARMY

Meanwhile, what was the French army doing? Philip, whose intelligence service was strangely bad, assumed that the English had retired to Crotoy, the smoke of which could be seen from the walls of Abbeville. If this were so he might yet coop up the English between the Somme and the sea, as he had hoped to do on August 24, only this time on the right bank of the river. Soon after dawn therefore he gave the order to his unwieldy army to advance along the right bank of the river heading for Crotoy. But when his leading troops reached Noyelle they discovered the mistake and informed the king accordingly. The leading units were therefore switched sharp to their right, while those in rear who had not advanced far, if at all, were put on to the Hesdin road that runs north-east from the city.[2]

The old road to Hesdin was even straighter then than it is today, passing through Canchy and Marcheville and leaving Fontaine and Estrées a short distance on its right. Even the longest and slowest march comes at length to an end, and just when the English were beginning to assume there would be no battle that day the van of the French army hove in sight, descending the gentle slope into the valley of the Maye. It is usually assumed that the army marched in a single column. If

[1] Jules Viard in his book queries the historical accuracy of the storm, but I feel that there are too many witnesses to it for it to be doubted, though I agree in doubting the French statement that the Genoese let their bowstrings get wet and thus could not shoot; this was a palpable excuse for their defeat.

[2] The only evidence for this faulty opening move is local tradition at Noyelle and the existence of a road from there towards Crecy, with the name "Le Chemin de l'Armée", but such will explain, as nothing else will, the tardy appearance of the French army on the battlefield. Noyelle is six miles from Abbeville and the detour added a good seven miles to the leading troops, giving them a 17 miles march, whereas those who went from Abbeville direct had ten miles.

that were so the leading troops would, by a rough reckoning, be on the battlefield ere the tail had left Abbeville, but it is unlikely that all units kept to the Hesdin road. Philip had strengthened "bridges", not "a bridge", over the Somme and no doubt this was with the object of marching on as broad a front as possible, thus shortening the length of the column. Allowing for the detour by the leading troops, it is likely that every village in the whole triangle Abbeville–Noyelle–Fontaine saw some French troops passing through it that day.

NUMERICAL STRENGTH OF THE FRENCH ARMY

It is time to say a word about the strength and composition of the French army. As to its strength, the investigation is hedged about with difficulties owing to the almost complete silence of the extant French sources in the matter. We are in the domain of inferences and conjecture. Subject to the above qualifying remarks, the following assessment is probably not far from the facts.

The French army that fought at Crecy was composed of three broad groups or categories of troops. First there come what may be called the regular contingents, consisting in the main of the king's personal retinue of household troops and the Genoese mercenaries – a composite well-trained body under their own commander, Ottone Dorian. They are usually assessed at 6,000 in number.[1] They had played a prominent part in what fighting there had been during the previous ten days, and had suffered heavily at the hands of the English archers. Next come the foreign notabilities, each with his own contingent. The principal of these were the grand old blind king of Bohemia, who had lived for years at the French Court, with his son Charles king of the Romans, and with his contingent of Luxemburgers; John count of Hainault, the turncoat brother-in-law of the English king; James I king of Majorca; the duke of Savoy, and various German mercenaries.

---

[1] Villani gives and Luce accepts this figure, but it is probably too high, though the French figure 2,000 is too low.

Their total contribution must have gone into the thousands. Lastly come the provincial levies, who answered the call of what amounted to a *levée en masse*. Even if we knew their total number we should still not know what proportion of them had actually joined the army in time for the battle; stragglers and distant contingents from the south were continually swelling the ranks, and the number present at any given time would be as difficult to assess as the numbers of Harold's shire levies that straggled on to the field of Hastings. The English chroniclers give figures, the favourite being the suspiciously round number of 100,000, but they are no real guide. The only point on which there can be hardly a doubt is that the French vastly out-numbered the English. Giving what amounts to no more than a guess, I would suggest that the French army approached 40,000 in number and was about thrice as numerous as the English army.

### THE FRENCH APPROACH

At about 4 p.m. the French army started to descend the slope from Marcheville into the valley of the Maye. Its leading elements were spotted by the look-out posted, no doubt, in the top story of the windmill. From there the news could be signalled direct to the king's tent, which would be between the ridge and the Crecy Wood. Edward, having rushed forward to verify that his enemy was indeed approaching, gave the signal: the trumpets sounded, the groups broke up, the knights donned such armour as they had temporarily cast off; and all returned to their allotted posts. The French army was coming at last.

But there was a wait of nearly an hour before the enemy came within striking distance. Throughout this period every movement of the French could be seen from the English position, and what the troops saw was calculated to inspire them with confidence. To explain, we must return once more to the French column—if it can be called a column.

It follows from what has been said above that good order

and march discipline was not to be looked for in the French
ranks. The inevitable disorder was accentuated by the sudden
change in direction of the march, and contingents jostled
against contingents, units bumped into one another and
crossed each other, while the king looked on helplessly. His
army was out of hand before a shot had been discharged.
Eloquent testimony to this initial disorder can be gleaned from
the astonishing discordance in the statements of the chroniclers about the formation of the French army. The number
of "battles" or divisions varies from three to over twelve; which
implies that they were never properly sorted out at the start,
still less toward the end, of a long march. When the English
position burst into view, just three miles away, Philip was
taken by surprise. His intelligence, which failed him right up
to the end of this campaign, had given him no warning and
any idea of fighting a battle that day was far from him. His
first action was to take hasty counsel with his leading officers.[1]
Should he accept the challenge that day, or should he halt
for the night? The predominance of opinion was strongly in
favour of postponement till the next morning; the troops were
wearied by the march, hungry, disordered and probably
dispirited after their wanderings; furthermore fresh contingents were known to be on the way: a few hours' delay might
enable them to join up. This advice was to the king's liking;
always when it came to the pinch he shrank from taking
decisive and irrevocable action. So much was at stake–his
crown, perhaps his liberty! Orders were therefore dispatched
along the line for all units to halt. But the order was only in
part obeyed; impulsive French knights, knowing the vast size
of the French army and supremely confident in their ability
to win a great victory, ignored the order and pushed forward
on top of those in front. Thus the Genoese who led were pro-
pelled forward whether they liked it or not and, if only in self
defence, attempted to deploy and march against that portion

[1] Accounts of the actions and conduct of the French king in the battle are more
discordant than almost any other feature of the battle, but the account that follows
seems the one most in accordance with inherent military probability.

of the English position that appeared opposite them. A glance at the map will show that the line of approach of the French army was oblique to the line of the English position. In order to form front to the position and march straight on the windmill which towered above it they had to turn through some 40 degrees. For a large body, nearly 6,000 strong, to change direction to this extent and simultaneously deploy, while being hustled by rude French knights in their rear, required a higher tactics dexterity than even the experienced Genoese were capable of. In spite of their efforts the line became hopelessly ragged and out of dressing and in the course of the mile or so to be covered before the Vallée aux Clercs was reached their commander was obliged to halt his men no less than three times.

## THE BATTLE

Meanwhile the English, now drawn up in position, looked on in grim and confident silence. Everything was ready, nothing had been overlooked and, although at extreme range the archers could reach the bottom of the valley with their shafts, orders were, it seems, issued that their fire was to be withheld till the Genoese were within decisive range. The Genoese slowly crossed the valley and started to ascend the gentle slope to the hostile position. As they advanced occasional shafts were discharged, as was the custom with these crossbowmen, but they all fell short. Not till they were within 150 yards of the motionless line in front of them did their enemy respond. Then a sharp word of command rang out and instantly the heavens were, as it appeared, black with the swarm of arrows discharged from the trusty English longbows. The result of this discharge, striking the closely-knit lines of the Genoese, was devastating. The ranks of crossbowmen staggered and reeled while, to add to their discomfiture, a series of thunderclaps and belches of flame, followed by the swift hurtling through the air of great balls of iron and stone, shook the men and stampeded the horses. It was Edward's "secret weapon"—those

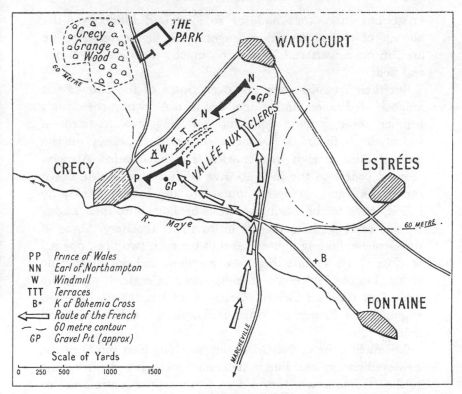

**Crecy Grange Wood**

**THE PARK**

**WADICOURT**

**CRECY**

**ESTRÉES**

VALLÉE AUX CLERCS

R. Maye

60 METRE

+ B

**FONTAINE**

MARCHEVILLE

| | |
|---|---|
| P P | *Prince of Wales* |
| N N | *Earl of Northampton* |
| W | *Windmill* |
| T T T | *Terraces* |
| B+ | *K of Bohemia Cross* |
| ← | *Route of the French* |
| ‒ ‒ ‒ | *60 metre contour* |
| G P | *Gravel Pit (approx)* |

Scale of Yards

0   250   500   1000   1500

IO. BATTLE OF CRECY

mysterious tubes that had for so long laid hidden on the bottom of the ammunition wagons—the first cannon to be fired in open warfare.[1] It was too much: the Genoese broke and fled.

But their troubles were not over. Some of the élite of the knights of France under the count d'Alençon, the king's brother, spoiling for a fight and crowding forward hard on top of the unfortunate Genoese, suspected treachery on the part of these foreign mercenaries. The hot-headed Alençon shouted orders to the men-at-arms behind him to ride down the traitors and, clapping spurs into his horse's flanks, he suited action to the word and drove his horse into their midst, fiercely reviling them the while for their treachery. Some of the Genoese, finding themselves thus between two fires, opened at close range against their new enemies, and an internecine battle began. Alençon's men-at-arms, relentlessly treading underfoot the "traitorous" Genoese, at length reached and engaged the Prince of Wales's division in a hand-to-hand mêlée.

Meanwhile the divisions in rear, brushing past the Genoese, deployed and formed line in succession on their right, wheeling to the left into line as they did so. Eventually a continuous line was formed roughly equal and parallel to the English line. They then closed with Northampton's division in irregular and spasmodic efforts. All along the battle line the French mounted men-at-arms, forcing their reluctant steeds up the hill in the teeth of a hail of arrows from the *herces* of archers, closed with their terrible opponents.

Multitudes fell by the way, but the remainder struggled on with typical French *élan* and fierce hand-to-hand conflicts took place between the mounted Frenchmen and the dismounted Englishmen. The scene must have closely resembled that of the third stage of the battle of Hastings, when the mounted French knights vainly attempted to penetrate the stolid and solid

[1] For evidence on the presence of cannon at Crecy see the appendix to this chapter.

"shield-wall" of the Saxon housecarls. It could not be done; the French horses, in spite of the monstrous medieval spurs worn by their riders, declined to face the human wall in their front, while a crossfire of arrows at close range assailed them from the flanks. Casualties rapidly rose, but whenever a man fell another was found to take his place from the apparently inexhaustible supply of the French host. The pressure on the English line increased, and was especially strong on the right. Godfrey Harcourt, feeling a natural anxiety for the safety of his precious *protégé*, took two measures: he ran across to the nearest unit of Northampton's division on his left—that commanded by the earl of Arundel—and begged him to put in a counter-attack across the slight re-entrant that divided the two divisions, and strike the Prince's opponents in their flank. This Arundel agreed to do. Harcourt's second step was to send to the king for reinforcements. By the time the messenger had reached the king, in his command post high up on the windmill, Arundel's counter-attack was beginning to take shape. It was not lost upon the king; this was not the moment to launch his precious reserve into the fight. "Let the boy win his spurs," he remarked briefly to the messenger. The latter returned with this ungracious message. But in the meantime the counter-attack had relieved the pressure on the Prince's division and the messenger arrived to find the Prince and his troops seated on the ground amid the heaps of dead Frenchmen, quietly awaiting the next attack. But the brief words of the king remained engraved on the memory of the messenger and, years later, he recounted them to a foreign cleric, inquisitive for information about the great battle, and his story is now immortalized in the pages of Froissart's *Chronicles*. In point of fact, the king did send his son a token force of 20 knights, probably under the command of the warlike bishop of Durham. The carnage opposite the Prince's division was particularly great. According to the testimony of the king, in a small space in front of the Prince's troops there lay no less than 1,500 French knights.

"The sun went down and the stars came out" far over the battlefield, but the fight went on into the night under the light of a rising moon. Everywhere it was the same story; the French chivalry boldly and gaily spurred up to the motionless English lines in wave after wave, till all men lost count of the number, but nowhere could a penetration be effected. Line after line "reeled back with their dead and their slain".

> "God of battles. Was ever a battle
> Like this in the world before?"

It is said that there were as many as 15 separate attacks on the English position. But they were not continuous. In all battles there are pauses, of varying duration. During these pauses we can picture the English archers running forward down the slope to retrieve their precious arrows from the bodies of the slain—just as they did at Poitiers ten years later. A little before midnight the battle-flame flickered and died out; silence, except for the groans of the wounded, descended upon the battlefield.

The English army, wearied with slaughter and gorged with victory, lay down on the spot and went supperless to sleep. The king had issued strict and sensible orders against any attempt at pursuit under those unusual circumstances, and his orders were obeyed. Indeed there can have been little temptation to disobey them.

The French army melted away silently into the night, each man selecting his own line of retreat, for there was no one left in command to give him orders, the slaughter among their leaders having been particularly heavy. Their king had shown signs of wishing to fling himself into the midst of the battle—no one could suspect a Valois of physical cowardice—but John count of Hainault, taking a firm hold of his horse's bridle, led him off the field (much as 300 years later the earl of Carnworth led the reluctant Charles of England off the doleful field of his greatest defeat). Both monarchs probably lived to regret that they had survived the battle. For the battle was in each case irretrievably lost. *La dolente bataille* (as the *Grandes Chroniques* calls it) was over.

The king of France rode, or was led, off the field, accompanied by a small band of faithful servants. At about midnight he reached the château of Labroye, three miles away in a north-easterly direction.[1] Here, with some difficulty, he obtained admission and refreshment. His subsequent movements have been slurred over by chroniclers and commentators alike, but they are full of significance. At dawn next day he set out again, not for Abbeville where he might expect to regain touch with a portion at least of his army, but to Amiens, a 43-mile ride to the rear, halting en route at Doullens for a meal. At Amiens he was eventually met by four of his allied chiefs: Charles of Bohemia, John of Hainault, the count of Namur, and the new count, Louis of Flanders. They all reported that their troops had dispersed. They then politely "took their leave" and returned to their respective homes. They had finished with the war; the great alliance had come to an end; the most powerful monarch in western Europe, the head, only a few hours previously, of a mighty army, was abandoned. He had lost in the battle his own brother the count d'Alençon, his brother-in-law John of Bohemia, and his nephew the count de Blois (elder brother of Charles de Blois). Moreover there had been a "clean sweep" of generals. The army was leaderless. The flower of the chivalry of France, as the *Grandes Chroniques* sorrowfully relates, lay dead on the field of battle.

The king was utterly dumbfounded: he dallied in Amiens for a few days, his only recorded activities being to request a three days' truce to bury the dead, and to execute some of the unfortunate Genoese for suspected treachery. He then set off for the château of Pont St. Maxence, situated in a secluded spot on the edge of the great forest of Hallate, 35 miles north of Paris. He arrived there on September 8 and remained in solitary retreat till well on in October, leaving his army and

[1] An extraordinary direction to take – square to the right flank instead of to the rear with the bulk of his army – was it intentional?

his country to fend for themselves as best they could. Philip of Valois was, to use a modern term, deflated.

*      *      *

Meanwhile John duke of Normandy was hastening north with the mounted portion of his army. Arrived in Paris (also on October 8) he made inquiries about his father's whereabouts, and then pushed on into the forest, and eventually tracked down the king. The meeting of father and son must have been piquant: Philip *père* had lost his army; just ten years later John *fils* was to lose both his army and his liberty. The duke persuaded the king to return with him to Paris.

*      *      *

We must return to Crecy. Sunday August 27 dawned with a thick fog spread over the battlefield, as if Nature was trying to throw a veil over the scars of war. It was useless for the moment to send out reconnaissance parties in search of the enemy, but two other measures could be taken. The valley was black with the bodies of dead and dying. The English king arranged for the monks of the nearby abbey of Crecy-Grange to tend the wounded and he sent Sir Reginald Cobham with his clerks to make a careful tally of the dead knights and men-at-arms (the "communes" were seldom included in a tally). The clerks carried out their task methodically, and the scene of their work is to this day known as the valley of the clerks. The tally of knights and men-at-arms amounted to 1,542. That is the only reliable data on which to calculate the total French casualties. As a pure guess the figure for the "communes" would be 10,000. It may be exaggerated, although it only amounts to about three notches to each archer.[1]

The exact figure matters not; whatever the total, the great French army had ceased to exist. The Genoese, receiving no pay—for the administration of the army had come to a standstill—for the most part wandered off to their homes in far-off

---

[1] At Agincourt the English archers made a notch in their bows for each Frenchman killed.

Italy (whence the news of the defeat spread through Europe). The remainder of the army dispersed to their own homes, just as did the defeated armies in our Wars of the Roses. The English losses were astonishingly light, though it is not necessary to accept the grotesque assertion of one chronicler that only two knights were killed.

The king of Bohemia was buried with special honours, Edward himself being present decked in funeral trappings, as no doubt was the Prince of Wales, who from then onward adopted his badge of the three plumes.[1]

Before the clerks had completed their gruesome task the fog lifted and Northampton and Warwick were sent out with a strong force, in search of the enemy–if there still was one. There was. At some undisclosed spot not very far from the battlefield a large hostile force was seen advancing toward them. They prepared to receive it. Here we get a rare example of that *friction de guerre* that must have been even more prevalent in those days than at the present time. The corps in question consisted of the levies of Rouen and Beauvais, hurrying forward to take part in the battle. It is hard to credit the assertion that they were unaware that the battle had already taken place for they must have passed some fugitives from the field. However that may be they spotted the English force and, in the foggy atmosphere, mistook it for French. Approaching without adequate precautions they were speedily made aware of their mistake; the English archers took a heavy toll of them and then the men-at-arms charged and drove them back several miles, accounting, it is said, for "several thousands" of them.

### CAUSE OF THE VICTORY

How are we to account for what appears at first sight to be an astonishing result to the battle of Crecy? Many explanations have been put forward and indeed the issue of all battles is

---

[1] The traditional spot where the king fell is on the road midway between Crecy and Fontaine and is marked by a cross. On the 600th anniversary of the battle the only gathering on the battlefield was a small party of Czecho-Slovaks, who held a service round the cross in honour of their revered monarch.

decided by many and complex factors. The combination of all these factors on the two sides, weighed against one another, decides the issue. Nevertheless in this case there was, as it seems to me, one supremely important factor which almost outweighed the total resultant of the remainder. It was the quality of the two armies. On the one side was a trained, disciplined, well-armed and confident army, fighting for all it knew with its back to the sea, with no hope of escape if it were defeated. On the other was a largely untrained army, hastily collected from differing lands, races and tongues, each unit unknown to and distrusted by its neighbours, lacking cohesion, order and respect for authority. Such an army was calculated to disintegrate when buffeted, and disintegrate is precisely what it did. There is no need to look further for some reasons or excuses for the French disaster in the *"dolente bataille de Crecy"*.[1]

# APPENDIX

### FRENCH NUMBERS AT CRECY

The last word, but not, it is to be hoped, the final word, comes from the historian Ferdinand Lot, writing in 1946 in his *L'Art Militaire et les Armées au Moyen Age*.[2] After computing the English army at fewer than 9,000 effectives, he writes:

"Everything leads us to believe that the French army was inferior in numbers to the English."

By what channels does he reach this rather startling conclusion—so utterly at variance with all the written evidence and the consensus of opinion from the day of the battle until the present time? The Professor produces two reasons. He prepares the ground by arguing that when Edward wrote that the French army numbered "more than 12,000 men-at-arms, of whom 8,000 were gentlemen, knights and squires" he meant that 12,000 was the whole French total. This would leave only

---

[1] Ferdinand Lot calls it, from the French point of view, *"le chef d'oeuvre de l'incoherence"*.

[2] Professor Ferdinand Lot died in 1953.

4,000 for the Genoese and infantry, country levies and allies, making the gentlemen-at-arms more than half the army. Edward was an experienced soldier, and he can never have believed that: when he said "men-at-arms" he *meant* "men-at-arms". It is to be noted that his confessor, Wynkeley, gives the same figure, 12,000 men-at-arms, as his master.

But let that pass, it matters not, for even were we to concede the point it would still leave the French superior in numbers according to Lot (12,000 French to "less than 9,000 English"). How does Professor Lot pare down the French numbers to fewer than "less than 9,000"? Philip had sent the bulk of his troops under the duke of Normandy to Gascony, "Philip could therefore only bring against Edward III improvised levies. The slowness of mobilization of the feudal contingents was such in those times that it is impossible that the king of France could assemble serious forces in the short time that elapsed between the landing of his enemy at St. Vaast, July 12, and the battle."

Let us see. The great English expeditionary force must have been signalled by French ships, who were on the look-out all along the coast. It might take them two or three days to put into Harfleur with the news, which should reach Paris within a week of the landing. As a matter of fact we know that Philip must have heard by July 19, for he returned from his country residence to his capital on that day, and presumably ordered what Ferdinand Lot calls "mobilization". This mobilization proceeded so rapidly that only ten days later he was in possession of an army so numerous that he dared confront his opponent with it. As we know, the battle did not take place for another four weeks, by which time considerable accessions had been made to the French army, notably in Amiens, whereas the English army had diminished in size owing to casualties and sickness. The probability is therefore *a priori* that the French army by August 26 was markedly superior in numbers to the English, quite apart from the written evidence pointing to that, both explicitly and by the *argumentum a silentio*; for is it to be supposed that, if the French army were indeed inferior in numbers, not a single French chronicler would have seized on that excuse to lessen the bitterness of defeat! "Only improvised levies" fails to take into account the 1,542 knights and men-at-arms dead on the field, and the numerous allied and mercenary contingents. Nor were the Genoese "improvised levies". Professor Lot asserts that "everything" points to the French inferiority. I assert that "nothing" points that way.

### DEFEAT OF THE GENOESE

Three excuses for the defeat of the Genoese have been variously given by French sources:

1. That the rain wetted their bowstrings;[1]
2. That they were outranged by the English and their arrows all fell short;
3. That part of their ammunition and personal armour had been left in the wagons in rear.

These excuses do not ring true. The rain "falleth on the just and the unjust" and it is not to be supposed that trained troops, such as the Genoese were, would be caught out by it any more than were the English archers. The same applies to their arrows falling short; they would not *all* have made this elementary misjudgment of the range; and even though the longbow had a greater extreme range than the crossbow, the fact is irrelevant since the English archers shot at effective, not at extreme, range. They may have been only lightly armoured, but so were the English archers; and no doubt their reserves of ammunition were not immediately available, but they were routed in the very early stages of the battle, before reserves of ammunition would be likely to be required; in any case excuse 3 invalidates excuse 2, for if all their arrows fell short it did not matter how many or how few they possessed.

No; the main reason for the defeat was inferiority of morale, induced by their recent experiences of the longbow, especially

---

[1] Given by one French chronicler and repeated by Froissart in his *Abrégées*.

at Blanchetaque, and accentuated by the surprise of the "new weapon"–the cannon–employed by the English.

## SOURCES FOR THE BATTLE

As may be supposed, the sources for the battle are much the same as those noted in the last chapter. We should however add Froissart, who took great trouble over his account of the battle, and undoubtedly did produce some fresh evidence, notably about the presence of English cannon. Jean le Bel still, however, remains our chief source for battle incidents. He was a friend of John of Hainault, from whom mainly he received his information on the French side. Le Baker is our next best source. One might expect that the three eye-witnesses who wrote almost from the field of battle–king Edward, Northburgh and Wynkeley–would produce a fund of details of the battle, but they do not. Edward, in his letter to Sir Thomas Lucy, had to cover the whole campaign, and had not much space left for the actual battle. He does however record the interesting fact that the army went to bed that night supperless and drinkless. Still, they had had a good meal in the middle of the day and one good meal a day should suffice a soldier. But drinkless on that summer night!

Neither Northburgh nor Wynkeley give details of the fighting, the reason no doubt being that they were herded into the park, out of sight and almost out of sound of the fighting. But le Baker can be depended upon for he wrote only a few years after the battle. The French chroniclers can hardly be expected to give long or reliable accounts, but their side of the story is well told by the Fleming, Gilles li Muisis. He was obviously at pains to give an accurate account, but complains pathetically that he finds it hard to know what to believe. Nevertheless his material came almost entirely from the French side, so his version reflects their side of the story only. Another valuable neutral account is that of "A Bourgeois of Valenciennes", printed by Lettenhove in his edition of Froissart as *Valenciennes Chronique*.

There are of course a large number of modern accounts. In 1844 F. C. Louandre wrote *L'Histoire d'Abbeville*, containing a fund of useful information, topographical and local, of which subsequent writers have made ample use. Two years later–the 500th centenary of the battle–the Baron Seymour de Constant established the exact site of the battle, and the road by which the French army approached. Lettenhove and Luce in their editions of Froissart added useful notes; in 1887 General Gustav Köhler in his great work *Die Entwickelung des Kriegswesen* produced an interesting account, but it would have been more weighty if he had shown himself better versed in the English chronicles and commentators. Of all the modern accounts I prefer that of the Rev. H. B. George, written in 1896. It is rather short but he was the first to suggest the formation of the English archers which is basically accepted nowadays. J. E. Morris supported this view next year in the *English Historical Review* as also did Colonel E. M. Lloyd, the only soldier to make a deep study of the battle. Little of note has been written since then in England.

### THE BATTLEFIELD

Within the past few years the local authorities have allowed a great sprawling beet factory to be placed right on the battlefield. It is at the lower end of the Vallée aux Clercs, precisely where the Genoese first came into action, and the scene of their discomfiture. In the last century vestiges of one of the grave-pits were visible here. The factory forms an ugly gash on the panorama of the field that can be seen from the windmill mound. The mill itself was deliberately pulled down by a "patriotic Frenchman" in 1898 in revenge, it is said, for the episode of Fashoda in that year. The foundations on the mound remain, but recently it has been selected as the site of a water tank. Whether this selection of site was another patriotic act is not known.

Apart from these "encroachments" the ground is quite unspoilt and, standing on the windmill mound, it is easy in imagination to follow every incident of the fight. Of the grave-pits dug after the battle two were still visible in 1844, one on the spot now occupied by the beet factory, and the other high up the Vallée aux Clercs where a slight ravine strikes north to Wadicourt. This indicates that the left of the English line was heavily engaged.

Of the old road from Marcheville by which the French army advanced few traces remain. It still is known locally as *le Chemin de l'Armée*.

French accounts emphasize the strong defensive line con-structed by the English, consisting of trenches, hedges and barricades of carts and wagons. The only partial corroboration from the English side comes from le Baker who speaks obscurely of "openings", or holes, being dug. I think these must have been pot holes dug by the archers, reminiscent of Bannockburn and more recently of Morlaix. If there had been any strong obstacle in front of the men-at-arms we should have heard something about it in the course of the fight. On the other hand, it would be a natural story for the French to circulate in explanation of their defeat. The wagons were parked in the rear.

The ground has never been accurately contoured, but a roughly contoured 1 over 20,000 map was produced in England during the 1939–45 war. Of modern maps, that of Ramsay in his *Genesis of Lancaster* is the best, though I do not entirely agree with the dispositions shown on it. Belloc's map would be more helpful than it is if the scale had been drawn correctly: it is only half the correct size.

## CONDUCT OF PHILIP VI

Few things are more difficult to ascertain regarding the battle than the actions and conduct of the French king. The most contradictory stories are told of him; he was too impulsive and from hatred of the English ordered his army to attack; he was surprised by the presence of the English and tried to prevent his army attacking at all; during the fighting he kept so far in the rear that he was obliged to enquire of John of

Hainault how the battle was faring; he was so forward in the fight that he had two horses killed under him, on one occasion being unhorsed by king Edward; at the end of the battle he tried to ride forward but was forcibly prevented. These stories contradict each other and most of them smack of propaganda, just as does the French story that the Prince of Wales was at one moment captured by a French knight but afterwards rescued. It is easy to see how such stories gain currency.

The conduct of the French king after the battle certainly seems to call for comment. The *Grandes Chroniques* confines itself to stating that he returned to Paris, but I do not think we can reject the circumstantial story told by the Bourgeois de Valenciennes (or the *Valenciennes Chronicle*), printed by Lettenhove. The chronicler was a neutral and his account does not seem to show conscious bias against the French. Philip, in fact, seems to have been so utterly shattered morally that for several weeks he just allowed affairs of state to take their own course.

## CANNONS AT CRECY

The long dormant controversy whether the English used cannons has reappeared. In 1942 M. Paul Schaepelynck read a paper before the *Société d'Emulation d'Abbeville*, which disputed the presence of cannons on the battlefield, and his views appear to have received favour with that Society.[1] The same point of view has also been voiced in the correspondence columns of the *Sunday Times*. It seems therefore desirable to review the evidence for and against the presence of the cannons in order to see if some final conclusion can be reached in the matter. I will first enumerate the arguments in favour of their presence and then examine those opposed to it.

---

[1] I sohuld perhaps add that I have recently had a very pleasant meeting with the leading members of that Society at which they expressed no definite opinion on the subject.

## ARGUMENTS IN FAVOUR OF THE USE OF CANNON

These can be grouped under three headings: A–documentary, B–inherent probability, and C–the evidence of the spade.

### A. *Documentary*

There are five apparently independent contemporary sources, the first two of which can be bracketed for the purpose of examination.

### 1. *Giovanni Villani*

"The English guns cast iron balls by means of fire. . . . They made a noise like thunder and caused much loss in men and horses. . . . The Genoese were continually hit by the archers and the gunners . . . (At the end of the battle) the whole plain was covered by men struck down by arrows and cannon balls."

### 2. *Istorie Pistolesi*

"The English knights, taking with them the Prince of Wales and many bombards, advanced to attack the French."

Villani certainly, and the author of the *Istorie* probably, died of the Black Death in 1348, two years after the battle. So both are absolutely contemporary sources. Both writers enjoyed a high reputation. Whence did they get their accounts? There can be little doubt that they emanated from the Genoese fugitives from the battlefield who, making their way back to Italy as no pay was forthcoming in a chaotic France, spread the first stories of the battle. The stories of nearly all fugitives are exaggerated and self-exculpatory, and the Genoese crossbowmen would naturally be tempted to make the most of the "new weapon" that had been used against them. On the other hand would not be likely to invent the presence of a new arm of which few, if any, of them had ever heard. There is nothing in common between the above two passages. The *Istorie* is in error in asserting that the English knights advanced with the Prince of Wales. This certainly shows that the author had received some erroneous information, but the very dissimilarity between his account and that of Villani shows also that they were working on different sources, both of which however agreed in asserting the presence of English cannons. The conclusion is inescapable that within two years of the battle stories were current in Italy, brought there by eye-witnesses, that the English had indeed used the New Weapon at the battle of Crecy.

### 3A. *Les Grandes Chroniques de France* (or of St. Denys)

"Thus the King, with all his people assembled, went to meet the English, which English fired three cannons, by which it happened that the Genoese crossbowmen who were in the front line turned their backs."

*Les Grandes Chroniques* was about the best contemporary French record, the monk of St. Denys being in close touch with the French Court when he wrote it.

### 3B. *Continuator of William de Nangis*

"Then the English began to shoot on our people and they fired three cannons so that the said crossbowmen were dismayed."

At one time I regarded this passage as but a slavish copy of the *Grandes Chroniques* and rejected it entirely; but a close examination of the original shows that only three words in the two passages correspond, namely "getterent trois canons". Admittedly these are the key words and they point to the strong probability that both passages are derived from the same source, but they can be independent passages and yet coincide in using those three words, for if the common source stated that the English fired three cannons, "getterent trois canons" would be the natural words for them both to use. I do not claim two sources, and for that reason have bracketed them 3A and 3B, but it does seem that two independent chroniclers at the same time heard and believed the report that the English used cannons. Or it can be put in another way: The *Grandes Chroniques* are corroborated or supported by another contemporary writer. Who was this writer? Auguste Molinier, the unrivalled French expert for the period, is correct in identifying him as Jean de Venette, whose work is "a chronicle of the first rank".

4. Froissart's *Chronicles* (Amiens MS)

"And the English kept quite still and discharged some cannons which they had with them in order to disturb the Genoese."

This version of the *Chronicles* only came to light in Amiens in 1839, previous to which date it was believed that Froissart had not heard of the presence of the cannons as he did not mention them in his first version. Various explanations of this silence have been put forward and the matter has been needlessly complicated by the fact that Lettenhove (followed, I regret to say, by Sir Charles Oman) wrongly placed the Amiens version earlier than the first version. This was rectified by Simeon Luce in his definitive edition of Froissart. The usual explanation of Froissart's silence in his original version is that as he was attached to the English Court he did not care to mention a new weapon whose intervention in the battle might take away some of the credit for the victory from the knights and archers. This may be so; but there is another and even simpler possibility–that Froissart had not heard of the cannons when he first wrote, but received the news before his second edition.

5. Froissart's *Chroniques Abrégées*

Late in life Froissart set to work to compile a condensed or abbreviated version of his Chronicles. This is known as the *Abrégées*. Strangely little notice has been taken of it, though Luce considers, in view of the new matter that it contained, that it deserves to be considered as a completely new edition. This applies to the passage about the Crecy guns which now reads in this version:

"The English had with them two of the bombards[1] and they made two or three discharges on the Genoese who fell into a state of disorder when they heard them roar (ruer)."

This account is more explicit than the Amiens version, to which it clearly owes nothing. It must represent a further item of information that had reached Froissart in the interval

---

[1] English writers without exception translate this "two or three bombards". The French original is *deul des bonbardieaulx*.

between the two editions. It is in close accord with the *Grandes Chroniques*.

To sum up the documentary evidence, we have six passages emanating from at least five different sources, but all testifying to the (then surprising) fact that the English were in possession of cannons at the battle of Crecy.

N.B. If it be asked why in the Rome edition of the *Chronicles* no mention is made of the guns, the simplest explanation is that Froissart was working on the first edition (there were probably only two copies of the Amiens version, neither of which was to hand) and he forgot to incorporate the rather vague passages in the Amiens edition. The new information that appears in the *Abrégées* probably reached him after he had compiled the Rome version.

## B. *Inherent probability*

This argument can be stated concisely. Edward III had suffered from the attentions of hostile artillery at the siege of Tournai, and had since exhibited great activity in amassing a force of cannons himself. I am informed by Brigadier O. F. G. Hogg that he has discovered documentary evidence that Edward III ordered some "gunnes" for use in France as early as 1339. Professor Tout has shown that he expressly ordered some cannons[1] to be constructed to take with him on his expeditions to France in 1346, and though there is no documentary evidence that they were actually embarked there is no reason to suppose that he left them behind. Unless we happened to possess an inventory of the stores actually placed on board we could hardly expect the contemporary chroniclers to relate the fact.

If the cannons were embarked but did not reach Crecy, what happened to them? It has been suggested that they were captured while crossing the ford at Blanchetaque, along with some of the baggage wagons. But this cannot be the case for the Prince's own division crossed the ford *behind* the baggage wagons.

[1] Some lead or iron balls were also made for them.

After his victory at Crecy, one of the first things that Edward III did was to write to England asking for all available cannons in the Tower of London to be sent to him before Calais. Evidently he had cannons in his mind, and if he had used some in the recent battle and had been pleased with their performance this action of his would have been eminently natural and inherently probable.

## C. The evidence of the spade

Two journals, Le Courrier de la Somme and L'Abbevillois, reported in September, 1850, within a week of the occurrence, the discovery of a cannon-ball weighing 560 grammes (about 1¼ lb.) and measuring 24 centimetres in circumference (about 79 mm. or 3 in. calibre), and that it was made of iron, and was badly rusted. The name of the farmer who found it on the battlefield was M. Douvergne, and the cannon-ball was placed on view in the café of M. Lejeune of the Rue de l'Hotel de Ville at Abbeville. M. Lejeune's house was destroyed by a bomb in May, 1940, and there is no trace of the cannon-ball.

The above details are circumstantial, and there can be no doubt that a cannon-ball as described was in fact found on the battlefield in 1850. One would expect such a ball to be of from 2 in. to 4 in. calibre. Also it agrees with Villani's statement that iron balls were fired. Thus the ball found accords with expectation, and it is scarcely conceivable that such a ball, found on the battlefield, had no connexion with the battle. L'Abbevillois stated that the ball came without doubt from the battle of 1346. Moreover it was found, according to the Town Clerk of Crecy, in the precise area that one would expect—namely, the area where the Genoese attacked the Black Prince's division. The only fact that could cause any lingering doubt would be if fighting had taken place on the same field at a later date. I have searched the history of Crecy for that purpose. This can be found in L'Histoire d'Abbeville by F. L. Louandre (1844). From this it appears that the only fighting in the neighbourhood occurred in 1625, during the Thirty Years' War. It was of a minor nature and there is no mention of cannons being present. Moreover the fighting seems to have been confined to the village itself, which is well to the flank of the Crecy battle-field. M. Ridoux, late Mayor of Crecy (and the local historian), corroborates that there has been no subsequent fighting on the battlefield of 1346.

But this does not complete the contribution made by the spade to the elucidation of the problem. At various dates in the period 1800 to 1850, at least four other cannon-balls were unearthed by farm labourers and collected by Madame Desjardins, the great-grandmother of the present M. Desjardins, who resides in Froyelles Chateau, three miles south of the battlefield. They are described as being found in the area between the Vallée aux Clercs and the monument to the king of Bohemia, which is about a mile further south. This is rather vague, and evidently no exact record was made of the dates and spots where they were all found. The natural presumption is that they were found in the Vallée aux Clercs alongside the 1850 ball, and perhaps subsequently removed to the king of Bohemia's monument as being the only spot identified with the battle.

I inspected these balls in July, 1950, and took a photograph of them. Two are of stone and two of iron. One of each has a calibre of 92 mm. (3·6 in.) and the other two of 82 mm. (3·23 in.) as compared with the 1850 ball of 79 mm. calibre. In those primitive days there can be no doubt that the 79 and 82 mm. balls would be fired from the same piece. It seems likely that the 92 mm. balls were fired from a slightly larger cannon, though there may have been only the one calibre: even as late as Peninsular War days cannon-balls of widely varying calibre were fired from the same piece.

We thus have strong evidence that at least five cannon-balls, three of iron and two of stone, were found in or near the Vallée aux Clercs during the last 150 years.

The chief argument, and the only one that requires detailed examination, is the argument from the silence of the English chroniclers. This argument was, till the discovery of the Amiens MS, strengthened by the supposed silence of Froissart. Michael Northburgh and Richard Wynkeley might have been expected to mention the cannons, but both were civilians and both, in the opinion of Maunde Thompson (whose name carries unrivalled weight in this matter), "probably watched the battle from the rear". Now, the battle took place just over the crest on the forward slope and consequently it was quite invisible from the rear. Our two clerks would be with the baggage which was half a mile or more in rear and they would from there see precisely nothing of the battle. It is therefore probable that these two clerks were dependent for their account on what the soldiers told them after the battle. But, it may be advanced, surely they would hear the discharge of the cannons? Not necessarily. It is a notable fact that nearly all chroniclers stress the noise of a medieval battle; the shouts of the soldiers, the clash of weapons, etc. What does Isaiah say? "Every battle of the warrior is with confused noise." Amid this confused noise of the warriors, a few—only a few—discharges of the cannons took place. The tiny charge for the crazily-constructed tubes would not make a loud report. Such report as there was, would be more audible in front of than in rear of the gun muzzles. Now, the clerks were in rear, and perhaps half a mile or more away with a ridge intervening between them and the guns. Thus they may not have heard the discharges, and even if they did, not knowing of the presence of the cannons, they would not connect any noise they heard with these new weapons.

But how could they be ignorant of the presence of the cannons with the army? Perfectly easily. These cannons must have been very small, they were simply tubes, perhaps as much as six feet long, each lying in a wooden crate. They would be carried in carts, lying on the floor of each and doubtless covered with a tarpaulin or spare weapons. Until occasion arose for action they would remain unseen and unsuspected by the great mass of the troops and Edward no doubt reserved his "secret weapon" till it could be employed in the decisive battle.

If, however, the clerks did know of the presence of the cannons, that silence can be explained in one of two ways. The letters that they wrote home were not very long, and when they come to the details of the actual battle they become exceedingly brief. Wynkeley has only 43 words on the actual course of the battle, which may be slightly condensed as follows:—

"The enemy, wishing to take the person of the king, thrust himself forward. The struggle was hard and long, twice the enemy was repulsed, and a third time. There was a great mass of men who fought strenuously."

He then goes on to recount the casualties.

Northburgh's account is even shorter, extending to exactly 30 words:—

"The battle was hard and long, for the enemy fought well, but they were defeated and their king fled."

Neither of these accounts, it will be noted, gives a single detail worth relating. There is not even mention of the vital work performed by the archers. By the *argumentum a silentio* we might assert that Edward III had no archers on the field, since neither of the eye-witnesses mentions them. But if the part played by the archers was not deemed suitable for mention in these letters *a fortiori* the action of the cannons was not.

There is another possible explanation for the silence of these eye-witnesses – that of motive. If the English victory had been due in the smallest degree to the use of the new weapon, and one not possessed by the enemy, there would be a natural reluctance to proclaim the fact; for artillery fire seemed to run counter to the tenets of chivalry, of which there was no more ardent supporter than Edward III. He above all would be anxious to keep the matter quiet, and it is at least conceivable that he positively enjoined his clerks not to mention it in their letters. The Germans have never boasted about their victory in the second Battle of Ypres when they used a "new weapon" – gas – and we had none. If it had been possible to keep its employment quiet they would undoubtedly have done so.

The same motive for silence would apply to the contemporary chroniclers also, assuming that they were cognizant of the presence of cannons. But were they? Let us now consider them. For practical purposes they were four in number, and I will deal with each briefly in turn.

First comes Geoffrey le Baker, whose account of the battle is the longest (excluding Froissart the Fleming of course). The actual battle is described in 50 lines of Latin. Geoffrey was a *clericus* living in Oxfordshire. He took Murimuth's chronicle as the basis of his account, adding a few details that probably reached him at second or third hand from eye-witnesses. Now, if our two eye-witnesses, Northburgh and Wynkeley, did not care to mention the new weapon in writing, other eye-witnesses may have been chary about mentioning it to writers in England. This would account for Geoffrey's silence without looking for any other reasons. Next we have Robert of Avesbury, a canon lawyer, who transcribed Northburgh's letter and only added a half-dozen lines of his own. The third, Adam Murimuth, was a canon of St. Paul's. He also contented himself in the main with transcribing Wynkeley's letter and translating Northburgh's from French into Latin (a significant sign of the rapid decay of the French language in England). Lastly comes Henry Knighton, a canon of Leicester. His account of the battle is almost equally short. He mentions three charges by the French and the wounding of the French king in the face by an arrow. This is the only reference to the archers in his account.

We can conveniently bracket these four chroniclers together, observing that all of them got their information at second or third hand, and that they omitted any detailed description of the work of the archers, the main feature of the battle, so that *a fortiori* they could not be expected to refer to the three small cannons which cannot have played anything like so important a part in the fighting.

Finally it may be observed that the motive for silence on the part of the eye-witnesses would apply in only slightly less degree to the English chroniclers. We can sum up by saying that our chroniclers were probably unaware of the presence of cannons at Crecy, but that if they were aware of it they preferred not to chronicle the fact.

## SUMMING UP AND VERDICT

We have seen that the documentary evidence for the presence of cannons at Crecy is strong and precise; that their presence is inherently probable from what went before and what followed, and that the evidence of the spade is what the French would call *frappant*. Weighing all these considerations together, and bearing in mind the weakness of the objections to their presence, I subscribe to the conclusion of that profound historian, the late Colonel Henry Hime, "The presence of our guns at Crecy is one of the best established facts of the Hundred Years' War".

## SOME TACTICAL POINTS

The dominant tactical point on the English side was the fact that every man in the army fought dismounted, and that the two arms–archers and men-at-arms–mutually supported one another all along the line. The French, on the other hand, concentrated their missile-throwers, *i.e.*, the Genoese crossbowmen, in one mass, directed against one portion only of the line. This was probably because the Genoese refused to fight except in a single body under their own leaders. The result was a complete lack of cooperation between the arms, with the disastrous results that we have seen.

The battle was a rare example of decisive results being obtained from a wholly passive defence. How is this to be explained? Undoubtedly the decisiveness of the French defeat was self-inflicted. It was largely due to the desperate and unthinking bravery of the French knights, who, undeterred by the awful fate that overtook each body in turn, still continued the unequal conflict till practically all the flower of the chivalry of France had fallen. It is, however, probable that the English king did not contemplate fighting such a purely defensive battle. He kept a large portion of his army in reserve under his own firm hand. He was chary about reinforcing his own son. It seems therefore likely that, like Harold at Hastings, he intended to launch his reserve in a great counter-attack as soon as the enemy should have completely shot his bolt, but as this did not happen until far into the night, Edward wisely retained his troops in hand.

Criticism has sometimes been directed against the French king for not undertaking a flank attack against the obviously strong position of the English. But his attacking troops were all mounted and a mounted charge through either of the villages on the flanks was impracticable. No doubt a wide enveloping movement right round Wadicourt followed by an attack on the English left rear might have produced good results; but such things were not done in the pitched battles of the time, and the French chivalry would have considered it rather derogatory to shirk a direct frontal attack against a numerically inferior enemy. (It required a woman to set the fashion–at St. Albans– of a flank attack delivered by the whole army.[1])

[1] This, of course, was Margaret of Anjou, the wife of Henry VI when she routed Warwick the Kingmaker.

# CHAPTER VIII

# THE SIEGE OF CALAIS

EDWARD III must have been a trifle dazed at the extent of his success on August 26, 1346. The great French army had ceased to exist: it had crumbled, as it were, into dust and the winds had swept it away. Clearly a review of his plan of campaign was now necessary.

Three courses seemed open to him. He could maintain his original plan of joining forces with the Flemings; he could attack Calais; or he could advance on the French capital. There was obviously no longer any urgency about joining forces with the Flemish army, for the danger threatening each had, for the time at least, disappeared. Moreover he had by this time probably heard of the abandonment of the siege of Bethune and the withdrawal of his allies toward their own base. Calais, on the other hand, presented a very tempting target. The English army was sadly in need of warlike stores of all kinds: boots and horse-shoes were worn out or worn thin; transport vehicles were in need of repair; above all, the stock of precious bows and arrows needed replenishment. But a wide stretch of water separated the army from a renewal of all those things, and a powerful French fleet roamed these waters; St. Vaast and Caen were now far distant—while Harfleur and the mouth of the Seine were in enemy hands. The same applied to Boulogne and the mouth of the Somme, and the little port of Crotoy was the sole link with England that the army possessed. The capture of Calais would secure not only a firm base for future operations, supported on its eastern flank by the friendly Flemings, but would provide the shortest possible sea route between the army and the home country—a big consideration in the days of sail. If France was to be conquered, Calais would have to be captured sooner or later, and the sooner this difficult task was tackled the easier it should be. But the third course – an advance on Paris – also had its attractions. The possibility of this course has been ignored by most commentators on the campaign, doubtless because there is a paucity of precise information about the strength and dispositions of the French military forces at this time. This is not surprising, because the internal condition of the country verged on chaos, and French sources skim lightly over this disastrous period. It is thus difficult for us, and must have been quite impossible for the English king, to "appreciate the military situation" with any degree of assurance. We are reduced largely to guess-work; but two fairly safe guesses may at least be made: the first is that Edward was not at first fully aware of the extent of the success he had achieved and the second that he was equally unaware of the strength and position of the army that the duke of Normandy was bringing north, though he must have guessed that it was approaching. There would seem to the king to be weighty reasons against making the attempt on Paris. His army, as we have seen, was badly in need of further supplies, and by marching on Paris it would be marching away from those supplies, even if the march was practically unopposed; it would be necessary to capture the French capital, which was strongly fortified and would almost certainly involve a long siege, for Edward had no siege engines capable of breaching the walls, with the army. It is significant that, on September 1, only five days after Crecy, he sent orders for all available cannons in the Tower of London to be sent out to him, but it would be weeks before they could be counted upon. The time that would elapse before the city fell would allow Philip to collect a new army. We know that he did manage to collect a large army before the siege of Calais was over, and he would have been able to do the same in the case of Paris. The situation of the English army, cut off from its base and surrounded by enemies, would have been desperate – or so it would seem at first sight. But that is not quite the whole story. There were some favourable factors beneath the surface. Let us take first the size of the army with which the duke of

Normandy was approaching. At first sight there is little inkling to be obtained of its strength or composition, and it is generally assumed that the great army of Gascony was brought north in its entirety. But that is probably not the case. In the first place, the duke left in Gascony certain garrisons. We know two facts about his northward march: he heard the result of Crecy at Limoges, and he arrived at Paris on September 8. The news of Crecy could have reached Limoges about September 1 at earliest. He cannot therefore have left till September 2, and he reached Paris seven days later. The distance is 220 miles, *i.e.*, he must have covered over 30 miles a day. This pace would be impossible for foot soldiers, so it points to the fact that the duke had only mounted troops with him. We get apparent corroboration for this from the Bourgeois de Valenciennes, who states that John pushed on from Paris "with a strong force of cavaliers". On meeting the king in his forest retreat, he did not persuade him to march north with this fresh army and either relieve or reinforce the threatened city of Calais; on the contrary the two quietly returned to Paris, and no attempt at relief of Calais was made for over six months. All this is good evidence that the duke of Normandy brought only a portion of his army from Gascony, and that he did not consider it strong enough to confront the invaders.

The English army should thus have had little difficulty in approaching and laying siege to Paris. Its shortage of ordnance stores would not become evident unless and until the French opposed it in the field: to the enemy it would appear to be simply a victorious and all-powerful army.

This brings us to the final objection, namely that the siege of Paris was bound to be a long one and before it was over Philip would have raised a large army and would have cut off the English from their base. The length of the siege of Calais, and later of Rouen and Orleans, may affect our military judgment here. Is it right to assume that Paris would have resisted the summons to surrender? The inhabitants had the awful example of Caen before their eyes: the English king had been uncannily successful in everything he had undertaken: he had overrun Normandy and twice when he appeared trapped he had eluded his opponent and had then administered an unheard-of defeat on an immensely larger army. The Parisians had murmured against their king when the English army had appeared outside their walls a few weeks before; Philip, though possessed of superior numbers, had shrunk from engaging his opponents until practically obliged to do it and, having been utterly defeated, had secreted himself in the forest, not choosing to face the wrath of the burghers of his capital. It was about the last straw. National sentiment was not fully developed in western Europe in the fourteenth century, the precise amount of French blood that a claimant to the throne of France possessed did not greatly interest Frenchmen; in any case Edward was half a Frenchman and many thought his claim to the throne was stronger on legal grounds than that of his rival. In short, it seems conceivable, if not probable, that the gates of Paris would have been thrown open to Edward, and that he would have been accepted as king.

If Edward, marching on Paris, had put down with a stern hand the senseless burnings that had marked and marred his march through Normandy, I believe it possible that the Hundred Years War might have been concluded in a single campaign. No doubt a second war would eventually have taken place, but militarily speaking I hold that Edward had it in his power, on the morrow after Crecy, to win for himself the crown that he sought.

ARRIVAL BEFORE CALAIS

By August 28 Edward III had made up his mind: Calais should be his next objective. The same day his army set out and, marching by easy stages via Montreuil, Etaples, the outskirts of Boulogne and Wissant, they arrived on the western side of Calais probably on October 4.[1] The commander of the

---

[1] Three sources give the date as the 4th, one gives the 3rd and one gives the 2nd.

garrison, a stout-hearted Frenchman named John de Vienne, closed the gates, and the siege commenced.

The outskirts of Calais have changed greatly since those days. An early map printed toward the end of the English occupation shows a broad belt of waterlogged country surrounding the town. Through it meandered the little river Hem, passing 1,800 yards to the west of the walls, and then bending to the right and entering the sea immediately to the north of the town.[1] This last stretch of the river formed the town haven, which provided a secure anchorage for a large number of ships. To the east of the town a line of low sand dunes stretched away toward Gravelines, while on the west another and higher line of dunes commenced about 3,000 yards from the walls and ran out to the sea in the headland of Cape Gris Nez.

A double wall and double ditch surrounded the town and there was a citadelle and several angle towers. King Edward cannot have possessed accurate information as to the defences of the town, but a glance of his experienced eye would show him that they were immensely strong, and that to take them by storm was, for the moment at least, out of the question. Nor did he wish to subdue the town by prolonged bombardment and extensive breachings of the wall, for he intended that it should henceforth be, not merely an English possession, but a part of England. It is true that he directed all the cannons in the Tower of London to be sent out, but these were not breaching guns; catapults were still the breaching weapon, and the marshy ground rendered the provision of steady platforms for these heavy engines impracticable. Edward therefore was driven to the lengthy procedure of a blockade. For this purpose he encamped his army on the west side of the town; his left flank stayed by the sea, his Flemish allies held the dunes on the east side and detached posts guarded the approaches across the marshes on the south side. It was thus comparatively easy to blockade the landward side, owing to the marshes that surrounded the town, but to prevent entry of supply ships was

[1] But see the note on terrain in the Appendix.

a more difficult undertaking. Though we cannot give the relative strengths of the French and English fleets in the Channel, it would seem that the English fleet could not maintain absolute command of the sea in the vicinity of the port. Enterprising Norman ships could, and did, run the gauntlet and enter the haven with supplies till late in the siege, thus prolonging its length. Another cause for its prolongation was that in the early days de Vienne expelled from the town 1,700 (according to Froissart) old men, women and children who were of no assistance to the defence but whose mouths had to be filled. Thus they became *bouches inutiles*—useless mouths to feed. In so doing de Vienne was following a very common custom, and indeed he may have had in mind the famous siege of Chateau Gaillard 150 years previously, when the English commander adopted the same procedure and Philip Augustus of France refused to allow the ejected civilians to pass, thus condemning them to a pitiful existence in the no-man's-land outside the walls of the castle. Edward, however, did not follow the example of Philip Augustus: he not only allowed them to pass through his lines but provided them with a hearty meal. It may be that policy rather than natural kindness of heart prompted this action, for if Calais was to become an English town it would be highly desirable that the French inhabitants of it should be well disposed to the English connexion. The inevitable result however was that, with fewer mouths to feed, the food lasted the longer, and the siege was thereby prolonged. Edward realized this, and when late in the siege de Vienne repeated the action, expelling another party of 500, the English king sternly refused to allow them to pass, and another tragic instance of *les bouches inutiles* was witnessed.

The siege was bound to be a long one—unless the French king attempted to relieve the town, and of this there was at first no sign. Edward therefore sat down to blockade it methodically. This provided a striking example of his thoroughness and foresight: he realized that it would be a lengthy operation;

14

autumn was come and winter was not far ahead. If his troops were to maintain their health during the winter months in that swampy neighbourhood, something better than canvas tents became imperative. A wooden town was therefore laid out in the space between the river Hem, the town walls and the sea. It was planned symmetrically, all roads radiating to the centre, where a large market square was formed—a nice example of town planning.[1] The town was even given a name—Nouville, or New Town. The king appointed two regular market days a week to which the inhabitants of the countryside were invited to bring their wares—an astute move from every point of view.

## FLEMISH FORCES

It is time to speak of the Flemish armed forces. We left them relinquishing the siege of Bethune two days before the battle of Crecy and falling back to Aire. After that, precise information about their movements becomes scarce, and—what is still more important—the nature of communications that were established with the English army is unknown. It is, however, clear that close liaison was established before long, for we find Flemish troops serving under the English king at Calais, and combined Anglo-Flemish bands operating inland in raids and operations. Thus Edward's primary object—a junction with the Flemish army—was eventually realized, and such delay as there was mattered little because of the upshot of the battle of Crecy.

But the future of the Flemish alliance appeared uncertain, and all through the winter and early spring of 1347 a pretty contest of wits between the kings of England and France took place, each paying court to the new and youthful count of Flanders. It will be remembered that the old count had been killed at Crecy, and his son Louis was only 15 years of age. Having a French mother, his sympathies were naturally French, but his subjects inclined to the English connexion.

---

[1] Cardinal Wolsey seems to have copied Edward's example at the famous siege of Tournai nearly 200 years later.

Both England and France aimed at inducing him to marry a wife who would favour their own cause, Edward's selection being his own daughter Isabella, and Philip's the daughter of the duke of Brabant, who was now openly on the French side. The youth must have felt flattered at the efforts of two powerful kings to provide him with a wife. At the outset he declared boldly for the Brabant marriage, but the Flemish government practically forced him to agree to the English marriage. At a meeting at Bergues with the king and queen of England in March, 1347, Louis signed an agreement to marry Isabella. Great was the joy at the English Court; but it was short-lived. Though practically a prisoner of his own subjects the boy count managed to give his gaolers the slip while out riding, in a manner reminiscent of Prince Edward's escape on the eve of the battle of Evesham. Louis fled to France and no more was heard of the English marriage.

Philip of Valois then addressed himself to the Flemish government and tried to bribe them into alliance by offering the restitution of Lille, St. Venant, Lillers and other towns. But the Flemings remained faithful to their English allies.

Apart from these diplomatic activities, Philip VI appeared to take little interest in the war with England and he took no steps to relieve the town of Calais.

INVASION AT HOME

Meanwhile the siege dragged on in an uneventful way. There were numerous skirmishes and feats of arms, but details are lacking and even Froissart could not work up his imagination sufficiently to retail them. There were also forays into the neighbouring country, some as far as St. Omer and Boulogne, but they were devoid of military significance. Much more significant operations were taking place in England and Scotland during the early months of the siege, in the shape of a formidable invasion of England by David II. This will be referred to in due course; here we are only concerned with the impact of the news on Edward III. One might suppose that,

having set under way the siege of Calais, which was bound to
be a long one, the English king would hurry home on hearing
of the invasion, or impending invasion, of his own country,
leaving the trusty earl of Northampton to carry on the siege.
Not so: Edward had had an elaborate headquarters constructed
in Nouville and there he remained. One may feel surprise at
this decision. The English king had been absent from his
capital for over three months, Philip was showing no signs of
attempting operations of any sort, while mortal danger loomed
at home. Why then did Edward persist in remaining in France?
The conclusion is inescapable: he had assessed the military
chances and outcome of the operations in the north of England
correctly, and he attached such importance to the capture of
Calais, and to the bad moral effect that would be caused if he
left his army before his objective had been gained, that he
decided to accept the risk: he would continue, in principle at
any rate, to share the privations of his soldiers outside the walls
of Calais. Edward had, to use a modern expression, appreciated
the situation correctly.

### FRENCH MOBILIZATION

On March 25, 1347, Philip of Valois at last bestirred himself.
He summoned a meeting in Paris of the leading persons,
political and ecclesiastical, and he asked them for support in
raising an army for the relief of Calais. Support was promised
him, and the summons went out for a fresh levy of troops. The
king appointed May 20 as the date and Arras as the rendezvous
for the new army.[1]

The king's vassals played up unexpectedly well, and contingents came forward from all parts of the country, while
Hainault and Brabant also sent contingents. But the concentration was deplorably slow and it was not till mid-July that all
was ready. The army, when it did collect, was however greater
in numbers than ever; one chronicler goes so far as to give the
phenomenal figure of 200,000. We have no real clue about the

---

[1] Amiens is usually but wrongly given as the rendezvous.

correct figure, but it must have exceeded that of the Crecy army. If we put it at over 50,000 strong that is by no means an impossible figure for a country whose population was several times that of England. It was however a badly balanced army, most of the Genoese having gone home. War-wearied, short of cash, and with the accusation of treachery hanging over them, it is not surprising if they "had no stomach for the fight". The army was also said to be lacking in infantry, for Philip had a contempt for foot soldiers – in spite of his experience at Crecy.

While the new French army slowly collected, events of some consequence took place around Calais. In the month of April a huge convoy, estimated at 300 ships, succeeded in running the blockade, and not only entering the haven without loss but in getting away also without loss, under the eyes of the English army who were helpless to prevent or even to harm it. Presumably the French ships kept to the centre of the fairway where they were out of range of the puny English cannons. What the English fleet was doing to allow this successful blockade-running is not recorded.

King Edward was naturally upset by this humiliating incident; he realized that if it were repeated the garrison of Calais might never be reduced by starvation, and he took energetic steps to prevent its recurrence. He constructed a fort, which he named Rysbank, on the spit of land between the sea and the haven, overlooking the Gullet (as the entrance to the haven was called) and on it he mounted the most powerful weapons he had. (Rysbank remained a permanent part of the defences throughout the English occupation). He constructed groynes or piers running out into deep water all along the shore towards Wissant, in order to prevent single vessels creeping inshore at high tide, thus eluding his deep-water fleet; and most important of all, he increased the size of the fleet, which enabled it to keep a closer blockade. At times he placed aboard the fleet some of his most trusty army officers, such as Northampton, Pembroke and Talbot, in order to keep his admiral – John de

Monte Gomery as the *Foedera* writes the name—up to his work.
He also called for reinforcements from England, prominent
amongst whom was Henry of Lancaster, who soon made his
presence felt in successful raids.

On June 25 a curious naval action took place. A portion of
the fleet with Northampton and Pembroke on board[1] was
cruising off the mouth of the Somme. A French fleet of 44 sail
tried to slip past them with supplies for Calais. The English
fleet gave chase, and the French ships scattered in all directions.
Not one reached Calais, and many were captured. One ship
in particular ran ashore and the captain was seen to attach
a paper to an axe-head and throw it overboard before sur-
rendering. The spot was marked and at low tide the axe-head
was found, with the paper still attached. It was indeed a find.
It was none other than a letter from John de Vienne to King
Philip describing the desperate state of the garrison and
imploring help before it should be too late.

"Everything is eaten up—dogs, cats, horses—and we have nothing
left to subsist on, unless we eat each other."

This illuminating letter was dispatched to King Edward who,
with grim irony, courteously forwarded it to the addressee.
This action shows how sure of himself and of his army the
English king was.

\*   \*   \*

The army that set out for the relief of Calais in mid-July
had nearly all its old leaders. There were the two sons of the
king, the dukes of Normandy and Orleans; the dukes of
Burgundy and Bourbon, the count de Foix, Louis of Savoy and
the ever-faithful John of Hainault. All being in order, the army
set out, marching *via* Hesdin to Therouanne. Philip had
intended to make for Gravelines and approach Calais from
the east along the dunes. This would have been sound strategy,
but he could not obtain the assent of the Flemings to this

---

[1] Historians generally show these earls as being in command, but the chronicle
does not state this: the relationship between them and the admiral was probably
a delicate one.

course, so he weakly decided to approach from the west. This submission to the wishes of the Flemings by the leader of an army 50,000 strong seems astonishing, but we are now past experiencing astonishment at any of Philip's actions, or in-actions. Be this as it may, the march was resumed, and on July 27 the French army camped on the dunes immediately to the south of the little fishing village of Sangatte, five miles west of the walls of Calais.

A look-out tower on top of the dunes (here over 300 ft. high) was captured by a *coup de main*, but that was the limit of the French success. Philip had got his army into a hopeless position, the sea was on his left flank, thickly lined by the English fleet; there were marshes on his right flank and in his front was the river Hem, with only one bridge, that at Neuillay,[1] which was strongly held by the earl of Lancaster. Philip recognized his position as hopeless, after a couple of days, and decided to get away with the least possible damage to his prestige. For this purpose, after three days of fruitless parleys,[2] he played his old card of challenging his opponent to engage in battle on some selected spot.[3] Edward, knowing his man, promptly accepted the challenge, and then, as usual, nothing happened. While the parleys–aided and abetted by the usual pair of cardinals sent by the Pope–were proceeding, Philip was making secret preparations to retreat, and on the night of August 1-2–the day before the battle was to take place–the whole French army crept silently away. There is indeed evidence which points to an actual panic having hastened and accompanied the movement, but we are left to conjecture its cause: it may have been some superstitious motive, caused by some phenomenon in the sky. Whatever the cause, the fact

---

[1] Now the site of Fort de Neuillay.

[2] The English Commissioners at the parleys—Lancaster, Northampton, Burgersh, Cobham and Manny—may be considered the five senior generals in the army.

[3] The appraisal of the eminent French historian Simeon Luce is probably the correct one. "It seems, to tell the truth, that the challenge had been sent scarcely more seriously by Philip than it had been received by Edward, and the king of France no doubt only proposed battle to his opponent in order to cover his retreat or at least to provide himself with a reasonable explanation for it."

remains that the army burnt its tents, left great quantities of food and stores *in situ* and retreated in such disorder that the pursuing English, under the dashing Henry of Lancaster, were able to make large captures of men and stores and to harry the retreating army for many miles. A great French army was for the second time within 12 months in ignominious flight.

### THE FALL OF CALAIS

Our commiseration must go out to the gallant defenders of Calais. From the summit of the towers in the town the relieving army could be seen, but all communication was cut off; only a rough-and-ready method of contacting their saviours could be extemporized. This was done in an ingenious way. On the first night of the relieving army's arrival a great beacon was lit on the highest tower, in full view of the relieving army: on the second night a similar but much smaller beacon was lit and on the third night only a mere flicker of a beacon could be seen—a dramatic and sure method of depicting the desperate position of the garrison.

But they had not lost hope; Philip's huge army covered many acres of ground, and its extent could be descried from the town walls; surely the French king would make a fight for it before tamely withdrawing! But the hope of speedy relief was cruelly dashed when on the morning of August 2 the Sangatte dunes were seen to be an empty smouldering heap, with English troops swarming all around. Philip had deserted his noble city of Calais.

There could be no doubt of what their next course must be. That which de Vienne had hinted at in his letter to the king must now be carried out; Calais must surrender at discretion.

The story of the surrender is one of the best-known episodes of the Hundred Years War, thanks mainly to Froissart's graphic account of it. But Froissart and le Bel are not our only evidence for the circumstances of the surrender. There can be no doubt that the English king intended the surrender to be accompanied by every circumstance of humiliation. Six of the leading burgesses with de Vienne at their head were required to come into the king's presence bearing the keys of the town and castle, bare-headed and footed, with halters round their necks. Le Bel states – and Froissart embroiders the picture – that the king would have had them executed but for the intercession of Queen Philippa, and the chroniclers assert that he was influenced by his hatred of the townspeople. It may be so, and modern historians seem to be satisfied with this explanation; but it is hard to see what good purpose could be served by thus gratuitously antagonizing the people who were about to become his subjects. Edward was a purposeful monarch, he was farseeing, astute, even crafty, and all his actions, so far as we can see, were directed to a single end – his establishment as the predominant power in France. He was not cruel by nature, and he later treated de Vienne graciously,[1] while a prisoner in England. Ramsay is probably right in describing the scene of the surrender as "a solemn pageant". Edward wished to impress not only the inhabitants of Calais but all other towns with a sense of his own power and of the terrible fate that, but for his royal clemency, would overtake any town that refused, as Calais had done, his summons to surrender.

Immediately after the surrender the king had food sent into the town for the relief of the starving population, after which he had everyone ejected whose adhesion to their new sovereign liege was in doubt. Calais, henceforth, was to be an English town and the king could not afford to allow inside it large numbers whose loyalty might be suspect; moreover he required space within its walls for the English settlers whom he designed to plant therein. Shortly afterwards a truce was made, to last till June 24 of the following year. The defences having been set in order and the administration settled to his liking, a task that occupied him for another two months, King Edward set sail on October 12 for the home that he had not seen for 15 months.

---

[1] A French historian goes so far as to assert that the king "overwhelmed him with gifts". Professor Tout agrees that "the defenders were treated chivalrously by the victor, who admired their courage and endurance".

NEVILLE'S CROSS

Reference was made above to the invasion of England by the Scottish king. This invasion does not strictly belong to the Hundred Years War, but strategically it affected the war, for Scotland was the ally of France, and King David, in invading England, was acceding to the request of Philip of Valois to make a diversion in his favour. A brief account of it must therefore be given. Early in October, 1346, David II crossed the Cumberland border at the head of a large army, and advanced toward Durham, laying waste many places as he passed, and burning the famous abbey of Lanercost. He expected an easy progress south, as the English army was far away oversea. But Edward, who never quite trusted his northern neighbour, had with careful foresight prepared for this very contingency before leaving the country. In recruiting his army for the invasion of France he had deliberately excluded all the country north of the Humber. Usually the task of defending the border against a Scottish incursion was the responsibility of the Prince Bishop of Durham, but the soldier bishop Hatfield was, as we have seen, fighting lustily with his king in France; his task therefore devolved on the archbishop of York, who speedily collected an army, and with it confronted the Scots at Neville's Cross, just outside the walls of Durham. On October 17, 1346, the Scots attacked and were decisively defeated, and King David was taken prisoner and lodged in the Tower of London, shortly to be the companion in adversity of Charles de Blois. Few tears need be shed over his fate. As Professor Tout observes: "In thus playing the game of the French, King David began a policy which from Neville's Cross to Flodden, brought embarrassment to England and desolation to Scotland. It was the inevitable penalty of two independent and hostile states existing on one little island."

The "desolation" was not long in coming. As punishment, the English king resolved on the subjugation of the northern kingdom, which he felt powerful enough to achieve, in spite of the fact that 30,000 English soldiers were campaigning in

northern France, with further armies in Brittany and Gascony.
His calculation, however, appeared to be justified; he had
Edward Baliol brought forward as king, raised two armies
and sent them across the border in the spring of 1347, while he
and his own army were still sitting before the walls of Calais.
Earl Percy led one army across the eastern border, the other,
under Baliol, marching by the western route. They speedily
overran Lothian but Percy, for some reason, did not attempt
to take Edinburgh. Instead he swung to his left, probably by
previous arrangement with Baliol, and joined forces with the
other army, which had been ravaging the Galloway country.
All southern Scotland now acknowledged Baliol as king. His
rule was to prove of short duration, but the important point
as regards the war with France was that danger of Scottish
aggression had definitely passed away, and Edward could draw
freely on the whole of England in his efforts to maintain the
strength of the army before Calais. To such good purpose did
he do this that his army eventually topped 30,000 in number.

ANNUS MIRABILIS

A truce having been signed with France, a survey of the
English achievements up to date will be appropriate. The
English king was received with acclamation when he returned
after a long absence to his capital, as well he might be. In
spite of the heavy taxation and the calls on manpower needed
to sustain the war in so many spheres, the country had pros-
pered materially, but—more important—it had been welded
and stimulated by the long series of victories achieved wherever
King Edward's armies had fought. The year 1346–7 may well
be called *Annus Mirabilis*, the year of victories. The Tower of
London was bulging with royal and noble prisoners from
Gascony, from Brittany, from Ponthieu and from Scotland.

There were almost simultaneous victories in four different
and widely separate theatres, for if we regard the earl of
Derby's victory of Auberoche in June, 1345, as a "curtain-
raiser", we get four victories in four different campaigns in

the space of five months in 1346: Aiguillon, Dagworth's victory of St. Pol de Léon, Crecy and Neville's Cross, while 1347 witnessed the victory of Roche-Derrien and the capture of Calais. To all this can be added the conquest of Poitou by Henry of Lancaster. Wherever men looked, there the soldiers of Edward III were victorious. In an astonishingly short space of time English soldiers had established a world-reputation, and had come to be looked upon everywhere as invincible. Little wonder is it that the inhabitants of Calais soon transferred their allegiance from a Valois to a Plantagenet, led by the man whom, only two months previously, Edward was credited with the intention of hanging—Eustache du Pont St. Pierre.[1]

How are we to explain these remarkable and sustained successes? The reasons may be comprised under two headings—strategical and tactical. Taking the latter first, it has come to be recognized that Edward's tactical methods were derived from his grandfather. Edward I had realized the advantage to be gained from the cooperation of archers and men-at-arms, between cavalry and infantry. The younger Edward carried this principle a step further and at Dupplin Moor his *protégé* Baliol, and at Halidon Hill Edward in person, employed dismounted men-at-arms and archers in skilful combination. The lesson was well learned by Edward's lieutenants, and Northampton at Morlaix and Derby at Auberoche employed the two arms in close cooperation. Crecy only put the seal on what had become an established practice. Needless to say, no method of tactics will avail unless the tool to be employed is sound and sharp. This was so. The English men-at-arms were the pick of the country, and the English archers had graduated by long training and practice at their craft.[2] The unanimity with which the French chroniclers emphasize the

---

[1] This action of the French hero of the siege has led some people to doubt the historical accuracy of the story of the halters.

[2] On many a sandstone village church the grooves are still be be seen where the archers sharpened their arrows after mass, preparatory to undertaking their weekly butt-practice.

skill and prowess of the English archers is significant of the deadly impression–literal and figurative–they had made upon their opponents. So, tactically, Edward had forged a sound and sharp weapon and employed it effectively.

Strategically the English king is assessed very low by most historians. It is said that his only idea in the realm of strategy was to embark upon aimless and purposeless raids. But Edward was the most purposeful of monarchs. Of that we have seen ample evidence. The siege of Calais was *par excellence* a strategical project, and the most outstanding feature of that famous siege is the tenacity of purpose exhibited by the English king: like a snake that has its fangs embedded in its victim, he never let go, jeopardizing everything for the attainment of his objective. And what a tremendous objective that was! A permanent base on French soil at the point where the Channel was at its narrowest fulfilled the triple function of facilitating a subsequent invasion of France, an increased control of home waters and a commercial pipeline, as it were, to the Continent. It was as useful as a Channel tunnel would be in modern days.

If anything is open to criticism in Edward's conduct of the siege it is the inadequacy of his measures to close the port until late in the day. As to this, it is a fact that such blockading was not as simple in the days of sail as in these of steam; the failure of the Spaniards, during the three-year siege of Ostend, to block the harbour, is a good example of this. Yet the fact remains that Edward did eventually find means to effect a total blockade, and there seems no reason why he should not have found them several months earlier.

But that is not the end of the matter. In another sphere his strategy was brilliantly successful, namely his conception of a concentric attack on France by means of exterior lines, possible to an island power that has command of the sea. It was largely as a result of this far-flung strategy that neither of the two great French armies was enabled to achieve anything. The army of John duke of Normandy had as its mission the expulsion of the English once and for all from Gascony. The duke had merely to march straight forward in order to drive the tiny English army into the sea, but instead he allowed himself to become involved in the siege of a petty town, and then he marched north, too soon to win Aiguillon and too late to prevent Crecy. Such transferences of armies when operating on interior lines are common, and Edward's operation on exterior lines thus produced a rich dividend.

The contrast between the strategical prowess of Edward of England and Philip of France was glaring. The latter, throughout his campaigns, exhibited no coherent, continuous military strategy or design; he wavered, fumbled and faltered, and may well go down to history as Philip the Fumbler.

# APPENDIX

### THE TERRAIN

No historian, as far as I can discover, has attempted to pinpoint the exact site of the English camp before Calais. It is described vaguely as "to the west of the town". Now, the country directly to the west of the town was all marshy,[1] to such an extent that the English could not find firm platforms for their siege ballistas. Are we to believe that the English army sat down for almost a year in this marsh? The nearest approach to an exact description of the site is contained in an anonymous work entitled *Le Siége de Calais* published in 1739, which states that the English camp was between the river Hem, the sea and the town.

The oldest printed map that I can discover dates from 1555, and this shows the course of the river Hem as I have described it above.[2] A still earlier map of 1547 in the MS room of the British Museum unfortunately does not clearly show the course of the river. If it then flowed, as indicated above, into the town haven, the English camp must have been situated on the marsh. But, in view of the fact that there was a strip of firm ground

---

[1] It is now built over, and excavations would not be likely to uncover any remains of "Nouville".

[2] In the map-room at the British Museum.

to the north between the marsh and the sea, it is contrary to inherent military probability that the English camp was sited anywhere else. It was the obvious place. It is however possible that the river Hem did not at the time of the siege flow into the town haven; there is a dip in the line of dunes immediately to the north of Neuillay, still covered with water channels, which may have been the old channel of the river Hem. If this was so, the statement that the English camp was between the river, town and sea becomes clear and plausible. Strength is given to this supposition by a phrase in King Edward's letter to the archbishop of Canterbury in which he states that the French king encamped "opposite the marsh". This implies that the English army was not situated on the marsh, but on firm ground beyond it. Since we know that the French camp was on the Sangatte dunes, the only possible place for the English camp must therefore be on the low spit of dunes between the town and the sea, though it probably extended as far south as the bridge of Nieullay on the west side of the town. This is where I have placed it in my narrative.

### THE SOURCES

The sources are naturally much the same as for the preceding chapter. Edward III's chaplains desert us, and Knighton becomes our chief authority. Rymer's collection of *Foedera* assumes increasing importance, showing the steps taken by the king to sustain the siege.

On the French side there is practically nothing of importance –if we perhaps except the *Continuation of Guillaume de Nangis*– but the *Bourgeois de Valenciennes* again comes to our help, as does *Gilles li Muisis* for the part played by the Flemings, though here we could wish for fuller and more precise information regarding the cooperation between the English and Flemish armies, which appears to have been closer and more important than historians have given credit for.

There is no extant account of the siege by a participant or even by an eye-witness of any nationality.

## CHAPTER IX

# BETWEEN CRECY AND POITIERS

THE truce of 1347 and the Black Death (bubonic plague) that followed it in 1348 might have been expected to bring the fighting to an end, and it certainly languished during those years, but it is far from the truth to maintain, as has been done, that there was little fighting and that of no particular interest between the battles of Crecy and Poitiers. On the contrary there was much fighting, and there were operations of considerable interest to military historians. Indeed, apart from the fact that the two kings did not lead armies in person against each other, the truce was a truce in name only. Moreover, the Black Death had a direct influence on the war. It was, curiously enough, more severe in England than on the Continent; indeed nearly half the population is said to have perished during those dreadful years (though this is probably an exaggeration.) This enhanced the already enormous preponderance of potential French over English soldiers, and made reinforcement of the many English garrisons in France ever more difficult. Recruits were drawn from all quarters, from Ireland, from Brittany, from Gascony even, from Flanders, from Italy, and from "Germany". But not from Scotland. England and Scotland—both sprung in the main from the same Anglian stock—remained the bitterest of enemies.

Though the Black Death ravaged the common people more than the upper classes, it carried off the king's youngest daughter, and also the queen of the French king. Philip of Valois married a young girl of 18 exactly one month after the death of his first wife, but did not live many months to enjoy his new spouse: he died on August 22, 1350, and was succeeded by his eldest son as John II, or John the Good.[1]

[1] The appellation "The Good" refers not to his moral qualities, but to his fame for being a "good fellow well met".

Almost constant warfare of one kind or another went on in Picardy, in Brittany, and in Gascony. In the latter duchy the English were steadily enlarging their conquests, and in the summer of 1349 the tireless duke of Lancaster (as Henry of Lancaster was now to become) carried a whirlwind "push", as we should call it, to the gates of Toulouse. Failing to induce the French to meet him in the field he fell back, ravaging the country as he went. In this operation he captured more than 40 towns and villages (many of which were subsequently retaken by the French).

In the same summer a notable battle took place in Poitou at a place called Lunalonge.[1] The allies, English and Gascons, were commanded by the Captal de Buch—shortly to become famous—and the French commander was Jean de Lisle. The allies, as usual, dismounted for the battle, parking their horses in rear. Jean de Lisle, thinking to take advantage of this separation of the English from their horses, sent a mounted party round the rear of the line to capture the horses, which they were completely successful in doing. They then attacked the English line mounted, from the front, with the remainder of their force, but met with the same fate as their predecessors at Crecy, their commander being captured. As Professor Tout observes, "the real interest of the battle lies in the effort of the French to seek out the weak points of the new English system". In this they were indirectly successful, for the English, though victorious, feeling lost and insecure without their horses, fell back on their base during the following night.

Meanwhile spasmodic fighting around Calais was incessant; the French were looking for an opportunity and a means to regain what a French historian has aptly called "the Gibraltar of the North", while the English were forever attempting to enlarge their "pale", thereby increasing their security and providing a surer and wider source of supplies. The French efforts culminated in the next year in an elaborate plot or ruse to capture the place. An Italian named Amerigo, who had

---

[1] Identified as Limalonge (Deux Sevres) by Denifle.

been made governor of the Calais garrison, was bribed by Geoffrey de Chargny, the French governor of St. Omer, to open the gates to him. However, Amerigo, thinking better of it, crossed in secret to England and informed the king. Edward was delighted at the news: it would give him the opportunity for an exciting adventure, wherein he might teach the Frenchman that it did not pay to work "underground" in an age of chivalry. He instructed Amerigo to return, continue with the plot, and on the appointed day admit to the castle the first contingent of French troops. But the king was determined to play an active part in the counter-plot himself: he faced the unpleasant sea crossing[1] and he allowed his eldest boy to come too, accompanied by the inevitable Walter Manny. They crossed in disguise, and on arrival at Calais the king made certain arrangements. . . .

On the last night of the year 1349 the postern gate was opened, as arranged, and a party entered, the main body remaining outside the main gate. Everything appeared to be in order, no English soldiers being in evidence. But on a pre-arranged signal, a false wall in the courtyard that the king had had constructed was thrown down and a party of English soldiers rushed out and overpowered the Frenchmen. At the same moment a watchman, posted on top of the tower over the main gate, hurled a great stone down on to the already weakened drawbridge and broke it. De Chargny and his main body were thus prevented from entering in support of their advanced party, and they could only look on helplessly. But that was not the end. The king had prepared two assault parties, one of which he himself led, dressed as a simple knight, while the Prince of Wales led the other. Simultaneously they sallied forth, the king by the east gate, the Prince by the west gate, and attacked de Chargny from both sides at the same moment. It seems to have been a beautifully prepared and executed operation—none too easy in the dead of night. The French were routed and Geoffrey de Chargny was captured.

---

[1] In nearly all his crossings of the Channel, Edward was caught in bad storms.

King Edward, on good evidence (by which I mean not merely on the "picturesque romancing" of Froissart), dashed into the thick of the fray and crossed swords with and captured Eustace de Ribaumont. That night the chivalrous element in the character of the English king was in evidence; de Chargny was now a prisoner, but, far from punishing him for his breach of the truce, Edward invited him and other prisoners to dinner and even loaded honours on his own captive, de Ribaumont, whom he afterward set at liberty.

## BATTLE OF WINCHELSEA

The interest of 1350 lies mainly on the sea. It is typical of the uncertain and uncharted relations between countries of the fourteenth century that, while England and France were formally at war, the fleets of Spain and of Genoa should plan an informal but important part therein. The narrow strip of water separating England from France formed a veritable lifeline to the English armies engaged overseas. If that lifeline were permanently severed, slow death to those armies would follow. None knew this better than King Edward, and he exerted himself to build up a powerful fleet. But the seas are wide and, as we have seen at Calais, ships cannot be everywhere at the same time. Castilian and Genoese galleys traded on this well-known fact and openly waged war on English shipping in the Channel. They went further and talked of actually invading the country. No doubt it was an idle threat, but their activities jeopardized the English forces in Brittany and even in Calais. Eventually King Edward decided that this nonsense must be stopped. Hearing that a great Castilian fleet was making up Channel for the ports of Flanders he planned to intercept it on the return voyage. For this purpose he assembled a fleet at Sandwich and went there himself with the Black Prince and his second son, John of Gaunt, now a boy of ten years. The *élite* of the country joined him, William Bohun of Northampton, Henry of Lancaster and Walter Manny of course; others included Warwick, Arundel, Salisbury, Huntingdon, Sir

Reginald Cobham and young John Chandos. The Spanish
fleet was commanded by Don Carlos de la Cerda, whose
valiant brother we met in Brittany in 1342. The English fleet,
50 sail in all including small pinnaces, put to sea on August 28,
the Spanish fleet being reported on its return voyage from
Sluys. Though it numbered only 44 ships it was more powerful
than the English fleet, for its great galleons towered over the
smaller English vessels as did those of the Spanish Armada
200 years later. But in this respect only did the battle that
ensued resemble that of the Armada. In the latter the two
fleets engaged in a running fight, thanks to their guns, but in
1350 if either side possessed guns they were too weak for this
purpose and the only method of engaging was to turn it into
a land fight by grappling the hostile ships and boarding them.
Therefore the men-at-arms donned their armour as soon as
the enemy fleet was sighted.

King Edward hoisted his flag in the *Thomas*, and the ten-
year-old John of Gaunt presumably accompanied his father.
Prince Edward on the other hand sailed in his own ship; after
all he was now in his 21st year, and may be considered a
grown man. Both father and son were in high spirits, in spite
of the fact that they were about to encounter a superior fleet.
The young John Chandos, accompanied by a minstrel, sang
before his master a war ballad. For there was a long wait in
front of them. The wind was in the east, and the Spanish fleet
was running before it. At 4 p.m. on August 29 the two fleets
came in sight of one another. By this time the English fleet had
dropped down-wind about 40 miles and was off Dungeness.
Large ships could not beat against the wind in those days and
we may picture the English as tacking backward and forward
across the Channel at its narrowest point during those 24 hours.
When the Spaniards drew near, the English admiral, Lord
Morley, so manoeuvred his fleet that his ships were dead in
front of the Spaniards, and a collision was inevitable.

If the English ships put their helms down and lay up into
the wind the enemy would sail past them at too great a speed

to grapple them; the only possible method was to put their helms up and run on a parallel course to their opponents, shortening sail the while in order to be overtaken, albeit only slowly. This required nice judgment and good seamanship. The skipper of the *Thomas* did not possess these qualities to the full, for he closed with the nearest Spanish ship as it passed at too great speed or at too sharp an angle; there was a mighty thud, the *Thomas* shivered and rebounded from the heavier and stronger-built Spaniard, and sprang a bad leak. According to one account the ship was even dismasted. This seems unlikely, for the ship was still navigable and the skipper was successful at his second attempt: a big Spaniard was grappled and after its stone-throwing crew had been silenced by the archers, a detachment of men-at-arms, with scaling ladders, swarmed up the sides of the loftier ship and fought on deck a similar land battle to that they had fought just a decade previously at Sluys. The other ships in the royal navy followed suit and soon the scene of Sluys was being repeated in the English Channel—and with similar results. By sheer force of arms, and superior skill, though the odds were against them, the highly trained English men-at-arms under their renowned captains brought off a rather astonishing victory. Ship after ship of the proud dons succumbed in turn, till no less than 17 had struck their colours and the remainder were in full flight down the Channel, with every stitch of canvas unfurled. After capturing his opposing vessel, King Edward transferred his own flag to her, as the *Thomas* was now in a sinking condition. Meanwhile the Prince of Wales was in a parlous situation. His ship, too, was badly holed and about to sink, but he had not been successful in boarding his opponent. Fortunately Henry of Lancaster was disengaged at the moment and managed to sail his ship up to the Spaniard on the other side and board her. The enemy was overpowered and the prince transferred to her in the nick of time.

While the fight was in progress, both fleets of course continued to sail before the wind and so passed within sight of

Winchelsea. Great was the excitement in that little harbour, and the cliffs were black with the multitudes, cheering wildly as each Spanish ship in turn was captured. Winchelsea had suffered sorely in the past from sea rovers and now its reward had come, and the great battle has rightly gone down to history as the sea battle of Winchelsea.

The Channel was cleared of its Spanish pests and safe communication with the armies in Gascony and Brittany was restored.

## BRITTANY

The scene now shifts to Brittany, where a new King's Lieutenant, or viceroy, had been installed. The gallant Sir Thomas Dagworth had been killed in an ambush near Auray by a Breton named Raoul de Cahours, who had been made viceroy of Poitou, but had quarrelled violently with Dagworth and at the same time was bribed by the French king to desert the English cause. Edward was about to relieve him of his command when his murder of Dagworth took place. Dagworth was succeeded by Sir William Bentley, another remarkable English captain, about whom it is time to say a few words.

Sir William Bentley was now 47 years of age. He had previously served in the wars in Flanders. Coming out to Brittany in 1342 he was placed in charge of the garrison of Ploermel, 26 miles north of Vannes. From this place he had made a lightning march and attack on the besiegers of Annesin, which marked him out for high command. This exploit won him, it is said, the admiration of his enemies. A man of forceful character, he had twice earned the displeasure of his sovereign by openly opposing him. But Edward had an unerring eye for character and military talent and Bentley was restored to favour. Thus, when Dagworth was killed, Bentley was his obvious successor.

Though we are not concerned with his civil government of Brittany, it should be explained that the English king was, in the absence of an adult member of the house of Montfort, directing and controlling the affairs of the duchy more and more. Whether he intended to retain his hold over it when the young John Montfort came of age it is impossible to say, but this English control naturally antagonized the Breton nobles, who were, as has been pointed out before, mainly of the Bloisian faction. Moreover, Edward confiscated the lands of these nobles and granted them to his English captains. This may not have troubled the common people, but the king's policy was "to make the war pay for itself" and this policy naturally led to exactions which rendered the English rule still more unpopular. It may well be that the French would have acted in the same manner, but this was not an argument that would carry much weight with those who suffered the exactions necessary to pay for the war.

All this may explain the Battle of the Thirty, which has been rendered famous by a Breton ballad. It has in itself no intrinsic importance, but is interesting as throwing a light on military manners during the age of chivalry, so it is worthy of relation. It took the form of a mounted mêlée between 30 Breton knights of the French faction and 30 nominally English knights. (Actually there were only 20 Englishmen, the balance being Bretons and Germans.) Accounts differ about the cause; French writers assert that it was due to exasperation caused by the exactions of Bentley; English writers give as the cause the anger induced by the murder of Dagworth. The French account is probably the correct one, for the "battle" which occurred on March 27, 1351, was fought over six months after the death of Dagworth. Whatever the real cause, the engagement took place midway between Ploermel and Josselin seven miles to the west. Two of the English knights were afterward to become famous, Hugh Calveley and Robert Knollys, both Cheshire gentlemen. The fight resolved itself into a series of duels, which lasted an astonishingly long time, with a break for refreshments in the middle. Eventually nine on the English side were killed and the victory rested with the Franco-Bretons.

## THE BATTLE OF SAINTES

Eleven days after the Battle of the Thirty a battle of a more orthodox character was fought. In the spring of 1351 the new king of France decided to make an effort to recover the province of Poitou and started making preparations. By some means, news of this intention reached the English king and he immediately took what counter-measures he could. Since the departure of Henry of Lancaster from Gascony there was no outstanding English captain of proved ability in Bordeaux. Someone must be sent there at once and Edward's choice fell upon Sir John Beauchamp, brother of the earl of Warwick and governor of Calais. As always, the king made a sound choice. Beauchamp hurried out to Bordeaux, and so slow were the preparations of King John that the English John arrived at Bordeaux in time to take steps to confront the impending invasion. But he was only just in time. From the moment of his arrival, messengers came one after another hot-foot from the north, imploring help against the invading French army. These invaders were under the command of two marshals of France, Guy de Nesle (Sire d'Offremont) and Arnaud d'Endreghem. Advancing slowly, the French drove back the slender English garrisons and laid siege to St. Jean d'Angelys. Sir John Beauchamp advanced north to meet them and in early April reached the province of Saintonge and entered the town of Taillebourg, between St. Jean d'Angelys and Saintes. According to one source a force under Sir William Bentley had joined the English army near the coast, and had advanced to Taillebourg, but this seems unlikely; Robert of Avesbury would scarcely have omitted to mention it had it been the fact.

The French were besieging Saintes at the time, and when the two armies approached one another near St. Georges-la-Valade, the English dismounted, as was their custom, and formed line of battle, leaving their horses in the rear. The French, on seeing this, did likewise, but retained two mounted bodies, one on each wing. Beauchamp had sent for reinforcements from Taillebourg and Fonnay-sur-Charente, and so slow

was de Nesle in forming up his army that they arrived in time
for the battle. The French then attacked on foot and, though
details are lacking, it is clear that they suffered a bloody and
decisive defeat, 600 Frenchmen being killed or taken, the
remainder fleeing to Saintes. Among the prisoners were the
two French marshals and 140 esquires and gentlemen. Guy de
Nesle was promptly ransomed for a large sum by King John
and was soon in arms again against the English.

The numbers engaged were not large and the results of the
battle were not great, but it is of interest as showing the growing
custom of the French to counter the English dismounted
array on foot.

### THE CALAIS PALE

The interest shifts north again. In May, 1351, the ubiquitous
and high-spirited Henry of Lancaster, newly created duke (the
second of that rank to be created in the English peerage, the
first being the Prince of Wales), landed at Calais on his way
to join a crusade in Prussia. As Ramsay expresses it, "Having
set foot in France he felt bound to do something". This "something" consisted in nothing less than an attempt to take the
strongly fortified town of Boulogne. He succeeded in capturing
the lower town, alongside the river and haven, but his attempt
on the upper town failed because his scaling ladders were too
short. He therefore contented himself with a great raid right
up to St. Omer, and then passed on eastward to his crusade.[1]

On June 6 following, Sir John Beauchamp, who had with
great promptitude returned to Calais, met a French army
under the count de Beaujeu at Ardres, midway between
St. Omer and Calais, in a pitched battle. Once again the
French followed the English procedure of fighting on foot, and
on this occasion were successful, and Beauchamp himself was
captured. Unfortunately details of the battle are lacking.

Throughout this period the English were gradually extending and strengthening their hold on the Calais pale. A notable

---

[1] On arrival in Prussia he was arrested, but eventually set free.

example of this was the capture of Guines, eight miles south of Calais, which occurred in the following January or February (1352).

## BRITTANY

The same year was marked by important events in Brittany. Shortly after the battle of Saintes, Sir William Bentley returned to Brittany (if indeed he had ever left it), recaptured the enormously strong castle of Fougeres, which had been seized by a young Breton named Bertrand du Guesclin, and installed as its captain Sir Robert Knollys. But signs of an approaching campaign of reconquest on the part of the new king of France were not lacking, and Bentley hurried home to implore reinforcements from the king. Edward would willingly have provided them were that possible, but the country was still suffering from the effects of the Black Death, and the number of possible recruits to the army had been almost halved. Bentley had therefore to return early in 1352 disappointed, bringing with him a mere handful of men-at-arms and archers of doubtful quality.

Meanwhile the threatened French offensive had begun to take shape, and Fougeres had been invested. Knollys was in sore straights, and Bentley dashed to his rescue. In this he was entirely successful: he drove off the besiegers and levelled the "bastides" or towers that they had constructed round the castle. A few months were still available in which to organize and strengthen the scattered defences of Brittany and Sir William Bentley took full advantage of this breathing space.

Meanwhile King John also was busy. He collected recruits from places far and wide. By August all was ready, and Guy de Nesle, in spite of his defeat and capture the previous year, was again placed in command, with the high-sounding but empty title of "Governor-General of Brittany".

Several of the barons and knights of Brittany served under him, and it is probable (though it cannot be proved) that the young Bertrand du Guesclin was also present with the army.

Early in August, then, Marshal de Nesle led his army over the French border, and directed his march on Rennes, his ultimate objective being Brest. Thus his plan of campaign was exactly the opposite of that pursued by King Edward just ten years before. Leaving Fougeres wide on his right hand, de Nesle pushed straight on and apparently had no difficulty in gaining possession of Rennes. Bentley was wisely husbanding his resources, well knowing that if you try to defend everywhere you are weak everywhere and likely to be defeated in detail. He therefore concentrated his whole available field army in the vicinity of Ploermel, the defences of which he had just strengthened. Ploermel is 36 miles west by south of Rennes and the direct road to Brest runs several miles further north. If, therefore, Bentley remained at Ploermel after news of the French capture of Rennes reached him, he might find his position turned by his northern flank, and his army might thus be cut off from Brest. Two possible courses were open to him. He could either fall back towards Brest or he could advance northward toward the Brest road in order to cut off his enemy and offer him battle. He decided on this latter course, though he must have been aware that he would be heavily outnumbered.

On August 14 the little Anglo-Breton army set out. Most of its senior officers were Bretons, but Sir William Bentley had as his right-hand man Robert Knollys. The route took the army through the small town of Mauron, 12 miles north of Ploermel, the Brest road being a further ten miles on. But either Bentley had miscalculated the time required (which seems unlikely) or the French had left Rennes earlier than reported, for they had already passed through Montfort, 12 miles north-east of Mauron, and had only to march straight on in order to by-pass or get behind the English army. But such was not de Nesle's intention; he desired an encounter and on hearing that the English army was on his left hand he turned south, leaving the Brest road, and marched straight on Mauron. Thus it happened that about noon on August 14 both armies were approaching

Mauron from opposite directions. An encounter seemed inevitable.

## THE BATTLE OF MAURON—AUGUST 14, 1352

The little town of Mauron is pleasantly situated on a low ridge about 150 ft. above the valley which sweeps round its foot to the east and south. This valley contains a tiny stream, the head waters of the river Ivel. A spur runs forward from the town to meet this rivulet 1,200 yards to the east, the highest point on this spur being 300 yards short of the rivulet. On the far side of the rivulet the ground slopes up very gently except to the north-east where it is for a short distance very steep.

A narrow belt of trees ran across the top of this spur. The country around was open, devoid of hedges, ditches or woods. Two roads now approach this ridge from the Rennes direction. On the right hand one there was till the last century a château named Brembili; it is now replaced by a warehouse on the side of the railway which runs along the foot of the ridge, between it and the rivulet. At the time of the battle the herbage was at its strongest and most luxuriant. From the top of the spur on the outskirts of the town a distant view can be obtained towards the east and north-east.

We may picture Sir William Bentley riding forward to the top of the spur on hearing that dust columns were rising in the distance to the north-east. From here he would verify the fact for himself. It could only mean one thing—the French army was approaching. Though it was greatly superior to his own in number, Bentley had already resolved to accept battle, and to accept it in what had now become the traditional English manner, that is, dismounted and in a defensive position. Such a position was not difficult to find, for the English commander must have been standing upon it at the time. It was not ideal—no position ever is ideal—but it had certain points in its favour. Though the approach was easy for the enemy (for the tiny rivulet offered no appreciable obstacle), it was on commanding ground and the long rank undergrowth immediately in its front would slow up the French advance, that is, if they dismounted for the purpose, as they were becoming accustomed

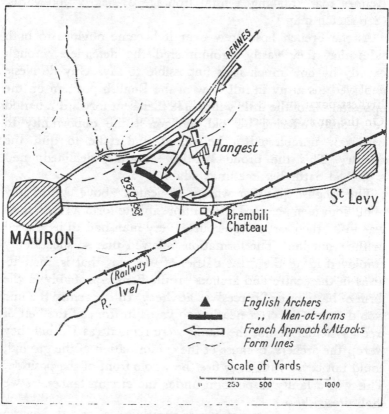

II. BATTLE OF MAURON

to do. Its weak feature was that it was over-extensive for his slender force, about 3,000 all told. For such a force a frontage of over 500 yards was on the large side. But this position required a frontage of over 600 yards, and because of the shape of the ground it must either be very curved, with flanks drawn back, or the centre of the position must be much higher than the flanks. But it was possible to compromise, and this is probably what Bentley did; he placed his centre midway between the belt of trees and the rivulet, while his right rested on the château Brembili and his left on the valley bottom at the main Rennes road, making a total frontage of nearly 700 yards. (See sketch map.)

As the French host drew near it became obvious to both sides that they vastly outnumbered the defenders, though exactly by how much it is impossible to say. Guy de Nesle deployed his army in full view of the English position on the opposite side of the little valley. He then sent forward a herald courteously offering his old antagonist the opportunity to withdraw unmolested if he would undertake to quit the country. This the proud Bentley scornfully declined; and a pitched battle became unavoidable.

The English position was as indicated above. With only about four men per yard it was impossible to form a reserve. As was to be the case at Agincourt, every man had to be placed in the front line. The formation followed that so successfully employed in all the great battles of the war, that is, men-at-arms in the centre and archers on the flanks–probably in the form of bastions or "herces" as at Crecy. In the centre the line would follow the crest nearly 200 yards in front of the belt of trees. Whether or not the flanks were refused (as I think they were), the archers, because of the conformation of the ground, could not cover with their fire the whole front of the position. This was a faulty disposition under the circumstances, as we shall presently see.

## THE ATTACK

It was a hot summer day, and during the pause while the parleys were proceeding the English soldiers could hear the hum of innumerable bees sucking honey in the flowering herbage to their front.

As the afternoon wore on, Guy de Nesle formed up his army in battle array. Somewhat surprisingly, considering his recent defeat, he formed his army in the same fashion, that is, all dismounted except a small body of horse. The only difference was that in place of two such bodies, one on each flank, he confined them to a single body of 700 men under the count Hangest, with orders to operate on the left flank. The nature of the ground on the other flank will explain this limitation for, as stated above, the slope here was very steep—in places almost precipitous for a few yards—and would handicap the heavily armoured men and horses.

It was the hour of vespers, about 4 p.m., before all was ready and the French advanced to the attack. The assault was delivered practically simultaneously all along the line. Hangest's cavalry, being on the flank, naturally came into contact with the right wing archers. The slope at this point is about the same as that at Crecy, but the upshot was quite different: the English archers gave way, and several of them—30 at least—fled to the rear. The consequence was that the men-at-arms on their left could receive little or no covering fire from the archers, even if the ground allowed it; their own right flank became uncovered and they fell back up the slope till they reached the belt of trees on the summit. This double setback boded ill for the English, but two things helped them. The archers on the left, having steeper ground to their front and no mounted attack to face, stood their ground and exacted such a heavy toll of their opponents that the French men-at-arms broke and fled down the hill. This in turn threatened the right flank of their advancing centre column. The second aid to the English was the belt of trees, which constituted a natural "anchor" for the men-at-arms who formed a firm line along its front edge. The same belt of trees handicapped the French horsemen, checking them in their pursuit of the fleeing archers, and brought them to a partial halt. But it was an anxious moment for the little English army and its commander, who was "horribly wounded" according to le Baker.

But he cried "Fight on! Fight on!" and the archers on the left, with that rare initiative and offensive spirit that was the hall-mark of the English archers throughout the Hundred

Years War, charged down the hill after their opponents, thus
still more exposing the right flank of the centre column of the
French army. Encouraged by the sight of this, the English
men-at-arms advanced once more, gradually pushing the
enemy down the slope. Into the valley bottom the French
knights were rolled and as they struggled across the valley they
were caught by the archers, to whom they presented an easy
target. Worse still befell the right wing of the French, for after
re-crossing the valley they encountered the steepest part of
the opposite slope referred to above. Here, loaded down by
their armour, exhausted by their flight in the heat of the
sun, they became practically immobile and were shot down
mercilessly.

Soon the French army had dissolved in flight, Hangest's
men alone preserving any order. The main body was leaderless, and it became a case of *Sauve qui peut*, for their commander,
Guy de Nesle, was dead on the field, and most of his senior
captains were dead or captured. Very few of the leaders can
have escaped, and Bentley, in his official dispatch, rolls off an
impressive list of knights and nobles. The dead included Raoul
de Cahours, the ambusher of Sir Thomas Dagworth.

The victory was complete and crushing. The French army
had ceased to exist as completely as that of Philip VI at Crecy;
2,000 dead, it is said, being left on the battlefield and the
remainder scattered to the four winds. No fewer than 89 of the
knights of King John's newly formed Order of the Star had
fallen, and this Order, intended as a rival to the Order of the
Garter, came to an early and inglorious end. The victory made
a painful impression in France, and its results were important.
For the next 12 years the French abandoned all attempts to
interfere in the English rule of Brittany. Yet the battle has
been allowed to fall into semi-oblivion. The French historian
of Brittany, A. de la Borderie, is candid enough to admit this.
"Our historians have in general ignored the importance of this
day; none of them say much about it although adequate
sources for the battle are not lacking."

## COMMENTS ON THE BATTLE

Apart from the important results of the battle of Mauron, it is a significant link in the contest between the English archer and the French man-at-arms – a conspicuous and continuous feature of the Hundred Years War. At first sight the defeat of the English archers on the right flank may puzzle some people and induce them to question whether the predominance of the archer that has been claimed for him is altogether justified. To this there are several replies. The first is of a general nature. Nothing is certain in war: there are no fixed rules by which one might calculate in advance the outcome of any engagement, for even though one has accurate information as to the material forces on each side there are two intangible, invisible and incommensurable factors: there is what the Baron de Jomini has named *friction de guerre*, or more simply the element of luck; and there is the morale factor, which, since it is not outwardly visible, can only be guessed at. Hence a single apparent contradiction of what may appear to be the general rule may prove nothing. In this particular case the morale of the English archers probably was not as high as the archers of Crecy. Bentley had scraped together his army from all quarters, they were far from being picked men, as were the Crecy archers, indeed the Black Death may have physically weakened a number of them. On the other hand, Hangest's horsemen may have been the *élite* of the French army; we have no information on the point. But putting aside these unknown factors, the terrain and the tactics employed by Hangest may alone have been responsible for the result. Why did de Nesle employ only *one* body of mounted men whereas at Saintes he had used two? The formation of the ground is, as I have hinted, one answer. On his right it was no place for mounted action, the slopes on both sides of the valley being much too steep. But his experienced eye may have indicated the possibility of an enveloping, flanking movement against the right flank of the English archers. Such enveloping movements, though the exception, were by no means unknown in medieval warfare:

indeed we shall see a conspicuous example of its employment
in only four years' time. The slope of the spur on which the
English were posted was at its gentlest in the neighbourhood
of Brembili château. If Hangest took the route indicated on my
sketch map he would have fairly favourable ground for
mounted action once he had crossed the rivulet; further, by
approaching the archers from the flank the French would
render about half the archers incapable of engaging them with
fire, for they would not only be facing the other way but would
be screened from view of them by their own comrades (always
assuming that the Crecy "herce" formation was adopted).
Looking at the problem on the ground such a manoeuvre
seems the obvious thing and quite sufficient to explain the
setback to the archers without invoking inferior quality in these
particular archers. It is true that on the day after the battle the
stern Bentley had 30 archers executed for running away.
Thirty, however, is not a large proportion of the whole, and
as Bentley was himself horribly wounded he was not in a good
position to appraise calmly and accurately the behaviour of
these men. Be this as it may, when we turn to the opposite
flank we see the lesson and experience of Crecy being repeated
most emphatically. Here the archers had things all their own
way, in spite of the rearward movement of the men-at-arms
on their immediate right. I think it may also help to explain
the sudden reversal of fortune in the centre of the line if we
suppose that a portion of the victorious archers, instead of
pursuing their own opponents straight down the hill, swung to
their right and attacked the hostile centre in flank – a winning
manoeuvre, as Henry's archers showed at Agincourt and
Cromwell's troopers showed at Naseby.

Properly viewed, therefore, Mauron is an interesting link between Crecy and Poitiers. It confirmed the predominance of the
archers in a frontal fight and passed on to Poitiers the idea of an
enveloping mounted attack. So the battle of Mauron can claim
importance both historically and technically, and it is strange
that it has been ignored by historians and soldiers alike.

EPILOGUE

Sir William Bentley was not the least notable in a notable line of English soldier-statesmen whom the war in Brittany threw up. He was soon to show a third example of his courage in opposing his own sovereign. Charles de Blois had been all this time an inmate of the over-populated Tower of London. For the sake of an enormous ransom King Edward now was prepared to grant him his liberty on very lenient terms. Under certain stipulations he was to be recognized as duke of Brittany and certain strongholds were to be given up to him. On receipt of this intelligence Sir William Bentley reacted so strongly that he returned home in order to expostulate in person with the king. On arrival he was clapped into the Tower and kept there for nearly two years. This was a rather rough-and-ready method of justice on the part of the king, but as Bentley met as Constable of the Tower his old comrade-in-arms and brother-in-law, Sir John Beauchamp, his sojourn was no doubt rendered as little irksome as possible. The proposed treaty with Charles de Blois eventually fell through, and de Blois, who had returned to Brittany on parole, surrendered himself once more; such was the binding power of chivalry in those days. King Edward at length realized his mistake, and Bentley was restored to favour. He returned to Brittany where the king granted him numerous possessions, including the tactful gift of Ploermel Castle. Bentley now took part in affairs of state; but he had never fully recovered from his desperate wounds and in the summer of 1359 he died. Within a few months two other great viceroys of Brittany also passed away—William Bohun earl of Northampton, and Thomas Holland earl of Kent. Brittany "bred a breed of mighty men".

# APPENDIX

## THE SOURCES FOR MAURON

There is little change in the sources for the foregoing chapter, but a word must be said about those concerned with the battle of Mauron. There are really only three sources for the battle, but they are all good ones and it is a relief not to have to go to Froissart for battle details. These sources were for a long time considered to be confined to the letter from Sir William Bentley to the Chancellor (printed in Avesbury) and le Baker's account. The latter relies on Bentley for the early portion of the battle, but adds some later details. But all the while there was a good account of the battle available in the *Chronique Normande du XIVe Siècle*, edited by Auguste Molinier in 1882. M. Molinier, one of the most eminent bibliographers then living, held it in high esteem where military information is concerned, and there is no reason to doubt the inherent accuracy of the Chronicle's account of the battle. To Professor Tout must go the credit for rescuing and applying this long forgotten account and for drawing the battle out of the oblivion into which it had sunk. This he did in an article in the *English Historical Review* for October, 1897. This was followed next year by A. de la Borderie's *Histoire de Bretagne*. But the fullest examination of the battle appeared in a curious book published anonymously in 1917, of which apparently only 100 copies were produced. It is called *A brief note upon the battles of Saintes and Mauron* and appears from internal evidence to have been intended as a memoir of Sir William Bentley. It is useful for biographical details. The publisher's name is not given.

### THE BATTLEFIELD

At first sight the evidence on which to fix the exact battlefield seems scanty. We know that the English were marching from Ploermel toward Mauron and the French from Rennes toward the same town; that the battle took place near Mauron, and (from the *Chronique Française*, quoted by Dom H. Morice in his *Preuves* . . .) that "the year 1352 was the battle of Mauron at the château of Brembili and the English won it". These facts do not appear to provide much to work upon, but if we place ourselves in the shoes of Sir William Bentley when he saw or heard the approach of the enemy, standing on the

Mauron spur, and if we apply the test of inherent military probability, it should be possible to pin-point the position with a reasonable degree of certainty. Indeed, if we accept the position suggested in the text above it seems to fit the description as a glove fits a hand. The position seems the natural, indeed the only, possible one; the whole course of events becomes comprehensible, especially the success of the French horse on the southern flank and of the English archers on the northern flank. Though the château of Brembili has long since disappeared (probably during the construction of the railway) its situation is known, and that seems to confirm the supposition, made on the grounds of inherent military probability, that the English position was on the spur to the east of the town.

The only battlefield monument or memorial is that erected to three American soldiers who were killed there on August 3, 1944.

# CHAPTER X

# THE BLACK PRINCE'S "GRANDE CHEVAUCHÉE"[1]

FOR three years after the battle of Mauron the war (or rather "truce") languished in all theatres. Prolonged negotiation for permanent peace, conducted under the aegis of the new pope, Innocent VI, at his palace at Avignon, finally broke down early in 1355 and both countries prepared once more for open war.

The plan of campaign evolved by Edward III followed closely that of 1346, which had been attended with such success; that is, it comprised a triple attack on France, directed from the north-east, the north-west and the south-west. That from the south-west–Gascony–was to be under the command of the Prince of Wales, and it will be described presently; that from the north-east was to be under the king and was based on Calais; while that from the north-west was to be under Henry duke of Lancaster, and was to be carried out in Normandy.

The last-mentioned campaign need not detain us long. While Henry of Lancaster had been conducting the negotiations at Avignon he met Charles "The Bad", king of Navarre. This monarch had been one of the claimants to the French crown, but had recently married the infant daughter of King John. He soon quarrelled with his father-in-law and came to Avignon, where he suggested to Lancaster a joint campaign against France in Normandy, where he held wide possessions. When next spring open war was resumed he undertook to join in the

---

[1] *Chevauchée* is translated by most English writers as a raid. The word literally means a procession of mounted men; thence, more loosely, a march or expedition of all arms, as here. An operation wherein the commander wished and tried to bring the French army of the south to battle is emphatically not a raid. A French historian describes this operation as an expedition, which it was.

Normandy campaign, and it was arranged that both armies should cooperate from Cherbourg. But when Lancaster set sail, after vexatious delays, Charles the Bad backed out of the undertaking without informing Edward and patched up his quarrel with the French king. The Normandy campaign was thus still-born.

## EDWARD III IN PICARDY

"What you lose on the swings you gain on the roundabouts." The troops earmarked for Normandy now became available for the Picardy campaign. For this campaign Edward amassed a considerable army. After incipient trouble with Scotland all seemed quiet on the Border, and Earl Percy and the bishop of Durham came south with their troops and joined the continental expedition. A third accession to the strength of Edward's army was a large force of mercenaries from Flanders and beyond. Edward took with him as his second in command his favourite general, Henry of Lancaster. His other principal officers were the earls of Northampton, Stafford and March, and Sir Walter Manny.

Because of various delays, inseparable from such an ambitious operation, the English army was not concentrated at Calais till October 26. It was strong in numbers – being possibly as numerous as the Crecy army. But the king of France had not been idle. Among other measures, he had concentrated an army under his own command in the area between Amiens and St. Omer, ready to confront the English invader. There is no means of computing the strength of this army, but it is reasonable to suppose that it was larger than that of the English king. After spending a week organizing his rather heterogeneous army, Edward moved off in search of his old opponent on November 2, very late in the year for the inception of field operations. Groping for the enemy, Edward made first for St. Omer. He reached this town on November 4, but did not attack it. Pushing on south to Blangy, he was met by an envoy from King John, who was then, it appeared, at Amiens.

Edward sent by the envoy a return message to the French king that he was ready to accept battle and would await him for three days with that object. John was not responsive; on the contrary he shut himself up in Amiens, first wasting the country in the path of the English army. At this stage he does not seem to have been much more aggressive-minded than his father had been when in the vicinity of the king of England. Evidently there was to be no fight, and Edward returned with his army via Boulogne to Calais, reaching it on November 11 after the shortest and most baffling campaign of the whole war.

It would be fruitless to spend time in vain speculation as to the reason for this sudden *volte face*, but the presumption is strong that news or rumours of a disturbing nature had reached the king at Blangy, the nature of which will shortly transpire.

The French army seems to have followed up slowly, and John sent an advance challenge to Edward to come out and fight a battle on November 17. A long and confused correspondence then took place, strongly reminiscent of the old verbal man-oeuvring between Edward and Philip. The fact is, as Sir James Ramsay suggests, that "neither king had any serious intention of fighting". If actions speak louder than words, this is certainly the case with John. As for Edward, the reason for his declining battle now becomes clear; whether or not rumours or presenti-ment had reached him at Blangy, he received at Calais definite news that the Scots were besieging the border castle of Berwick.

Edward took prompt and drastic action. He paid off his mercenaries, ordered up his ships and took his army back to England. How came it that his reaction was so different from that of ten years previously when a Scottish king and army penetrated to the walls of Durham? The answer is that the Border was this time defenceless. "Rashly relying on an armistice concluded with the Douglas", Percy had, as we have seen, led away the Border defence force to France and the Scots had, as usual, taken advantage of the cat being away to come out and play the Border game.

The accounts that reached Calais may have been exaggerated; we cannot say; but there can be no doubt that the safety of northern England was in jeopardy, and the course taken by the king was the only possible one in the circumstances.

## THE SCOTTISH CAMPAIGN

In order to explain the situation that had arisen we must hark back to the spring of that year (1355). While the king of England was busy with his plans and preparations, his French rival was no less busy. One of his measures took the customary form: Scotland must be induced to make trouble in the north. To this end he sent an envoy offering–and indeed bearing–money and troops, if the regent, William Douglas, would take the offensive.[1] Douglas took the bait, but Percy had not then gone south, and the regent soon signed the armistice mentioned above. But as soon as Percy and the king were safely oversea, egged on again by King John, the Scots made the attack on Berwick recorded above.

Edward was, not unnaturally, furious, but the Scots advanced no further and the king was able to make methodical preparations for the delivery of his retributive blow. While concentrating an army at Durham for the purpose, the king sent forward Sir Walter Manny to relieve the garrison of the castle, which was still holding out. In the dead of winter, about New Year's Day, the English army set out toward the Border. A few days later the Scots evacuated Berwick and the regent sued for peace.

It was too late, for Edward had "taken the bit between his teeth". An unexpected turn of events now seemed likely to ease the task of the English king. Baliol, still in Edward's eyes the nominal and rightful king of Scotland, came to the English king, who had then reached Roxburgh, and surrendered to him his kingdom of Scotland, in respect of which Edward granted him a life pension. Douglas then professed friendship and asked for a truce of ten days, on the pretext that he re-

---

[1] The northern Irish were also inveigled into taking offensive action, but were speedily subdued.

quired time to consult his government. Edward granted this, but on discovering that it was not asked in good faith he resumed his advance. Meeting with practically no opposition he moved north, bearing the twin banners of England and Scotland, and burning the countryside as he passed. He entered Edinburgh without difficulty. Here he expected to be recognized as king, but his savage and senseless burnings and devastation had so incensed the people that he met with no response. Recognizing the futility of obtaining recognition as king by force of arms, he, as suddenly as he had made his *volte face* in Picardy, marched back to England and disbanded most of his army.[1]

Sir James Ramsay sums up this unedifying campaign in the following words:

"The inroad was one of the worst experienced in Southern Scotland. For many a day the horrors of 'Le Burnt Candelmas' marked an epoch in the national memory; and for it Scotland had again to thank the French alliance."

Two of Edward's three campaigns for the year 1355 had crashed. There remained the third–that of the Black Prince in Gascony. And that was of a very different complexion.

### THE GRANDE CHEVAUCHÉE

For two years Count Jean d'Armagnac, the French king's lieutenant in Languedoc (the southern province of France), had been nibbling away at the territory won by the earl of Derby. The Gascons applied for help to England, and the expedition of the Black Prince was sent out ostensibly in response to this appeal. But there were other reasons of a strategic nature. Not only was it desirable to restore the waning English prestige in Gascony and to punish d'Armagnac for his harsh treatment of the people and land that he had lately overrun, but a diversion in the south would, it was thought, help the campaign in the north just as it had so signally done in the year of Crecy.

[1] He was also short of supplies, his ships having failed to keep their rendezvous at Dunbar.

On that occasion the army of the duke of Normandy, torn between two objectives, was successful in neither. And there was another way in which a punitive expedition in Languedoc might help the general war effort. It was one of the richest parts of France, and the king was wont to draw plentifully upon it for military resources in supplies, money and men. If the province could be systematically devastated this source of supply would dry up and the French war effort be correspondingly reduced. Great hopes were therefore placed in the new expedition.

After the usual delay, chiefly because of foul winds, the Black Prince set sail from Plymouth on September 9, 1355, with 3,500 troops. By September 20 he had disembarked at Bordeaux, where he was greeted with enthusiasm. He was not only to be commander of the army but the king's viceroy in the duchy, endowed with the widest powers.

After his installation as the king's deputy, he summoned a council of war, and to it he wisely called the Gascon lords. It would seem that they took the lead in preparing the plan of campaign, and the prince showed his good sense in following their advice. The Gascons were insistent on vengeance against Jean d'Armagnac. He was not at the moment in the field, having presumably gone into winter quarters. But this did not deter the eager young prince, now for the first time, at the age of 25, enjoying a command of his own. There were two methods whereby d'Armagnac might be brought to battle: by advancing straight toward him or, if he did not react to that, by devastating his country, until he was forced to take action in its defence. The plan formed envisaged both these possibilities. The army was to march as one complete integrated body, ready to fight, with all forces united, at the shortest notice; at the same time systematic devastation was to be carried out while inside the enemy's territory. It was hoped to march through Languedoc from end to end, from sea to sea.[1] For this purpose elaborate

[1] The original Languedoc had stretched across the whole of southern France from the Atlantic to the Mediterranean.

preparations were made. For instance, the march would take the army close to the foothills of the Pyrenees, where numerous swiftly flowing rivers would have to be crossed, and the enemy might be expected to break down the bridges; so a number of portable bridges were constructed and carried on the line of march.

The prince pushed on with his preparations with all speed and by October 5, 1355, the expedition set out. The army was about 5,000 strong, mainly English, but with a backing of Gascons. Marching south-east at a leisurely pace at first–for the army had to get into its stride–the frontier at Arouille was reached on October 11. It had so far been a peace march, but now battle formation was adopted, the vanguard being under the earl of Warwick with Sir Reginald Cobham of Blanchetaque fame, as Constable; the main body was commanded by the Prince in person, with Oxford and Burghersh the leading English officers, while the Captal de Buch (Jean de Greilly) and the Sire d'Albret were the chief Gascons. The rearguard was under the two earls, Salisbury and Suffolk.[1]

On entering enemy territory the work of devastation began. The orders were that the maximum amount of destruction to crops, stores and buildings (churches and monasteries being spared) was to be carried out. Now the speediest, simplest and surest method of destruction is by fire, and it was by fire that the bulk of the damage was done, a work, we are told, in which the Gascons showed the greatest zeal. The slight feeling of embarrassment that we sense when trying to excuse or explain the burnings in the Normandy campaign have no place here, for the work had a clear military object, which had not been the case in Normandy, which was an old appanage of the English crown, and which it was hoped would become so again. But Languedoc was a foreign country and it met the fate of most invaded countries in the Middle Ages.

In any case, the soldiers were only carrying out their orders, and offences against the persons of the inhabitants seem to have

---

[1] Le Baker curiously omits the name of Sir John Chandos.

been few. A modern biographer of the Black Prince speaks glibly of the butchery of "men, women and children", a stock phrase of that reckless romancer, the Canon of Chimay. If there had been such outrages it is fairly certain that they would have been recorded in Father Deniflé's definitive work *La Désolation des Églises*. . . . But he records none; his complaints concern the burning of religious houses. This was contrary to the Prince's general policy, and in at least one case he tried in vain to save such a building from the flames. Most likely such burnings were accidental; when a fire gets out of control religious buildings are not immune, as we all well know in England, and on one occasion the very house in which the Prince was asleep caught fire by accident.

I have said that these burnings were much to the liking of the Gascons, to whom they were a form of revenge; but the English soldiers no doubt enjoyed them too–there is something exhilarating about a bonfire–in fact the whole army enjoyed the expedition enormously. The weather was fine, the country was beautiful and rich, the inhabitants for the most part abandoned their houses and possessions, which were given up to unlimited looting, and the danger to life and limb was practically nil. Early in the march the count de l'Isle was killed, but that was in a quarrel. There was no enemy to quarrel with, for Jean d'Armagnac and his army took care to keep well out of the way. In short, the army must have enjoyed itself as much as did Sherman's army "marching through Georgia" in 1865.[1]

After marching a hundred miles to the south (see sketch map), the army turned east, and 80 miles further on came opposite Toulouse, the capital of Languedoc. It was a fortified city and it was not the policy of the Black Prince to spend time and blood in capturing places that he had no intention of

---

[1] Perhaps I may be permitted to quote what I have written elsewhere: "Sherman exhibited his intention to 'make Georgia howl' by destroying the country on a sixty-mile band. This march was in effect a peace march. The average day's march was 15 miles." The Black Prince's average was 14 miles. Otherwise the parallel is startlingly close.

holding. He therefore by-passed Toulouse by the south. To do this he was obliged to cross two large rivers, the Garonne and the Ariège, on both of which the bridges had been destroyed. Much to the astonishment of the inhabitants living on the far side of the Garonne, a ford was discovered and the army waded across.[1]

It was not till they were past Toulouse that they learnt from prisoners that d'Armagnac with his whole army had shut

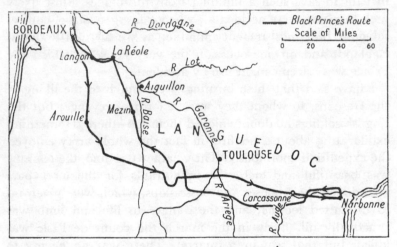

12. THE GREAT CHEVAUCHÉE

himself up in that city (like the other Jean who had shut himself up in Amiens at the approach of the Black Prince's father). This inactivity of the king's lieutenant in the south so incensed the citizens that they threatened his life and eventually galvanized him into action, as we shall see. Meanwhile opposition remained negligible, and the Anglo-Gascon army continued merrily on its way, its face ever to the east. Five marches and one rest day brought them to the wonderful city of Carcassonne, the sight of which still seems to transport the visitor into the Middle Ages. The old walled town is situated

[1] The season was abnormally dry and the water lower than it had been for 29 years.

on a hill, and the outer town nestled at its foot (as it still does). After some feeble resistance in the lower town the population took refuge in the upper town. The citizens then tried to avoid the destruction of the lower town by offering a large ransom, to which the prince haughtily replied that his father did not require gold, it was justice that he was after. With that, he set fire to the lower town and departed, for the walls were practically unscalable and he possessed no siege engines for breaching them. The army had spent three days at Carcassonne, and on November 2 they departed, crossing to the south bank of the river Aude and reaching Narbonne, 30 miles further east, on November 8. The English were now within ten miles of the Mediterranean, and all southern France was in a whirl of excitement and apprehension. Some English scouts appeared outside the walls of Bezières, 30 miles to the north-east; Montpelier, another 60 miles on, began looking to its defences, and even in Avignon, over 100 miles away, the Pope barricaded himself inside the gates of his fortress-palace, and sent an urgent embassy to the English prince begging for peace. Prince Edward, after keeping the envoys waiting for two days, sent them back with the message that the Holy Father must apply to the king of England, news of whose landing at Calais had just reached the army—a nice example of what is sometimes called "passing the buck".

Meanwhile there was at last some serious fighting to be done, for the outer town was held and resistance was at first fairly strong. It was captured, but the citadel held out. Before he had decided what course of action to adopt the Prince received more news from the outer world. Two armies were reported on the move in his direction. D'Armagnac had at last been stung into action, or an appearance of action; the second army was that of Jacques de Bourbon, who had been collecting an army at Limoges for the assistance of d'Armagnac, and was now drawing near. According to Froissart their intention was to hem the English between the Garonne and the Pyrenees, and the chronicler may here be right. The truth is, we know very little about the two French armies, their movements and their plans, nor about a force of militia that was reported approaching Narbonne from Montpelier.

The Prince of Wales summoned a council of war to consider the new situation, though the course to be adopted must have required little debating. To remain at Narbonne, where the storming of the citadel might take several days, whilst possibly three hostile bodies were drawing near, would be foolish. If forced to retreat the English would be driven into the sea. On the other hand a prompt advance against d'Armagnac before he could unite with Bourbon offered obvious attractions. The decision was therefore taken to withdraw from Narbonne and to seek battle with d'Armagnac. On November 10 the return march began. But instead of taking a westerly direction towards Toulouse, whence it may be assumed the Limoges army was approaching, the prince marched due north for eight miles and halted at Aubian where he crossed to the north of the Aude. The reason for this move is puzzling. This, no doubt, is because we know so little as to the French movements; their armies appear from time to time and disappear like ghosts. This paucity of information does not appear to worry the historians, but it worries me. Without more knowledge on the point it is impossible to descry the strategy, or to assess the ability of the Black Prince in the field. The northern move may have been intended, as Ramsay suggests, to mislead the enemy, but as the prince's aim was to bring them to battle, not to elude them, it seems more likely that d'Armagnac, having joined forces with Bourbon to the north of the Aude (and possibly with the Montpelier contingent also), was preparing to bar the advance of the English in that direction. What however is clear, is that on the approach of the invaders the French fell back westward toward Toulouse, and next day the English followed them in that direction. But the French were a day's march ahead: the next night the Prince's headquarters were in the place occupied by Jean on the previous night. The pursuit through the hilly country was an arduous one; the drought continued, there was a shortage of water, and even the horses had to drink wine—in some cases with rather ridiculous results.

But the French showed a clean pair of heels, and after covering 23 miles in two days the English made another sudden turn, this time to the south. The Aude was recrossed and the march continued well to the south of it. Again we must resort to conjecture; the reason may well be that to continue on the northern bank of the Aude would mean retraversing the country already devastated in the advance; the south side was virgin land and the prince had no intention of abandoning his devastation policy. The work of destruction—and the march—therefore went on, leaving Carcassonne well to the right and crossing the Garonne 20 miles south of Toulouse by another opportune ford. In the course of this march the Prince had been greeted by the young Gaston de Foix, later to play a prominent part in the war.

When the English army was safely past Toulouse, d'Armagnac ventured forth from that city of refuge as if to pursue. Prince Edward turned to meet him, sending a reconnoitring party forward under John Chandos, James Audley, and Lord Burghersh. By the time they had obtained contact, any resolution that Jean might have made to confront his opponent now deserted him; he turned and started on the return journey to Toulouse. Chandos and his little party charged boldly into the retreating rearguard and returned with 200 prisoners.

Prince Edward made another sharp turn, this time to the north, in the hope of regaining contact with his elusive opponent. But another incomprehensible turn of events supervened. On the next day, November 21, the French army again came in sight—not on the side of Toulouse but to the west—on the far side of the river Save down which the English were now marching. The French had put the river between the two armies and broken down the bridges. There was nothing for it but to continue on down the valley until a crossing became possible. This was effected at Aurade next day, after which the army pushed on for Gimont. D'Armagnac was now march-

17

ing on a parallel road, making no effort to close. During the day contact was, however, obtained and the French were roughly handled. But their main body marched on and reached the strongly defended Gimont that night. Edward encamped in the vicinity on the south side, fully expecting a battle next morning. Before daylight he arrayed his army in battle order, but when it got light it was seen that "the bird had flown": the combined armies of d'Armagnac and Bourbon, which must have heavily outnumbered that of the Anglo-Gascons, had brought the farce to an end by slipping away to Toulouse in the night.

*   *   *

Thereafter it became a peace march once more, and on December 2 the weary troops entered the friendly and historic La Réole—a town that witnessed the departure of Richard Coeur de Lion on his famous crusade and the return of the Black Prince from his *grande chevauchée*. After resting a day or two in La Réole the army resumed its homeward march, and entered Bordeaux on December 9, nine weeks and five days after setting out.

There were great rejoicings in the city when the Anglo-Gascon army entered with its huge train of booty and long column of prisoners. The Prince of Wales had every reason to be pleased with himself, according to his own lights. He was only 25, the commander of an army already become famous. He had set out on a bold and ambitious project and had accomplished all that he had set out to do. He had diminished the French war effort by an enormous and incalculable amount; he had restored the prestige of the English name, and had removed all danger to the frontiers of Aquitaine; his main body had marched, as nearly as I can compute it, 675 miles, as far as from London to the north of the Orkneys, averaging 14 miles a marching day on the outward and nearly 17 miles on the return journey. And all this had been accomplished at practically no cost in human lives. Thousands of the unfortunate inhabitants had lost their homes and sustenance, but not their lives; indeed the conduct of the army seems to have been correct throughout and they had humiliated the armies of their opponents in the eyes of the populace. The *chevauchée* was of good augury for the future.

*      *      *

Christmas was at hand and the army and its leaders must have looked forward to a period of rest and recuperation in the great city of Bordeaux. If so, they were to be cruelly disappointed. So far from resting, the already stern and implacable young prince sent off detachments under his chief officers to strengthen weak places and extend the frontier in all directions. This went on throughout the winter and spring and by May, 1356, over 50 towns and castles of the old English dominion had been recovered.

## APPENDIX

SOURCES

There are only three real sources for the Languedoc expedition, but they are good ones. On Christmas Day the Prince wrote a letter, which may be called an official dispatch, to Bishop Edinton of Winchester, the Treasurer (as he believed the king to be still in Picardy). A few days earlier his secretary, John Wingfield, had written a similar but longer letter to the same address. Our third source is le Baker, who managed to obtain possession of a detailed itinerary of the Prince's main body throughout the march–an invaluable document, though the spelling of names is mostly phonetic and some of the places named cannot be identified. One would expect that one of the Prince's many biographers would have annotated this itinerary and produced a detailed analysis of the march, but no; it has been left to the editor of le Baker to do the work and to do it very thoroughly. Maunde Thompson's notes to his edition, written in 1889, are as useful for this campaign as were his notes for the Crecy campaign. Of French writers, again one must go to an unexpected source for the most detailed account; it is contained in Father Deniflé's *La Désolation des Églises* ... which has already been frequently referred to. It is a valuable guide on sources throughout the war.

In the brief account of the Scottish campaign I have followed Sir James Ramsay closely.

# CHAPTER XI

## LANCASTER'S "CHEVAUCHÉE" IN NORMANDY

HISTORY does not record the feelings of Edward III on the results of the opening year, 1355, of the renewed war, nor his views and plans for the second year. But disappointment cannot have been entirely absent. The Languedoc expedition, it is true, had been unexpectedly successful, but it was too far distant to produce any immediate effect on the operations in the north. Here everything had gone wrong: both his expeditions had ended in fiasco and the king of Navarre had been reconciled to his French overlord.

But human events are always unpredictable, for luck and chance play a sometimes decisive part. An unlooked-for chance came the way of the English king in the spring of 1356. Charles of Navarre had again fallen out with the king of France, and it came about in the following way. Because of increased taxation, unrest became rampant in the Norman possessions of the king of Navarre, an unrest that Charles the Bad secretly encouraged. Rumours of this reached King John, and he suddenly put in an appearance at a banquet given at Rouen by his eldest son Charles, who had recently succeeded him as duke of Normandy. The guest of honour at the banquet was the king of Navarre. The story goes that John rushed into the hall at the head of 30 armed men while the banquet was in progress, seized Navarre by the collar, and exclaimed "Abominable traitor! You are not worthy to sit at my son's table. By the soul of my father, I will neither eat nor drink as long as you live." John was not quite as good as his word, for whereas he had the count of Harcourt summarily beheaded, he sent the king of Navarre to imprisonment in Paris.

The upshot was what might have been expected. Philip, the younger brother of the arrested monarch, declared war against John and appealed to Edward III for help. Nothing could have fitted the English king's purpose better. The appeal reached him on May 28, when he was in the process of fitting out a small expedition to Brittany under the duke of Lancaster, who was to be the king's new lieutenant in the duchy. The young duke of Montfort, who had now come to man's estate, was to accompany the expedition and presumably assume some share in the government of his father's duchy. Quickly Edward switched the expedition to Normandy. Henry of Lancaster embarked his troops at Southampton on June 4 and on June 18 he landed at La Hogue. Here he was met, by arrangement, by Philip of Navarre with a token force, and soon was joined by "the famous Robert Knollys" as Froissart calls him, or "the terrible Robert" as a French historian dubs him.

Henry was about to undertake one of his breathless *chevauchées*. We fortunately know nearly all the essential facts about this expedition, thanks to an official report drawn up by one of his staff officers only three days after the return of the expedition to its base. We know the exact composition and strength of his army, his orders, his marches and his timetable.

First, the army. The duke brought with him from England 500 men-at-arms and 800 archers; Robert Knollys brought from Brittany 300 men-at-arms and 500 archers; Philip of Navarre brought 100 men-at-arms "of the country"; *i.e.*, Normans. The total was thus 900 men-at-arms and 1,300 archers. To this must be added a small advance guard that had preceded the main body. The total cannot have exceeded 2,500, a small force with which to carry out the orders given him. These were to relieve and revictual the three Navarre towns then being besieged by French troops. They were Evreux, Pont Audemer and Breteuil, and all three were over 130 miles distant from La Hogue. Practically all the fighting men in the English army were mounted, but the victualling train, etc., would be on foot.

Let us now look at the French plans. Unfortunately, because of the dreadfully inadequate French records and chronicles of the period we know little of the French king's movements and still less of his strength. As for his movements, we do know that he immediately answered the challenge thrown down so courageously by Philip by sending forces to besiege the chief towns in the Navarre territories—the three above-named—and that he then set to work to collect an army and lead it in person into the field. It is quite evident that this was a large army. The *Grandes Chroniques* merely says that it was a very great assembly of men-at-arms and foot soldiers. We know, however, that it included his son the duke of Normandy and his brother the duke of Orleans, and most of the leading soldiers of France.[1] In other words it was the main French army.

The English official report, it is true, gives the figures for the French army with some precision, making them 8,000 men-at-arms and 40,000 others. Simeon Luce accepts this figure without demur, but I do not find it acceptable. The English staff officer cannot have been in a position only three days after the return of the expedition to compute the strength of the French army. He probably accepted unquestioningly figures given him by one of the prisoners. It is not of course literally impossible that the French army was 48,000 strong, but utterly unlikely. But even if we reduce it to a quarter of that figure it leaves it many times larger than the English army. Indeed, when fully concentrated, it may quite well have been ten times as large as Lancaster's little army.

When the campaign opened the French king was at Dreux, 25 miles east of Breteuil and the same distance from Evreux. The latter town had already surrendered, so Lancaster's objective was thus confined to Pont Audemer and Breteuil. On conclusion of this task the duke was evidently intended to pass on into Brittany, taking with him young Montfort, who was in the meantime presumably left at the base. This base was

---

[1] *Les Quatre Premiers Valois* gives an impressive list of these leaders, and frequently emphasizes the great strength of the army.

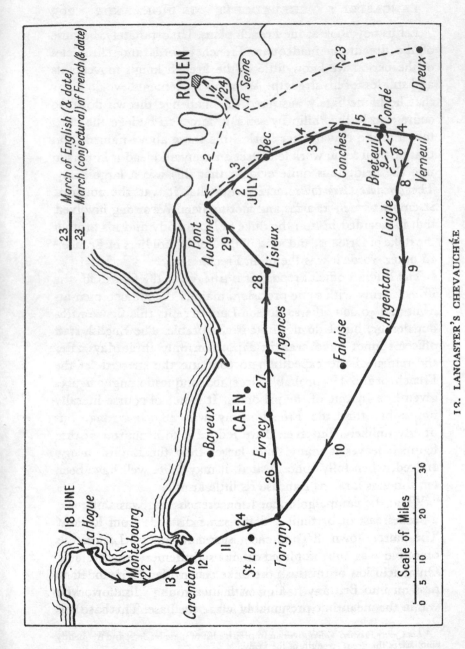

12. LANCASTER'S CHEVAUCHÉE

264

the abbey of Montebourg, seven miles south-east of Valognes. Robert Knollys was also left here, somewhat surprisingly.

The expedition set out on June 22, only four days after landing. (The march can be followed on the sketch map.)

The first day's march took the army to Carentan, 16 miles, where a day's halt was allowed in order to sort things out. The next march took the army past St. Lô, which was garrisoned by the French. Henry of Lancaster kept his eye steadily on his objective and had no intention of incurring delays by attacking strongly defended towns. He therefore skirted to the north of St. Lô, marching rapidly in order to avoid becoming involved with its garrison. That evening he reached Torigny, a 30-mile march. On June 25 the army halted, but the next four days saw marches averaging 21 miles per day. The first three marches to Lisieux were in an almost dead straight line, reminding one of Edward's marches through Normandy ten years previously. As on that occasion, we no doubt see the experienced hand of Godfrey Harcourt as guide, for he had again thrown in his lot with the English. He was the chief landowner in the Cotentin, and his château of St. Sauveur-le-Vicomte,[1] situated in the centre of the Cotentin, dominated almost the whole peninsula. The route followed also had the merit of avoiding Caen.

Approaching Lisieux a slight detour to the north had been necessary in order to cross the marshy valley of the river Dives. The bridge at Corbon was held by a French post who fled on the approach of the English and the crossing was secured, much to the satisfaction of the staff officer, who described it as "a very great stronghold, the strongest pass in the realm".

From Lisieux on June 29 the army marched direct to Pont Audemer, 23 miles. They encountered no opposition on the way, and entered the town without sighting any enemy. The explanation is that the post at Corbon had fled to Pont Audemer, where they had given the warning. This so worked upon the besiegers, who guessed what was coming, that they

---

[1] This château afterwards came into the possession of Sir John Chandos and underwent one of the most famous sieges of the war.

fled incontinently during the night, leaving "all their engines, artillery, crossbows, bucklers and other divers harness". The fugitives met strong reinforcements on their way, coming out from Rouen, who were so impressed by the exaggerations of the fugitives that they also turned and returned to the city. Henry revictualled the town from his train, according to instructions, and also left 50 men-at-arms and 50 archers from his scanty force for their additional protection. He remained in the town for the next two days, a curious reason being given for it, namely "to fill up the mines which the enemy had made right well and strong, so close to the castle that they were but four feet from the wall". One would have supposed that the townspeople could do the necessary spade-work themselves, and there must have been some other reason, the nature of which we cannot guess.

Half Henry's task was now accomplished, and still there was no sign of the king of France, or even of a detachment of his army. On July 2, therefore, the march was resumed and in 16 miles they reached the famous abbey of Bec, whence two great archbishops had come to England, Anselm and Lanfranc. Here they were placidly received, though most of the army must have camped outside in the open. It was near midsummer and mattered not. On July 3 a 23-miles march brought them to the French-owned town and castle of Conches. A prompt attack was made on the castle; an entry was effected into the outer ward and the place was then set on fire. This is all the staff officer says, but as the army spent the night there we may presume that all opposition was overcome.

Still no news of King John and his great army, yet he could not be far off. The next day, July 4, was indeed an eventful one. Setting off due south the army reached its second objective, Breteuil, again without opposition, after a ten-mile march, while it was still quite early. Once again the French abandoned the siege on hearing of the English approach and the army entered without losing a man. Extensive victuals, calculated to last the garrison for one year, were here unloaded and stored.

But though his double objective had now been accomplished, Henry of Lancaster evidently felt he must "do something more". His gay spirit cried out for adventure and he decided to try and capture the moated and walled town and castle of Verneuil, then considered by some the capital of Normandy. This venerable city is still outwardly strong, and the gaunt keep of Henry I, called not inaptly *le Tour Gris*, and as grim as its builder, might be expected to offer strenuous resistance.

Revictualling Breteuil must have occupied most of the morning, and eight more miles had to be covered before Verneuil was reached. During the afternoon, however, the English appeared before its walls and summoned it to surrender. But the gates were closed and an assault became necessary. This was successful; that is all we know, but it is reasonable to suppose that the change in procedure from avoiding defended towns before Audemer was reached may have sprung from the fact that siege equipment was captured at that town, which thus simplified, and indeed made possible, the assault of walled towns. Thus we see the speedy fall of two of them, Conches and Verneuil.[1] The assault on the town walls was successful, but a tower in the castle held out obstinately, and it was not till 6 a.m. two days later that it fell into English hands. Many troops were wounded in this assault, but none killed.

By this time the tiny English army had pranced through Lower Normandy, relieving two important towns and taking two others by storm, and still no army had appeared against them in the field. It could not go on much longer; Verneuil is only 20 miles from Dreux where the French army had been on the opening day of the *chevauchée*. Where was it and what was it doing? Henry did not know, and it was tempting fortune to dally another day at Verneuil, badly though men and horses wanted rest. But it was in Henry's nature to take risks.

[1] The army marched across the battlefield-to-be of Verneuil, just outside the town—that of a great victory of the duke of Bedford which the French have called "une seconde Agincourt".

July 7 was, therefore, devoted to rest and refreshment, and the following day the army set off on its long return journey. The direct route would take it through Laigle, 14 miles to the west. Thither the duke set his face. The march was uneventful to start with, and the headquarters had reached the town when word came that the French army was in contact with the rearguard. At Tuboeuf, four miles east-south-east of Laigle, the French army, coming from the direction of Breteuil, had bumped into the English.

King John had at last got within striking distance of his unpredictable and elusive opponent. Now was the chance to crush this disturber of the peace of Normandy. And how did he set about doing it? The answer is that he followed the trail so clearly and so disastrously blazed for him by his own father, Philip VI: he resorted, not to actions, but to words. He halted his army and sent two heralds to the English army with a solemn challenge to battle. Goliath challenged David. Such a gesture from the French king could hardly take the English duke by surprise, knowing his antecedents as he did. Henry was ready for it and he returned an adroit answer. His staff officer was evidently so pleased with the wording that he gives it fully. "Whereupon my lord gave answer that he was come into these parts to do certain business, which he had well accomplished, thank God, and was returning back to the place where he had business, and that if the said King John of France willed to disturb him from his march he would be ready to encounter him."[1] No reply was received.

Darkness fell, the two armies still sitting opposite one another. A report ran through the French lines that evening that the formidable duke of Lancaster was about to attack. A near-panic was caused, and the troops hurriedly stood to arms. No attack followed, but a battle seemed inevitable next day, July 9. Early that day trumpets sounded in the French camp, banners were unfurled and the marshals made busy to set out the troops

[1] There is a "Froissartian" twang about this message, but the author of the *Chroniques* had nothing to do with it.

in array. The English could be dimly descried, but they showed no sign of coming out into the open, nor did they send out a herald to inform the French king what they intended to do. Odd! After some time it was observed that the English became less and less visible and eventually there was not a man to be seen. Patrols were sent forward. They came back and reported that Laigle was empty. The English army had vanished.

The English commander had no intention of being so imbecile as to engage the huge French army in battle, but his astute answer to the herald, though containing a *suggestio falsi*, was not a downright lie; it contained a hidden element of truth. For Lancaster calculated that, with a little skilful management, he could get clear away, even though he was now weighed down with prisoners and loot. His plan to this end was simple (as war plans should always be). He deployed a small force of picked men along the front, just in view of the enemy, with orders to keep them amused next morning as long as possible, and then to slip away, mount and follow after the army as fast as possible. Meanwhile in the dead of night the main body was assembled in silence, a witness to the high state of discipline the troops had attained to under Lancaster's firm and experienced tuition. The army moved off shortly after midnight. It "swiftly and silently melted away".

By the time the ruse was discovered by the French their opponents were well on the way to Argentan, and pursuit would have been useless. The author of the *Grandes Chroniques*, in his anxiety to excuse the ineptitude of his king, produced an absurd story that someone unnamed had told the king when the English army was first sighted that there were vast forests in front and that it would be useless to attack. The real truth of the matter is stated bluntly by Simeon Luce: "The king of France, instead of falling on the English, sent heralds to offer battle to the Duke of Lancaster, who profited by this warning to escape."[1] John had not learned from Philip's example: in

---

[1] Delachenal writes that John "showed as much incapacity as chivalrous naivety".

fact one is tempted to liken the early Valois to the Bourbons—
they learnt nothing and they forgot nothing.

Argentan[1] was reached that evening, a distance of 35 miles
having been covered. Of course this was done in two stages,
a night march and a day march. Even so, it was a fine achievement for the dismounted men left in the army. I put it that way
because in the course of the *chevauchée* over 2,000 horses were
captured, sufficient to mount the whole army, train, prisoners
and all. But it is probable that the big haul of horses was made
in Argentan, for next day the length of march suddenly shot up
to the prodigious figure of 52 miles, which, coming on top of
one of 35 miles, must be considered phenomenal. Lancaster
must have believed he was still being followed (and he may
have been, by light forces). But after Torigny, which was
reached on July 10, the pace slackened. Delay was caused at
the crossing of the river Vire at St. Frommond. Since their
outward journey the bridge had been cut by French troops,
who laid an ambush at the spot. But something went wrong;
To quote the official report once more: "Sixty men-at-arms
and other soldiers lay in ambush, to do what mischief they
might to our people, and with them 15 of our English men-at-
arms fought and killed them all, which thing was held for
a miracle."

But even better was to come! Next day the army reached
Carentan in home country, and on the morrow they got back
to Montebourg. Robert Knollys, who had been left in charge
of the base camp, hearing of the advent of the army, rode out
to meet them and lead them into the quarters that he had
prepared for them. He had but seven armed men with him
and they ran into an ambush of 120 Frenchmen. "And the said
Robert and the said seven men-at-arms slew them all except
three which were taken at ransom." The "terrible Robert"
indeed!

The army had covered, according to my reckoning, about

[1] The duke must have lodged in the forbidding-looking castle in which Henry II,
200 years before, had uttered the fateful words: "Who will rid me of this turbulent
priest?"

330 miles in 15 marches and 22 days, at an average distance of 22 miles a march–a remarkable record. The summing up of the expedition by Roland Delachenal in his *Histoire de Charles V* reads:

"Complete success crowned the enterprise. The soldiers of Lancaster had captured or secured several fortresses, they brought back numerous prisoners, 2,000 horses taken from the enemy, an enormous booty, and they themselves had had very few casualties."

As a result of this expedition, Philip of Navarre crossed over to England and did homage to Edward III for his Norman possessions. The alliance was sealed and for some years English and Navarre-Normans fought shoulder to shoulder.

The achievement of Henry of Lancaster speaks for itself. Not so the lack of achievement of King John. This is due to the regrettable lack of written evidence. In order to assess his operations we must try to fill in the gap between June 22 when he was at Dreux and July 8 when he appeared before Laigle. I believe it can be done with a fair degree of plausibility.

If we make one big assumption everything seems to fall into place and fit into the picture. That assumption is that Rouen, not Dreux, was the concentration point for his army. Dreux was not a large town, and the record does not state that the main French army was there, or was going to concentrate there, though most writers seem to assume that. The natural place would be Rouen. It had obvious administrative and geographical advantages and it was in keeping with the policy of both John and his father before him to order such concentrations at large towns: Amiens, Arras, Chartres, Rennes, etc. Moreover, Rouen would be the best possible strategical centre, for it faced the heart of the Navarre territories, and was almost equidistant from the two towns then being besieged, Pont Audemer and Breteuil. Let us assume then that John left Dreux for Rouen on June 23 or very soon after, and see how the picture of the campaign can be filled in. He arrives at Rouen on June 25 and for the next four days is busied with the organization of his army as contingents arrive, one after the other. During the night of June 29 fugitives from the besieging force at Pont Audemer arrive. They are full of excuses for the abandonment of their post, and in self-defence wildly exaggerate the numbers of the English army that is approaching. John takes this seriously, not realizing that the stories of fugitives from the battlefield must ALWAYS be heavily discounted. He therefore makes careful and deliberate arrangements to march toward Pont Audemer with his whole army, not realizing the need for haste against such a slippery opponent. Two ponderous marches bring him to the vicinity of Pont Audemer where he arrives on the evening of July 2, only to find that the English army have departed that morning in a southerly direction. The pursuit, of which the *Grandes Chroniques* speak, then begins. Following in the tracks of the enemy, John reaches the vicinity of Breteuil on July 5 – a day and a half behind his enemy – and encamps at Condé, three miles to the east of that town.

The king is now separated by only ten miles from the English and as Henry is going to stay another two full days at Verneuil there is ample time and opportunity to bring him to battle. But John for some reason remains halted at Condé during those two vital days. Our evidence for this is a curious sentence (which seems to have escaped notice) in the message of the heralds: "The said king knew well, by reason that . . . my lord had tarried so close to him at Verneuil. . . ." This remark implies that both sides had tarried. We know why Henry tarried; the only reason we can suggest for John tarrying at this juncture was that as soon as he arrived within striking distance of his famous opponent, of whom he had unhappy recollections in Gascony, his professed desire to measure swords with him evaporated and he waited to bring up all the stragglers in his host before risking a battle. Hence he tarried two days, July 6 and 7, at Condé, and when he was on the point of setting out for Verneuil on the morning of July 8 news reached him that the English were on the march along the road to Laigle. He therefore cut the corner, marching along the river valley towards Laigle, and at Tuboeuf, as we have seen, he obtained contact with the rearguard of the English army at last. The rest we know.

The French king did not pursue with his main army, but turned back to resume the siege of Breteuil which had been so rudely broken off. Here he met with a determined defence, and had to resort to all the known methods of reducing a fortress. An enormous *beffroi*, or moving tower, was constructed that would overtop the walls and enable the attackers to set foot from it on to the parapet. But when it approached, the cannons in the town opened fire and set it alight.[1] This episode, combined with the mention of artillery at Pont Audemer, is interesting evidence as to the progress of artillery in siege warfare, of which we have heard little since the siege of Tournai 16 years previously. Contingents of Scottish troops joined the French army here under the command of Lord William Douglas, whom King John took into his paid service.

In mid-August, disturbing news was received from the south. That young son of the English king was again on the warpath, and this time was reported marching straight for Paris. It was therefore essential to bring the siege of Breteuil to a speedy conclusion and John granted it easy terms and departed in haste with his army to Paris.

# APPENDIX

**SOURCES**

The main sources are the Official Report, printed in Avesbury, the *Grandes Chroniques*, and the *Chronique des Quatre Premiers Valois*, which is steadily becoming more important for the French side. Subsidiary sources: in English, Knighton; in French, the *Continuation* of de Nangis; neutral, Froissart. The campaign has been scarcely even recognized by English writers with the exception of Mackinnon (two pages) and Ramsay

---

[1] During the famous siege of Ostend in 1601, Spinola, the Italian, constructed a similar tower which he named "Pompey". It was the wonder of the day, but the English gunners fired at its wheels, broke one of them, and brought it to a standstill. History repeats itself.

(one page) both of whom, however, ignore the *Quatre Premiers Valois*. The best account, as usual, comes from a Frenchman, Roland Delachenal, in his *Histoire de Charles V.*

## LENGTH OF A FRENCH LEAGUE

The staff officer in his report gives the interesting information that the French league was twice as long as the English league. He does not say how long that was, but as he gives the length of most of the day's marches, it is possible to calculate it approximately. Only an approximation is possible because of our ignorance of the exact roads traversed. One can, however, strike an average and my calculations made it equal to about three modern miles. M. Delachenal calculates the league as only 4,200 metres, say two and a half miles, but he evidently measures each stage in a straight line, *viz.* map miles, whereas the staff officer who presumably had no map must have judged the distance actually travelled along the road. The length of a league at any given period or place must be the bugbear of military historians (though they usually evade this difficulty by merely using the word "league" without defining it).

# CHAPTER XII

# POITIERS

THE king of France had brought the siege of Breteuil to a premature end because he received a report that the Black Prince was heading north for Paris. The report was in its essence true. The Prince of Wales and his army were heading not for but toward the French capital. It was part of another of those wide strategic plans that distinguish the warfare of Edward III.[1]

What then was the plan on which the Black Prince had set out? It was in essence a replica of the Crecy plan of campaign, which had worked so well. There were to be two, if not three, simultaneous and widely separated operations, acting on exterior lines; that is, facing inward as it were, and directed toward the Loire, where it was hoped they might join hands. No attempt was made to concert synchronized plans: experience had taught that the elements–that is the weather on the various sea passages–made any such plans impossible. The greatest latitude was therefore left to each commander and no great hopes of complete success were entertained: the subsidiary aims might at least be carried out–the ravaging of the enemy's territory and the defeat of his forces in the field.

The first part of the plan–an invasion *via* Calais by the king– was, as we have seen, still-born (if it was ever seriously contemplated) and the second–an invasion from Brittany *via* Normandy by Henry of Lancaster–had been delayed by the operations in Normandy. But in mid-July Henry had passed on into Brittany and in a few weeks this indefatigable soldier

---

[1] Most historians, both English and French, find little trace of strategy in any of the king's campaigns, probably because the documentary evidence for it is slight. But actions may be more convincing than words, and the actions of Edward III, which have been and which will be described in these pages, point to the fact that the English king was in advance of his time as a strategist. Indeed he may be described as the Father of English strategy.

was again in the field, marching toward the Lower Loire. His advance took him through southern Normandy where he captured the strong castle of Domfront and other castles on the border of Maine. Thence he advanced south on Angers, hoping to cross the Loire south of that city and to join forces with his second cousin, the Prince of Wales.

The third army was that of Gascony, still under the Black Prince. During the spring of 1356 he had extended and steadily strengthened his dominion and his task had been rendered the easier thanks to the number of Gascon nobles (who had held aloof from the previous expedition) now coming forward with their retinues. For nothing succeeds like success. It was therefore with an army nearly, if not quite, double the size of the previous one that the Prince marched out of Bordeaux on July 6. Making his first headquarters at La Réole, he took active steps for warding off a possible attack by Jean d'Armagnac, who had been showing unwonted activity of late. For this purpose the Prince detached approximately half his troops, nearly all of them being Gascons, for the defence of his borders during the absence of his main army. As a matter of fact, d'Armagnac's activities were of a purely defensive nature, but it would have been unsound for the Prince to march over 200 miles away from his base without first rendering it secure.

By the beginning of August all was ready and an Anglo-Gascon army about 6,000 strong set out on its second great *chevauchée*. The prince used this word *chevauchée* to describe it; it was a word with a wide connotation (for the French vocabulary was small in those days) and it covered the three aims of the expedition, *viz.*, to carry fire and sword into the heart of the enemy's country, thus showing that he was not master in his own domains; secondly to meet and defeat his armies in the field; and thirdly to join hands, if possible, with the king or with Lancaster, or both, somewhere on the line of the river Loire. Sketch map 14 (p. 282) should here be consulted.

On August 4 the army passed through Bergerac, and advanced by easy stages of about ten miles a day, *via* Périgueux,

Brantôme, Rochechouart (leaving Limoges on the right hand), Lussac (where Sir John Chandos was afterwards to meet his death), Chateauroux and Issudun. Up to this point the army was heading for Bourges, where the count of Poitiers, one of the sons of the French king, was believed to be lying. But Bourges did not hold him, and the English army continued on its way, leaving Bourges on its right hand. At Vierzon the border from Aquitaine into France proper was crossed and destruction of the countryside was systematically carried out. It did not, however, reach the height of the Languedoc devastations, and Father Deniflé (whose reconstruction of the itinerary is accepted by all) records the burning of only a few religious houses.

Next day, August 29, French patrols sent out by King John's approaching army were met for the first time. They were chivvied back to the castle of Romorantin, where they were shut up and besieged. The main castle fell next day, but the keep held out for another three days. Eventually it was set on fire[1] and captured.

Some information was obtained from the prisoners, to the effect that the French king was approaching and that one of the sons of the king was in Tours. The Black Prince went in that direction, marching westward down the right bank of the Cher for 40 miles to the Loire, which he struck near Amboise, 17 miles short of Tours. The Prince seems to have had a hope that his father might be not far off on the northern bank of the river. His aim was therefore to cross and join him, but no crossing could be found; all the bridges were either cut or strongly defended and the river was in spate and unfordable. The prince, who had taken up his quarters at Montlouis Castle, near the river, now turned his attention to the city of Tours. The vanguard of his army, on arrival opposite its walls, found that fresh defences had been

---

[1] No doubt with Greek Fire. I do not credit the report that cannons were used. If it were so the *Eulogium*, which notices the use of arrows in the siege, would hardly have remained silent. There is no record of the presence of cannon at any other time during this campaign.

thrown up and that there was a numerous and vigilant garrison. In default of a siege train, and in view of the approach of the French army, an attempt to capture the town would be fruitless, and the Black Prince was reduced to sitting down, in the hopes that the Valois prince might be induced to come out and fight. For four days, therefore, the English army sat down and rested. They had need of it. They had marched some 320 miles in 32 days, an average of 10 miles a day, including halts. Some of their wide-ranging foraging parties had, of course, covered very much more.

But prospects appeared gloomy. The broad river was uncrossable, the enemy was beginning to swarm everywhere, forage was becoming increasingly difficult to procure, the French main army was now within striking distance, and, worst of all, there was no news of either the king of England or of the duke of Lancaster. Evidently the Prince's army could not hope to push further into France unless one or other of the northern armies could get to him, which now seemed unlikely. Meanwhile his train of booty had become rich and lengthy[1]; parties of the enemy were reported crossing the river both above and below Tours, while the duke of Normandy, if he really were in Tours, had evidently no intention of venturing out. Would it not therefore be wise to set his face toward home?

Such may well be the thoughts that passed through the mind of the young Prince during those critical and anxious days. By September 10 his mind was made up; and orders were issued for the army to proceed to Montbazan, 12 miles south of Tours, on the following day. The reason given by the Prince for this move was that he wished to join the duke of Lancaster, and this may truly have been one reason, as we shall shortly see.

### THE FRENCH MOVES

It is time to follow the movements of the rival army. We left King John in mid-August abandoning his Normandy campaign

---

[1] The extent of his booty has probably been exaggerated. There are no exact records.

and repairing to Paris in order to take steps to repel the greater danger from the south. Unfortunately, the French chronicles are as scanty and as vague as ever during this period; all we know for certain is that the king ordered a great army to concentrate at Chartres, whither he went himself, arriving not later than August 28. His old army must have formed the nucleus of the new one, for operations in Normandy had practically ceased with the departure of the English army to Brittany. The orders convening the new army were as widespread as ever, all parts of the country except Languedoc being bidden to send their levies. The size of the army that collected at Chartres must therefore have been about as large as any the king had previously commanded, if not larger.

Through the latter half of August, then, detachments of French troops were hurrying toward the city of Chartres, whilst the Anglo-Gascon army was wending its leisurely way through the heart of the country. In the first days of September, King John set out for the Loire, on receipt of the intelligence that the Black Prince was approaching. His army was not fully concentrated, indeed it is doubtful whether it ever was, for we have the extraordinary fact that whereas he himself crossed the Loire at Blois on September 6, some of his detachments crossed at Orleans, Meung, Tours, and even Saumur—the latter obviously being Breton and Norman contingents—that is, on a front of 110 miles in a direct line. If the king believed a hostile army to be somewhere in the centre of this line his dispersion was either an extremely rash act or, if exactly co-ordinated and synchronized, a skilful strategic operation. But such synchronization was practically out of the question at that date. However that may be, on September 10, John crossed the river at Blois, and next day reached Amboise, a 21-mile march.

The following ten days are easily the most controversial ten days of the whole Hundred Years of War, and the reader is advised to consult sketch map 15 closely and to construct for himself a simple march table, showing the two armies in parallel columns. The sources are puzzling and conflicting and in attempting to establish the true course of events I shall have to make great demands on inherent military probability. The famous German military historian, Delbrück, when he examined the sources for the battle, gave up the task of describing it in despair–which was *grand pitié*–as Jean Froissart would have said.

There are two main problems: the first concerns the preliminaries of the battle and the second the conduct of the actual battle of Poitiers. The first problem may be simplified in the following terms: What was John's object in marching round the flank of the English army, and did the Black Prince seek to cross swords with his opponent or try to elude him? For convenience I will give a *précis* of the ascertained facts first and then go over the problem in detail.

The ascertained facts for the preliminaries are that on Monday September 12, the French were halted at Amboise, the English at Montbazan. On Tuesday the English marched to La Haye (30 miles) and the French to Loches (24 miles). On Wednesday the English marched to Chatellerault (17 miles), the French to La Haye (16 miles). On Thursday the English halted, the French marched to Chauvigny (33 miles). On Friday the English continued their halt, the French also halted.[1] On Saturday September 17, the English went to Chabotrie, four miles south-east of Poitiers (30 miles), the French to Poitiers (18 miles), the English crossing the path of the French and colliding with their rearguard near Chabotrie.

What construction are we to put on these curious marches and halts? The two opposing schools of thought may for convenience be called the French and the English, though this is by no means an exact definition. The French school avers that during these days the Black Prince was continuously retreating from King John who, by a brilliant flanking manoeuvre, put his army right behind that of his opponent and had it in his power to cut off the English

---

[1] That is, the main body. The king seems to have pushed on with his vanguard towards Poitiers, though the statement that he spent the night of September 16 at Chabotrie is most unlikely.

retreat. These critics stress the fact that when the Prince
heard at Chatellerault that the enemy had got past him and
were at Chauvigny he made a hurried retreat, being prepared if necessary to sacrifice his booty-train in his desperate
effort to get out of the net. The English school, on the
other hand, avers that so far from trying to avoid the
enemy in that hurried march of September 17, the Black
Prince was hastening to set a trap for his opponent on the
road from Chauvigny to Poitiers, and that it nearly came
off. Most of the chroniclers support the French school, only
three supporting the English; but these three happen to be the
three most reliable sources we have. Moreover until Father
Deniflé wrote his *Désolation des Églises* . . . in 1899 two out of
these three sources were, incredible though it may sound,
unknown to the French historians, so their adherence to the
French school is understandable. These sources are two letters
written by the Prince on October 20 and 22 to the mayor of
London and to the bishop of Worcester respectively. There is
also the Chronicle of Geoffrey le Baker de Swynbroke. Both
these sources state that the Prince throughout was anxious to
engage the French king in battle and that his march from the
Loire to Poitiers was a manoeuvre for that purpose, not a
retreat. Father Deniflé himself accepts this claim, but he has
not been followed by subsequent French historians. Professor
Tout and Sir James Ramsay are the chief exponents of the
English school, though biographers of the Black Prince seem
generally to side with the French school.

THE PRELIMINARIES

The ground is now cleared for an examination of these rival
contentions. If in the course of it I constantly refer to *L'Histoire
de Charles V* by Roland Delachenal it is because it contains what
is on the whole the most detailed, thorough and well-docu-
mented examination of the problem in print, and because
Professor Delachenal's views have been in the main accepted
by subsequent French writers since the book was published

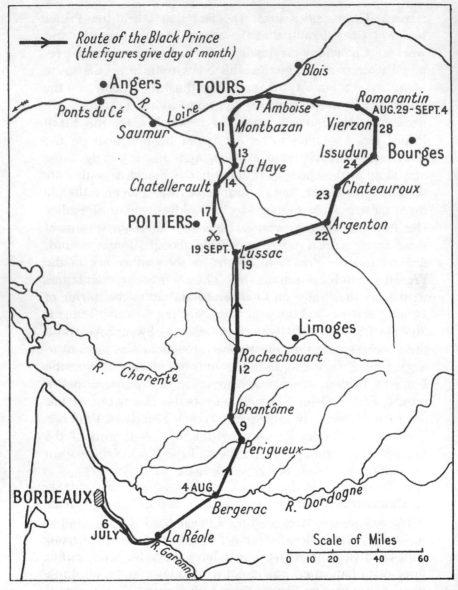

Route of the Black Prince
(the figures give day of month)

Angers

TOURS

Blois

Ponts du Cé

R. Loire

7 Amboise

Romorantin
AUG. 29 - SEPT. 4

Saumur

11 Montbazan

Vierzon 28

13 La Haye

Issudun 24

Bourges

Chatellerault 14

23 Chateauroux

POITIERS 17

Argenton 22

19 SEPT. Lussac 19

Limoges

R. Charente

Rochechouart 12

Brantôme 9

Perigueux

4 AUG.

BORDEAUX

Bergerac

R. Dordogne

6 JULY

La Réole

R. Garonne

Scale of Miles

0  10  20      40      60

14. THE POITIERS CAMPAIGN

(1909) till the appearance in 1946 of Professor Ferdinand Lot's
*L'Art Militaire et les Armées au Moyen Age.*

Let us open this examination on the morning of Monday
September 12, when the English army was halted at Montbazan
and the French at Amboise, 20 miles north-east of it. That day
the two inevitable cardinals appeared in the English camp,
beseeching that an end be put to hostilities. Prince Edward,
who had his mind full of other things, treated the cardinals
civilly but explained blandly that he was not authorized to
negotiate a truce, and that they should refer to his father the
king. It was either on this day or on September 11 that he
received a message from his "dear cousin" Henry of Lancaster.
The faithful Lancaster was doing his best to carry out his
instructions. It is a pity that we have few details of them, but
it is clear that he had reached the river Loire at Les Ponts
du Cé, due south of Angers, where he also was held up.[1] One
would give a good deal to know the exact nature of the information that the Prince received: it is reasonable to suppose
that it was to the effect that Henry was trying to get across the
river but had not yet succeeded. If he did eventually succeed
where would be the best junction point? Midway between the
two armies lay Saumur, which was in hostile hands. Lancaster
would therefore have to give it a wide berth. This would take
him through Montreuil (a dozen miles south of Saumur) and,
continuing the same line, he would converge on to the Black
Prince's road at or near Chatellerault. It may indeed well be
that the Prince sent back a message making this suggestion.
The latter resumed his march next day, through La Haye
to Chatellerault, where he arrived on September 14. Meanwhile he had lost touch with the French army. Had it stopped
at La Haye, 17 miles in his rear? He would send to ascertain
this; for though he would sooner have the battle after joining
forces with Lancaster, he did not wish to lose sight of his opponent. As far back as September 5 he had warned his troops to

[1] Ramsay is candid enough to say that he cannot find the place on his map,
which is a pity, for he might have developed the point I am about to make.

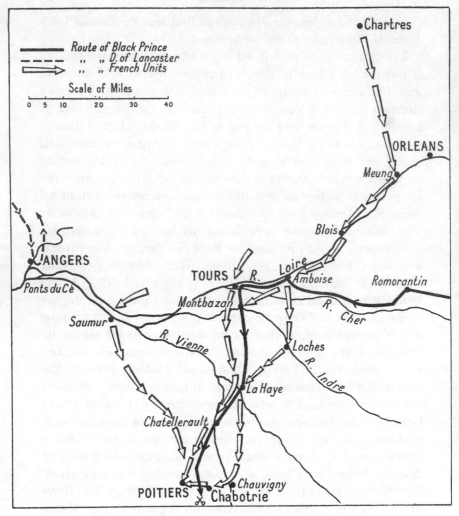

## 15. FROM THE LOIRE TO POITIERS

"prepare their harness" for the coming battle. He therefore halted on the next day, September 15, at Chatellerault. But why did he also halt the following day, too? This has puzzled all commentators and worried some of them. He was still without information of his opponent's whereabouts and he gives this as his reason for remaining halted for a second day. But if he was also waiting for more news from Lancaster it was natural that he should dally as long as he dared at Chatellerault. It was thus not surprising that he should halt for two days running. But on the evening of the second day he at last received definite news of the French army: he could not remain halted any longer, unless he was to abandon all hope of meeting his opponent. In that case the latter might in his absence devastate Gascony in revenge for the Black Prince's devastations. King John was reported halted in Chauvigny. The Prince judged that his immediate destination was Poitiers, where there was a strong French garrison; John might even shut himself up in it as he had done at Amiens the previous year. Was there time to cut him off and perhaps even capture him by taking up position on the road along which he would have to pass! The most likely, indeed the only possible, place for effecting this would be as far removed from Chauvigny as possible yet out of sight of Poitiers, in other words near Chabotrie. The distance was nearly 30 miles. By disengaging his baggage-train, getting it across the river Clain during the night and marching at dawn, it should be possible for the mounted portion of the army to reach the Chauvigny road by early afternoon. Orders were issued accordingly, the baggage crossed the river bridge during the night, and at dawn on September 17 the march began. The baggage was left to follow on, and after marching down the Roman road towards Poitiers for about 12 miles[1] the vanguard turned off the road and pushed on across country, leaving the baggage to its own devices, far in rear. It was an exciting race, and everything had to give way to the main consideration.

[1] Following Hilaire Belloc here.

As the vanguard reached the Chauvigny-Poitiers road, the French rearguard was just passing. It was promptly charged and received a rough handling from the English men-at-arms, many prisoners being taken, including two counts. But King John had escaped the trap, and was already safe in Poitiers. The English army was now short of food and water, especially water. The Prince therefore decided to go no further, he would give time for his baggage to catch up. So the night was spent in the forest near the little village of Chabotrie.

That, at least, is how I reconstruct the motives of the Black Prince, based on his known actions and his own statements.[1]

As to whether the Prince really wished an encounter with King John, Ferdinand Lot implies that his actions belie his words. Let us see. The crucial date is the Friday evening, when the Prince learnt that his opponent was at Chauvigny. If he had wished to avoid an encounter with the French king would he have remained halted for two days out of touch with his pursuers? Would he not rather have seized the opportunity to get his booty-wagons further toward Bordeaux and safety? His opponent had vanished. When on the second day his opponents were still unlocated, would not the Prince have grown apprehensive? Two days ago they were at La Haye; where might they not be now? Again, when, that Friday evening, the Prince learnt that King John had reached Chauvigny, 20 miles in his rear, would he not have looked for some way of escape? It was a very obvious guess that the French king would join forces with the Poitiers garrison; therefore the Chauvigny-Poitiers road would probably be in enemy hands ere now. Would not that line of escape offer the least likely chance of success? Would it not be better to march south-east, making for Lussac and then returning home by the same road that he had traversed in his outward march, or, better still, work to the south-west, leaving Poitiers on his left hand, and thus placing it between himself

[1] His statement that he wished to cross swords with King John has been questioned in many quarters, but that fair and indefatigable historian, Father Denifle, though bitter against the prince for his devastations, accepts his statement here at its face value.

and the French army? Surely the answer to all these questions
is in the affirmative, unless the Black Prince, and his experienced
generals, were imbeciles. Yet he did none of these things. So
it seems that when the prince told the mayor of London that
he had wished to cross swords with King John he was speaking
the truth.

### KING JOHN'S MOTIVES

Now let us consider the motives and generalship of the
French king. At first sight the generally held view of his march
to Chauvigny seems the natural one; *viz.*, that he wished to
turn the English flank and cut off their retreat to Bordeaux.
But there are some awkward questions. On what grounds did
he calculate at La Haye that he could outmarch the English
and get in their rear? To cut them off near Chabotrie his army
would have to march over 45 miles if it went, as it did, *via*
Chauvigny; whereas the English army had less than 30 to
traverse, as we have just seen. How could he foretell that the
English would halt for two whole days running at Chatellerault? Moreover the English troops were in harder condition
than his own, having been campaigning for over six weeks.
Even with the two halts included, the English, as we have seen,
nearly won the race. That is the first awkward question, and
I do not know the answer, nor how it showed "brilliant
generalship", as a modern English biographer of the Black
Prince has claimed.

Next, admittedly the king made a rapid and unexpected
march to Chauvigny; but if speed was essential why did he
throw away its fruits by halting at Chauvigny next day?[1]
There are two possible explanations for this. The king may have
found on the morning of the Friday that so many of his troops
had straggled that he did not feel strong enough to continue
with his plan until they had all caught up the main body. This
would certainly apply to all his infantry, who had marched

[1] Most historians slur over this, some of them even asserting that he only reached
the town on the Friday, but the evidence on the point is clear.

62 miles in four days, but it should have been an easy stage for his mounted troops.

The other possible explanation is that, as the prospect of crossing swords with the redoubtable and so far ever-victorious English army appeared more likely, he relished it less and less. King John was by no means a physical coward: he fought with magnificent bravery at Poitiers, like a true Valois, but his past record seemed to indicate a certain shrinking from the "final argument" when the time for it drew near. Those are the two explanations that I hazard, and the true explanation may well be a combination of the two.

There is, however, an entirely different view that may be taken of John's famous flank march. It may not have had an aggressive intent; its real intention may have been to get into Poitiers before the English could either get there first or stop him getting there at all. There is a good deal to be said for this theory. Let us go back to September 10, when the French army was crossing the Loire on a 120-mile front. How did the king manage to collect these widely dispersed detachments on the southern side of the river? A glance at the map shows that the English army was sitting down between him and the Tours and Saumur contingents. He could scarcely expect them to get past the vigilant English scouts during the next four days. Hence, if he was to obtain their services in a battle near Poitiers, they must march direct on that city instead of attempting to join him and accompany him to Chauvigny. Thus he would order Poitiers rather than Chartres as his concentration point as far as the Normandy and Brittany contingents were concerned (and we know he had both). If this be the correct explanation it means that the Chauvigny march, instead of being intended to hold up and bring to bay the English army, was on the contrary an attempt to keep well clear of that army until John had completed his concentration, which would be in Poitiers. In favour of this view is the fact that, whatever his intention, that is what in fact happened. The French army during those famous and critical ten days was spread out over a huge area of country, with the minimum of control and communication between the component parts. As an example, a few hours after the English had marched out of Chatellerault on that Saturday morning, a French detachment marched over the same bridge in the same direction, a fact which seems to have puzzled Delachenal.[1] An objection to this view is that, had the king desired to get into Poitiers first, he would not have made the wide circuit *via* Chauvigny, but would have cut the corner from Pleumartin onward, and ridden into the city on the Thursday.

If none of the above speculations is the truth it seems we must fall back on the view, expressed tentatively by one French commentator, that after his arrival at Chauvigny King John hesitated and wobbled for some time before deciding on his next step. If his opponent was in the dark, so also was he. The French chroniclers who might be expected to assist here throw no light on the king's motives. The problem will therefore never be finally solved. My own view, on balance, is that King John, in making his flank march, hoped by some means to shake off and evade the English army until he had fully concentrated his own army at Poitiers. If the facts are as suggested above, note how exactly they are corroborated by the Prince's letter to the mayor of London, which may be translated as follows:

"(King John) came with his army to Chauvigny, in order to pass to Poitiers; on which we decided to hasten towards him, on the road by which he must pass, intending to meet him on the road to Poitiers. . . ."

Here the Black Prince makes a definite statement as to the king's intentions. Did John tell him this when a prisoner!

SUNDAY, SEPTEMBER 18

The second great point of controversy concerning the battle of Poitiers centres round the events immediately preceding the battle and the nature of the battle itself. Was the Black Prince attacked while holding a position or while in the act of retreat-

---

[1] He calls it "fort singulier".

ing? The French school asserts the latter, the English school the former. As before, we will first give a *précis* of the events up to the moment in dispute. Early on Sunday, September 18, the English mounted units filed away to water in the Moisson stream, at Nouaillé, four miles due south of Chabotrie, while the marshals presumably reconnoitred the ground for a suitable position covering the river line and facing Poitiers, Nouaillé being distant eight miles from that city. Warwick's division led, followed by the Prince's, while Oxford's brought up the rear. At Nouaillé there was a narrow stone bridge. In order that the two leading divisions could water their horses simultaneously, Warwick's division would cross over the bridge and water on the southern bank. The rear division probably found sufficient water in Chabotrie and the neighbouring farms, and would then proceed direct to the selected position. Here it would be joined by the leading two divisions when watering was completed, the Prince's division doubling back up the road by which it had descended to the river, Warwick's division recrossing the river by a ford 600 yards further west (see sketch map), which was the direct line of approach to its portion—the left—of the selected position.

Meanwhile the two indomitable cardinals had put in another appearance. It is generally said that they spent the day "passing backwards and forwards between the two armies". This is hardly correct. They came from the French camp to Edward, who listened with courteous patience to their tearful pleadings for a truce. He ultimately agreed to a conference between delegates from the two armies, which accordingly assembled with the cardinals in no man's land. Discussions went on most of the day, but without result. The terms proposed by King John were too humiliating for the Prince to accept, and he fell back on the plea that he was not authorized to arrange a truce and that reference must be made to his father the king. Darkness fell, and both sides lay on their arms, the outposts, according to one source, being within bowshot of each other.

During the night the English held a war council, for the question had to be faced—supposing King John declined to attack the English position indefinitely, what was to be done? There were three possible courses. First, to take the offensive themselves. This was not in the English tradition, and as it had now become clear that the French army had attained great proportions such an attack was not likely to succeed. Second, to remain in position. But if the French remained stationary also there would be an impasse, which would redound to the advantage of the enemy, for the king could continually increase the size of his army whereas the Prince could not. Third, to retreat to Bordeaux. Such a move must sooner or later be carried out, for there was no longer any question of joining up with either of the two English armies to the north of the Loire. Might it not be advantageous to slip away quietly and so obtain a good lead for the slow-moving baggage and booty-wagons? The council decided upon the third course, provided the French king showed no signs of attacking next morning. The Prince, however, took the same preparatory step that he had taken before the withdrawal from Chatellerault: he passed his booty-wagons over the Nouaillé bridge during the night.

MONDAY, SEPTEMBER 19

Early in the morning the cardinal of Périgord again approached the Prince (who probably had pitched his tent on the ridge top in full view of the ridge held by the French outposts 1,500 yards distant). His keen eye detected continual movement from rear to front in the hostile lines: the French were evidently utilizing the unofficial armistice to bring up reinforcements and to collect stragglers after their hasty march. His own army was concentrated and ready for action. Any further delay would be in the interests of the French king. Indeed, the Prince is said to have accused the cardinal of working in the interests of King John. The Black Prince would listen to him no longer; the armistice was at an end. The die was cast. The Prince invited battle, and passed along his line, addressing encouraging words to all within earshot. It is noteworthy that, so great an importance did the English commander place on the moral effect of this harangue, that he instructed his subordinate commanders to pass on the gist of it to all.

The above narrative is, in general, common to both schools of thought up to the dawn of Monday. After that they diverge. The English school holds that no retreat took place before the battle and that the whole English army was drawn up awaiting battle when the French advanced. The French school asserts that the retreat had already begun, that Warwick's division had already crossed to the south of the river and, with the baggage, was on its way toward Bordeaux when the attack was launched. Roland Delachenal, who may be said to represent the extreme French school, asserts that while Warwick was on the south side of the river the remainder of the army was also on the march, quitting the position and heading for the Gué de l'Homme.

This divergence of view arises from a famous passage in the Chandos Herald's poem, which states:

"The French book says, and the account likewise, that the earl of Salisbury ... discomfited the (French) marshals ... before the vanguard could be turned and brought across again, for it was over the river." (The herald had previously stated that Warwick was in command of the vanguard.)

Written at approximately the same time, *i.e.*, some 30 years after the battle, the *Anonimalle Chronicle* states that Warwick's division crossed a narrow causeway, but later, when the French vanguard approached the English position, "Warwick and his people, passing the marsh, found a good passage which had not been found before", and attacked and worsted the French vanguard, after which Salisbury with the rearguard came to the aid of Warwick so that the French were defeated.

Thirdly, le Baker. He narrates how the Prince addressed his whole army and then, turning to the archers, gave them a special harangue. Thus saying (*talia dicens*), he looks up and notices a hill; and le Baker proceeds:

"Between us and the hill was a broad deep valley and a marsh, which was fed by a certain stream. At a fairly narrow ford the Prince's division crossed the stream, with its carriages, and occupied the hill. . . ."

Le Baker then describes the position held by the other two divisions, one flank of which rested on a marsh.

The above three accounts agree in one thing, *viz.*, that at some time before the battle a portion of the English army was on the opposite side of a valley from the position to be held. This has led the French school to believe that the herald's story is substantially true, and that the English army was in the act of retreating when the French attacked them. I hold to the traditional, or English, school. I must here support my case by examining the above passages.

Let us first take le Baker, easily the most reliable of the three sources. Though not himself present at the battle he must have obtained his story from eye-witnesses–indeed from several, for a single one could not have given the full coherent and detailed account that le Baker retails. But the author gives no indication of his division of sources: they merge into one in a flowing narrative that reflects the accomplished historian. Let us see whether we can break down into its components the story related by him. I suggest that the above passage originates from at least two informants, one in the Prince's division and one in Warwick's. Number one was present when the Prince made his harangue (probably an archer). The fiery harangue made a vivid impression on him, and in giving his story of the battle he starts off with it. Number two had crossed the river with Warwick, and had halted on the far side to water and feed. From here he well remembered looking across the valley toward the ridge up which he was shortly to toil on the way to the allotted position. This he retailed to his auditor, and then described in detail the position, how one flank rested on a marsh, etc. Le Baker no doubt heard other accounts, but having neither map nor photograph of the field was not able to form a clear and correct picture of the terrain. He did his best to piece the accounts together, but his chronology was the weakest part (as it nearly always is when relating battle or any exciting episode, or when listening to the accounts afterward). Thus in his effort to merge his various stories into one smooth-flowing account, he joined them into one continuous narrative with such conjunctive phrases as *talia dicens*. But is it conceivable, on the ground of inherent military probability, that the Prince should decide to stand his ground and announce the fact formally to his troops with the greatest publicity *before he had decided on the position to be held*, or had even reconnoitred the ground? Thus we are bound to place the speech after, not before, the scene in the valley. The speeches must have been delivered on the actual position occupied by the troops, either on the Sunday evening or, more probably, the Monday morning.

Thus regarded, le Baker does not lend any support to the herald's story. The *Chronicle Anonimalle* must be tackled in another way. The only essential point on which it supports the herald is in the statement that immediately before the battle, Warwick's division was on the far side of the river. In other respects it directly contradicts the herald, for it brings Warwick's division into action before, not after, Salisbury's. According to him, though at one time Warwick was over the river he returned in time to encounter the French vanguard, in other words, at the very beginning of the battle. This agrees with the other chroniclers, and with the English school. Incidentally, the *Anonimalle* account is full of obvious errors[1]; indeed, only one original statement in it "rings true", *viz.*, that some wagons retiring during the night over what is evidently Nouaillé bridge caused a traffic jam—a very likely occurrence before the days of traffic policemen—and even since their appearance for that matter. The episode is, however, of importance as showing that during the night the Prince prepared for an eventual withdrawal, by getting his booty-wagons clear of the river crossing

---

[1] A statement by the Chronicler regarding the siege of Romorantin is characterized by his editor, Professor Galbraith, "a wilful perversion of the truth".

overnight—just as he had so wisely done at Chatellerault a few nights before.

We must now consider the French school, which accepts implicitly the herald's statement quoted above. How can it be "explained away"? First, we must allow some licence to a poet who for the sake of rhyme and scansion must at times use an inexact word. Thus "rivière" was used by him irrespective of the size of the stream in question in order to rhyme with "pière".

But apart from this, whence did the herald obtain his information? In the first place it was already known that there was talk of retirement, and indeed that preparations had been made for it. Such preparations are evidently alluded to by Froissart when he makes the French marshals argue as to whether what they saw indicated a retirement or not. Then we are now all agreed, I hope, that at one time a portion of the English army had indeed crossed to the south side of the river (in order to water). But, allowing for all this, whence did the herald obtain his assertion that Warwick was actually in retreat when the battle opened? The herald himself tells us (though, rather surprisingly, his statement seems to have been overlooked by the commentators). Twice when describing the battle he informs us that he owes his information to "the French book", and the story of Warwick's retreating division is one of the occasions. So it was a French source—now lost—not a very good source for what was going on "the other side of the hill" to the French. We can safely attribute it to a patriotic and imaginative Frenchman anxious to impart a gleam into the gloom of that dolorous day and for this purpose inventing an English "retreat". Such a book would probably not come into the hands of the herald till after the death of his master, Sir John Chandos. It is generally and naturally supposed that the herald obtained his story of the battle from that master, with a view to his poem. But the idea of the poem perhaps occurred to him after the death of his master, when it was too late to question him. How often does one regret not having questioned the actor in a scene while he was still alive!

Let us now examine the theory of the French school, as portrayed by Roland Delachenal in his *Histoire de Charles V* and adopted by J. Tourneux-Aumont in *La Grande Goule* for 1935 (in reply to an article from my pen in the same issue).

The theory of M. Delachenal is that the battle took place in the bend of the Moisson river at Champ d'Alexandre where the English army was attacked while "en plein marche" toward the south, the English right being near Bernon and their left approaching the Gué de l'Homme. In other words, the English faced west and the French east. His ground for placing the French army in such a curious position is that the Champ d'Alexandre is described in a sixteenth-century MS as the place where certain French soldiers who had fought in the battle died. But Professor Lot has shown that this passage is wrongly transcribed from a fourteenth-century MS which refers to "plusieux des bons et loyaux amis du Roy qu'ils fussent ou non de sa bataille". Thus "bataille" means battalion or unit—not battle. But apart from the weakness of the written evidence, Delachenal's theory is open to attack on six grounds of inherent military probability.

1. In order to reach this position the French king would have to make a flank march across and in sight of the English position and then form line to his left, having altered the direction of his front by almost a right angle. This would be a hazardous and difficult manoeuvre for a badly trained medieval army, especially as the ground was wooded and hilly.

2. The French army would form up in line, facing east, the bulk of it on a narrow-backed ridge sloping down so steeply to both front and rear that the horsemen of that day would have found it practically unnegotiable—hardly an ideal place for an army that relied to a large degree on its mounted men.

3. The southern half of the army would be confined by the narrow loop of the river, with that river only 250 yards to its front and to its rear. In the event of being defeated it would be driven into the marshy ravine.

4. The position would thus have no depth; it would be

impossible to station any reserve behind the centre of the line, still less could the army approach in three or four columns, as we know it did.

5. If the French army had been seen approaching such a position and it had been the intention of the Black Prince to retreat he would scarcely have selected the Gué de l'Homme for that purpose, but would have taken the natural one–the Nouaillé crossing.

6. The Valois princes who fled at the end of the battle could not have gone in an easterly direction to Chabotrie (as they did) for that would have taken them right through the enemy army.

Even if King John had seriously proposed to occupy such a position he would have been dissuaded by his experienced generals, or if he had persisted in it and the manoeuvre had been attempted it would have foundered in the course of execution.

Whatever possible sites there may be for the battlefield there is one impossible one–Delachenal's.

In short, the conception is one that is refuted by inherent military probability. It is hard to believe that Professor Delachenal can have ever visited the terrain.[1]

THE ENGLISH POSITION

The English position can be easily defined, for it ran along a hedge–the famous hedge mentioned by three of the chroniclers–which faced north-west, and the centre of which was 500 yards due south of La Cardinerie farm. Portions of this hedge are still in existence. The hedge crosses two roads from Poitiers, that to Nouaillé and that to Le Gué de l'Homme, and the two roads, interrupting the line of the hedge, formed two gaps in it. That on the Nouaillé road was left open, but that on the Gué de l'Homme road was barricaded with carts and

---

[1] Since penning the above pages, I have read Ferdinand Lot's account of the battle in his *L'Art Militaire*. He appears to abandon Delachenal's theory, but though he says that my article in *English Historical Review* (1938) subjects it to "*des critiques les plus vives*" he does not specify how far he agrees with them.

brushwood. The lower, or left-hand, end of the hedge rested upon marshy ground in the slight "Depression" (so marked on the sketch map) that runs down to join the Moisson river. The upper or right-hand flank rested on open ground on top of the plateau, and was strengthened by the construction of a leaguer made of the war-stores wagons, surrounded by a trench.[1] Behind the position lay the wood of Nouaillé, which stretched down the slope for about 50 ft. to the winding narrow valley of the river Moisson. At the highest point of the ridge, on the edge of the wood, are two tall trees, which probably mark the approximate situation of the Black Prince's command-post during the battle. From it there is a good view of the position, and of the parallel ridge 800 yards beyond it (which I call the North Ridge) on which the French troops deployed for action.

The English army was about 6,000 strong, and the French over 20,000. The English army took up its position along or close to the hedge, Salisbury's division being on the right, Warwick's on the left, while the Prince's was in reserve in rear. The archers were for the most part drawn up in the Crecy formation, that is, on the two flanks of their respective divisions, in wedges slightly in advance of the line of men-at-arms. (They were, as usual, dismounted, but the Prince retained a small body of mounted men, as a reserve.)

The French army was formed into four bodies. In the van were two small contingents of mounted men-at-arms, about 250 in each, under the command of the two marshals, Clermont and Audrehem. Next came the division of the duke of Normandy, then that of his uncle, the duke of Orleans, and last of all that of the king. All except the van were dismounted. They had left their horses in the city of Poitiers, and for convenience in marching had cut off the long toes of their riding boots and had removed their spurs, and they had also shortened their lances to about five feet.

[1] Vestiges of this trench were still visible in the seventeenth century, and an air photograph might still disclose them. I made an ineffectual effort to obtain such a photograph in 1946.

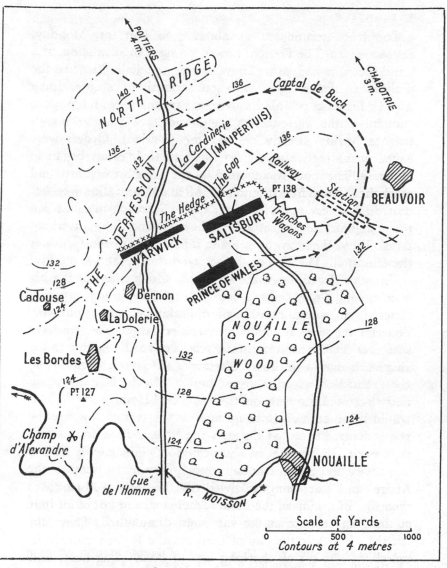

The map labels, reading across the figure:

POITIERS 4 m.

CHABOTRIE 3 m.

NORTH RIDGE

140

136

Captal de Buch

136

La Cardinerie (MAUPERTUIS)

136

132

The Gap

Railway

THE DEPRESSION

The Hedge

PT. 138

Station

BEAUVOIR

WARWICK

SALISBURY

Trenches
Wagons

132

132

128

Cadouse

124

Bernon

PRINCE OF WALES

La Dolerie

NOUAILLE

128

WOOD

Les Bordes

124

132

PT. 127

128

124

Champ
d'Alexandre

124

NOUAILLÉ

Gué
de l'Homme

R. MOISSON

Scale of Yards

0          500          1000

Contours at 4 metres

16. BATTLE OF POITIERS

299

THE BATTLE

The truce terminated at about 7.30 a.m. on Monday,
September 19. The French showed no signs of advancing, and
the Prince who had, as we know, during the night discussed the
desirability of slipping away, began seriously to consider doing
so. The first step was obviously to get on the move the wagons
containing the personal baggage and tentage (the booty-
wagons having already cleared the position). Orders were
issued accordingly and the wagons and their escort began to
move off. The move was spotted by the French vanguard, and
received different interpretations.[1] After an altercation whether
the English were really retiring, the two French marshals led
the vanguard to the attack.[2] They advanced by divergent
paths. Why? The terrain seems to afford the answer. Consider
the situation. The French horses were heavy and unwieldy;
their course led through the vineyard, which constituted a big
obstacle and would tend to break up the line formation into a
series of small columns, each column taking a track or pathway
between the vines in "follow-my-leader" style. Now we have
seen that there were two distinct tracks or roads, leading to the
English hedge in divergent directions. Clermont's column on
the French left would tend to "bunch" on the Nouaillé road,
and that of Audrehem on the Gué de l'Homme road. This
would bring both columns up against the two gaps where the
respective roads passed through the hedge. That confronting
Audrehem was barricaded and occupied; consequently he had
no success and was in fact captured (probably by jumping the
hedge and not being followed by the less well-mounted
troops); but that of Clermont met with more immediate
success, for it came up to the open unguarded gap on the

---

[1] Just as at the battle of the Aisne, the sight of German transport moving to
the rear led some to believe that it was the beginning of a general retirement.
I have here accepted the herald's account, but it is possible that Villani's statement that smoke from some burning wagons precipitated the battle is the
correct one.

[2] I cannot accept Froissart's unsupported statement that the battle began at
"prime" and ended at "nones": more likely it began at "nones" (noon) and ended
at vespers (4 p.m.).

Nouaillé road, and the leading files passed through it and swung to their right in support of Audrehem, already held up opposite his gap. It was only the prompt manoeuvre of Salisbury that frustrated this well-devised operation of Clermont's. Quick to sense the danger, he advanced his line right up to the hedge, thus effectually closing the gap and scotching the flank attack on Warwick's division.

Meanwhile on the English left some of our archers were carrying out a noteworthy manoeuvre. As the French cavalry approached, the bulk of them moved still further to their left into the marsh. Here they were comparatively safe from the hostile horsemen, and were able to gall them with a flanking fire. An obscure passage in le Baker[1] describes how the cavalry advanced direct upon the archers hoping to protect themselves by their breast armour and at the same time protect the infantry following behind them. The English arrows ricocheted off the French breastplates and the archers were consequently at a disadvantage till the earl of Oxford, appreciating the situation, ran down from the Prince's head-quarters and directed the archers to fire obliquely, not at the armoured riders, but at the unprotected hindquarters of their horses. It was in order to do this that the archers moved to their left into the marsh. This action was completely successful and the French attack was repulsed. The struggle had, however, been severe and in some places (probably in the centre) some cavalry had managed to break through the hedge.[2] Rigid discipline reigned in the English ranks, and no pursuit was allowed. It was recognized that only the vanguard had as yet been encountered.

The Dauphin's column now advanced, on foot.[3] Their horses had been left in the rear, as already mentioned. The English men-at-arms had also dismounted, with this difference,

[1] Omitted by Stow in his translation.

[2] No doubt making use of the "*pluseurs brèches*" mentioned by the *Chronique Normande du XIVe Siècle*.

[3] King John has been blamed for dismounting the bulk of his army, but he was well advised to do so. It was no innovation in the French army, as we have seen.

however, that they had kept their horses at hand, and did not remove their spurs.

The *élan* of the oncoming column cannot have been increased by the spectacle of disaster that had befallen the vanguard. Nor would the impact with the panic-struck horses of the vanguard, galloping to the rear, add to their order and cohesion.[1] But the column came stolidly on, in spite of all that the archers could do, and engaged the men-at-arms in hand-to-hand fighting. At this stage the hedge vanishes almost completely from the story. There are two possible explanations. Either it was by now so battered down that it ceased to be an obstacle for the dismounted French, or the English advanced slightly beyond the hedge for the hand-to-hand contest that ensued. The archers were running short of arrows, and the major credit for the defeat of the Dauphin's column goes to our men-at-arms. During the course of this fight the Prince reinforced Warwick's portion of the line with the bulk of his own column; but he was careful to keep a small mounted force in his own hands, which he later used to good purpose.

It is useless to attempt to compute how long the struggle lasted; but that it was prolonged is evident from the extreme state of exhaustion to which it reduced the English army. The accounts are clear and frank on this point. When at last the Dauphin drew off, defeated but in good order, the English heaved a sigh of relief, believing the battle was over. From this it is clear that the two remaining columns of the French army were still out of sight behind the North Ridge. A lull now descended on the battle, which the English utilized to replenish ammunition, exchange broken for sound lances, recover spent arrows and tend the wounded. Water was no doubt brought up from the river, as they must have been very thirsty by now— especially the men-at-arms. The pause was happily increased by the failure of the duke of Orleans' column to engage. What exactly happened to it is obscure, but it appears to have been seized with panic and to have fled toward

[1] A similar impact at Agincourt had serious results.

Chauvigny.[1] The duke of Orleans has, of course, been unmercifully blamed for this; but it must be remembered in his defence that, though the uncle of the Dauphin, he was himself under 21 years of age. Moreover the fugitives from two defeated columns had passed through his ranks and such people are not prone to underestimate the strength and hitting power of their opponents.

## THE KING ATTACKS

The column of the king of France alone remained. King John had to make a momentous decision. Should he attack, or should he cut his losses and retreat while yet there was time? Retreat would certainly be the more prudent course to adopt, but in those days considerations of chivalry were held of greater account than those of strategy. King John therefore ordered his column to the attack.

All the indications point to the fact that during the battle of the Dauphin the king's column was a long distance in rear.[2] This curious aloofness from the battlefield of King John's column is one of the enigmas of the battle. Whatever the cause, it was undoubtedly the gravest fault committed by the French king in his conduct of the battle, though it has been almost universally ignored by the commentators.

There was a long distance to traverse and no doubt the advance was slow as the knights moved forward on foot. But when the column topped the rise and appeared all along the North Ridge, it presented a formidable spectacle to the exhausted and depleted English ranks.[3] For it was the largest of the three columns, and superior in numbers to its opponents, besides being fresher.

[1] Ramsay's assertion that the column fought and was defeated is directly refuted by Villani's statement that it "had fled for fear without taking or giving a blow".

[2] The *Chronique Normande* expressly says so and it is implied in Villani's statement that "the Dauphin's column was defeated and dispersed before the king had news of it".

[3] Some of the English were still absent in pursuit of the Dauphin, and perhaps also of the duke of Orleans. Le Baker and Chandos Herald agree on this point.

The English chroniclers are strikingly frank about the disturbing moral effect the unexpected apparition of this huge and well-appointed column had upon the Anglo-Gascons. Historians, with that wisdom that comes after the event, have a tendency to regard the defeat of King John's column as fore-doomed and inevitable. But there seems no warrant for this. In the first place the extreme exhaustion of the Prince's army has not been sufficiently emphasized. Next comes the moral exhaustion, and reaction after a hard-fought fight.

"The great number of the enemy frightened our men", le Baker says bluntly. The *Eulogium* confirms that "many of our men were frightened; nor is it to be wondered at". Le Baker adds the interesting detail that at this juncture many of our wounded began to leave the field[1] (no doubt "escorted" by unwounded comrades, as the custom is!). Other men were heard to grumble that the Prince had left more than half his army behind to defend Gascony. No wonder Prince Edward offered up a fervent prayer to heaven! The depth of discourage-ment that reigned about him, contrasted by the Prince's own high courage, is well reflected in le Baker's story of how a prominent member of the Prince's staff cried out: "Alas, we are beaten!" and the Prince's stinging retort: "Thou liest, thou knave, if thou sayest that we can be conquered as long as I live!"

It was the critical moment in his career. Let us consider his perplexing position. He could not at the moment be aware of the flight of Orleans' column, which would be hidden by the North Ridge. He would imagine that he had the main body of the French army still in his front. Should he, in view of the weakened state of his own array, rest content with the blow he had struck against the Dauphin and now fall back? His horses were handy and there yet was time if he was prepared to sacrifice some of his foot men and wagons. Or should he accept battle in his defensive position? Or, thirdly, should he take the offensive himself?

Somewhat unexpectedly, when we consider all the circum-

---

[1] Discreetly omitted in Stow's translation.

stances, he chose the third course. Probably two considerations induced this decision.

1. He had already noted that his defensive position was more effective against mounted than dismounted men. The latter had fought upon fairly even terms. No benefit was therefore to be gained by awaiting attack behind what remained of the hedge.

2. At the crisis of a battle, moral superiority may just turn the scale. His men were then experiencing that reaction after a fight, that *lassitudo certaminis* that so frequently supervenes toward the end of a fight when physical and moral powers are at their lowest ebb. If he was content merely to sit still and await attack, the moral of his troops would scarcely be higher–it might indeed be lower–than that of the enemy. But if, with splendid audacity, he ordered an attack–and a mounted attack at that–the old moral superiority of mounted over dismounted men would assert itself and compel victory. The French were in the open, and on the move; they were deficient in archers, and dismounted; and would not be in a good posture to protect themselves against a mounted attack. Some such reasoning as this probably led the son of Edward III to the dazzling decision which stamps him for all time as a great captain.[1]

It is to be noted that the English attack was not to be the wholly frontal operation customary in those days. Combined with the frontal attack, the prince arranged a flank attack by the mounted reserve to which I have already referred. This he placed under the Gascon leader, the Captal de Buch. The force was small in numbers, but the ground was admirably suited to the operation. From point 138 the ground slopes down gently in all directions. Thus, from the northern edge of Nouaillé wood it is possible to skirt round to the east of the (present) railway station and swinging to the left approach the North Ridge unobserved. Such was the manoeuvre that was

---

[1] Ramsay is fully justified in claiming that "the daring attack on the king's big battalion is one of the finest things in military history".

entrusted to the Captal. No exact synchronization of the two
attacks was probably either hoped for or aimed at. The final
struggle was bound to be prolonged; a few minutes either
way would be immaterial, though it was desirable, but not
essential, that the frontal attack should slightly precede the
flank attack.

From a study of the ground, and the identification of the
place-names, the final clash must have taken place in the dip in
the immediate vicinity of La Cardinerie.

The scene must have been a striking one. The English men-
at-arms sprang to the stirrup, as they had done 23 years before
at Halidon Hill, and charged down the hill upon the slowly
oncoming column of dismounted men. A homeric contest then
ensued in which the French crossbowmen were prominent. In
the midst of the fighting and above the din was heard the
familiar English battle-cry "St. George!" and from the right
a body of mounted troops was seen galloping into the un-
suspecting flank of the French column. It was the Captal de
Buch with his gallant band. The result of this sudden onslaught
was probably out of all proportion to the numbers of those
engaged. Indeed it may have been the deciding factor—"the
last straw" which so often settles destiny.

The contest was long, but yard by yard the sturdy English
men-at-arms forced their way forward, as they had done across
the decks of the French ships at Sluys and the Spanish ships at
Winchelsea, while the mounted archers, having exhausted their
arrows, put aside their bows and drawing their swords, entered
the mêlée. The great French column, attacked on two sides,
gradually crumbled, then disintegrated and fled from the field,
leaving its king a prisoner in English hands. So much attention
has naturally been lavished on this resounding and world-
famous capture that the subsequent remarkable English pursuit
right up to the walls of Poitiers has been generally overlooked.
But it was yet another of the unusual features of the battle.
The pursuers no doubt got out of hand, as all pursuers do, and
the Prince had no means of reassembling them, save by hoisting

his banner on one of the bushes on the hill-top, as recommended by Sir John Chandos.

There, amid the dead and dying, the Black Prince pitched his pavilion, and there, when darkness descended, he sat down to supper with the king of France as his guest.

The losses in the French nobility were staggering—nearly 2,000 knights and men-at-arms were prisoners and over 2,000 of them lay dead on the field. Of casualties to the infantry levies, no record was attempted. A great charnel-pit was made for the corpses, and it would be interesting to know the exact spot where it was sited. As for the English, their casualties were slight, but they included the dashing Lord Audley. That evening he was found lying half-dead on the field, and was carried on his shield to the pavilion of the Prince of Wales, who was at that moment at supper with King John. The Prince interrupted his meal to tend the wounds of one of the staunchest of his captains.

\*　　　　\*　　　　\*

Next day the Anglo-Gascon army resumed its homeward march, and entered the city of Bordeaux some days later in triumph—while the Anglo-Breton army sorrowfully retraced its footsteps to Brittany. Henry of Grosmont, Derby and Lancaster had failed for the first and only time in his military career.

CAUSES OF THE VICTORY

It is not surprising that French commentators have pondered deeply the problem of how the English came to win this sweeping victory against such odds, adding one more to the line of consistent English victories during the previous 16 years of warfare. Simeon Luce, in the notes to his edition of Froissart, writes: "The incontestable military superiority of the English in the 14th century resided above all in the dexterity, the good weapons and the large proportion of their archers to other arms." Professor Delachenal starts with very similar words, but comes to different conclusions: "The intrinsic quality of the English army largely made up for its weak numbers. The military superiority of the English was established in the first encounters of the Hundred Years War, and it was maintained throughout the 14th century. Du Guesclin himself recognized this, for he never risked a set battle against them." But Delachenal finds other causes for this superiority than those given by Luce. In general he attributes the English success to superior organization, recruitment and training. Neither of these authors, in my opinion, gives the most fundamental cause. While recognizing that battles and wars are won, not by one single factor but by the resultant of several, it is usually possible to single out one factor as predominant in any given case. In this case I believe this factor to be *morale*— that mysterious quality that induces one man to persevere in the fight longer than another. An army, or a nation, gains a victory by certain means; its morale is thereby raised, with the result that a second victory is gained; this in turn still further strengthens the morale of the troops by the reverse of the "vicious circle" and until some greater antagonistic factor supervenes the army goes from strength to strength. The English army started the Hundred Years War possessed of a fairly high state of morale, born of their recent success against the Scots, with the victories of Edward I as a background. They went "from strength to strength" just as, for example, did Napoleon's *Grande Armée* 450 years later, or as did the British Eighth Army after its victory at Alamein. By the time of Poitiers the English morale was at its zenith.

### THE TACTICS

A word regarding the tactics, that is the dispositions and handling of troops in the battle, on the part of the rival commanders. As for the Prince of Wales, I can find no flaw at any stage. The only really difficult problem is to decide how far the young Prince really "took charge" in the battle and how far he was swayed or indeed governed by the counsel of others. It is clear that he was wont to hold a war council before making any important decision; but this was in accordance with the normal procedure of medieval times, and indeed of later times; even the duke of Marlborough conformed to this practice. As regards advice given by individuals, the only name mentioned is that of Sir John Chandos. At one time I was disposed to regard this famous knight as what we should call chief of staff to the Prince. But this is doubtful. Sir John Chandos at times roamed far from the main column, once at least as much as 25 miles; at such times he could be of little help to his master. The earl of Warwick was probably the most experienced soldier in the army and his high rank and station indicates him as the nearest in the line of succession to the Black Prince; but we hear nothing specific about this rather shadowy commander. The matter cannot be resolved on the available evidence; but it is reasonable to suppose that the Prince relied wholly upon his advisers in the early stages of his first campaign, but became progressively independent of them, until when the day of Poitiers dawned he was as much the commander-in-chief as his father had been at Crecy.

Though Poitiers was at the outset fought in the Crecy tradition, two important differences should be noted – the ascendancy of the men-at-arms, and the success of mounted versus dismounted troops in the final phase of the battle. In these two respects Poitiers was a hark-back to the previous century.

As for the king of France, we possess no account by an eye-witness from the French side, so must judge as best we can, solely from the evidence of the facts. This evidence shows no indication of control by one supreme commander. Indeed there seem in essence to have been three armies, if not four, for the two marshals with their mounted troops acted on their own initiative in opening the battle. These armies fought entirely separate battles (when they fought at all). This disconnected-ness was the weakest feature in the French tactics, and must be attributed to the king who, during the greater part of the battle, was far in rear of the field. His decision to fight dismounted was taken, we are told, on the advice of a foreigner, Sir William Douglas, and that is the only decision we hear of. As far as one can see, the battle would have been fought no worse had the French army possessed no commander at all.

As the unfortunate French king passed down the Bordeaux road into captivity, he passes out of these pages. What are we to say of him? Jean le Bon, John the Good Fellow, a man of stainless honour, during his military career encountered little but disappointment, defeat and disaster. He was more consistently unsuccessful than any captain of his century–with the possible exception of his own father. Some leaders are born so, some are made. John was neither born so nor made. The French nation was unfortunate, from a military point of view, in its first two Valois kings.

# APPENDIX

SOURCES

No battle in the Hundred Years War is better supplied with sources than that of Poitiers.[1] There exist over 20 fourteenth-century sources, some, of course, very brief. Here I will only list the dozen that I consider the most useful in elucidating the many problems of the campaign and battle.[2] I list them in roughly chronological order:

1 and 2. *Letters of the Black Prince to the mayor of London and to the bishop of Worcester*, dated respectively October 22 and 20. The first is the longer, and is particularly valuable for the campaign; the actual battle is passed over in a few words.

3. *Letter from Lord Bartholomew Burghersh*, who was present throughout the campaign. This letter also is more concerned with the campaign than with the battle, of which he gives only the strengths and losses.

---

[1] For a more complete list see my article in the *English Historical Review* (1938).

[2] The old-fashioned English pronunciation "Poy-teers" is nearer how our ancestors pronounced the word than the modern French pronunciation now taught in schools. English writers of the period spelt proper names phonetically: the Black Prince spelt it Peyters, and another Englishman Petters.

4. *Eulogium Historiarum*. Written by a monk of Malmesbury, but believed to be the record of an eye-witness. In it is what is called the *Itinerary of the Prince of Wales* in the campaign. From it Father Deniflé was able to compile a day-to-day journal of the march. It fortunately gives some space to the battle, and is incomparably the most reliable account of the battle, so far as it goes.

5. *Chronicle of Geoffrey le Baker de Swynbroke*. The author was not present, but most of his facts were probably gathered from eye-witnesses. His is the most detailed account of the battle except that of Froissart. Stow translated it in parts, quietly omitting difficult passages. Maunde Thompson, in his edition (1889), reproduces some of Stow's translation.

6. *Scalacronica*, by Sir Thomas Gray. The author served in the Black Prince's division in the 1359 campaign, whence he obtained most of his information. Unfortunately it is a muddled account, marred by some obvious errors, and written in execrable French – almost as bad as that of the Black Prince himself.

7. *Istorie Florientine*, by Matteo Villani, an Italian banker. Unbiassed, independent and contains some interesting details, but Villani naturally could not discriminate between true and false reports.

8. *Chronicles of Froissart*. Jean Froissart is here in his most tantalizing mood. He intersperses obviously genuine information received from participants with gross embellishments of his own. But it is an intellectual delight trying to sift the chaff from the good grain, of which there is plenty. The *Amiens* edition (never translated into English) should be consulted wherever possible.

9. *Chronicle of Henry Knighton*. Useful for the later stages of the battle.

10. *Le Prince Noir*, by Chandos Herald. A long poem by Sir John Chandos' herald, written some 30 years after the battle (with English translation in the edition of Pope and Lodge, 1910). The necessity for scansion and rhyming tells against it as exact history. All we can safely say is that here and

there it contains accurate statements not found elsewhere. The lines dealing with the battle have caused all historians many sleepless hours.

11. *Chronicle Anonimalle*. Written about the same time as the last-mentioned, and is about as unreliable. But it contains at least one statement not found elsewhere that rings true–the story of the traffic jam in the night at Nouaillé bridge. It has not been used by modern historians, having only been edited by Professor V. H. Galbraith in 1927 (though the MS was used by Stow).

12. *Chronique Normande du XIVe Siècle*. Written by a French soldier, not by a monk, consequently its military information is always of interest and no doubt fairly reliable. His is the best French account of the battle that we possess.

The other French sources help us very little, nor do the remaining English chronicles, or le Bel.

It is a regrettable fact that the only sources of which we possess a full modern rendering in English are the Prince's letter to the mayor of London, the *Scalacronica*, and the poem of the Chandos Herald. The others have to be studied in their original medieval French or Latin.

### THE NUMBERS

#### English Army

It has been established that the army that went to Gascony in 1355 was 2,600 strong. To this figure must be added the number already serving in that country, plus the reinforcements received in 1356. From this total must be deducted wastage by death, sickness, etc., and troops left behind to guard Gascony. Unfortunately, none of these figures is known. Another unknown quantity is the number of Gascons in the army. There are indications that a large number joined up in 1346 as a result of the successful campaign of the previous year. Indeed the total field force that the Black Prince led out of Bordeaux in July, 1356, has been estimated as high as 12,000. But a large portion of this, almost entirely Gascon in composition, was, as we have seen, left behind watching the Armagnac border. Thus our original figure of 2,600 is no guide, except as setting a kind of scale of values on which to work. The total numbers were evidently very small. The estimates given in the chronicles do not vary greatly, 7,000 being an average figure. I see no reason for not accepting the figure given by Burghersh, who was in a position to know the facts. He gives 3,000 men-at-arms, 2,000 archers and 1,000 sergeants, making a total of 6,000. The only estimate well below this is that of Ramsay, who suggests 3,500, on the unwarranted assumption that there were less than 1,000 Gascons in the army.

*French Army*

This is, as usual, a more difficult problem. Figures vary between 11,000 and 60,000. In default of reliable figures I will approach the problem from four different aspects.

1. There is ample evidence that the appearance of the French king's division on the battlefield dismayed the English because of its vast numbers. It must therefore have outnumbered the victorious English nearly, if not quite, twofold. If the English were 6,000 the king's division would thus be at least 10,000 strong. The other two divisions were much smaller than the king's. Stragglers and late detachments joining the army on the morning of the battle would be hastily drafted into the rear division, which was the king's. In addition, some of the stouter-hearted soldiers in the duke of Orleans' division joined that of the king, which we can thus assess at about twice the strength of each of the other two. Thus the total would amount to about 20,000, excluding the 500 mounted troops of the marshals.

2. King John had a large army in Normandy. Coville in Lavisse's History computes it at 50,000. We can scale this down to perhaps 20,000 but scarcely lower. As no operations were going on when John left for Chartres, he presumably took the great proportion of this army with him. To it he added levies from all over France—the chronicles are emphatic on the point.

At least another 5,000 must have joined his army from this source, making a total of rather more than 20,000.

3. Burghersh states that the French had 8,000 men-at-arms, 3,000 foot soldiers, totalling 11,000. He must have obtained these figures from French prisoners (who would be tempted to scale down the numbers from obvious motives) for neither Burghersh nor any other Englishman saw the whole French army, since Orleans' division never came in view of them. But if Burghersh was given some official French figure the only one available would be that of the permanent force (what we should now call regulars) that accompanied the king on his campaigns. The numbers obtained by the nation-wide levy called for so insistently by the king could not be known, for the simple reason that detachments were still arriving right up to the day of the battle, and after the battle the king was a prisoner and all internal organization of the army had vanished (and with it the records). It is, however, reasonable to suppose that the total of the levies equalled, if it did not exceed, that of the regulars. This would bring the grand total to something over 20,000.

4. Approximately 2,500 French are reported killed, and 2,000 captured. If we allow two men wounded for one killed that would make the total casualties including captured about 8,500. In so heavy a defeat as this one might expect the casualties to amount to nearly 50 per cent. of combatants, which would thus be 17,000. To this we must add the 5,000 or so of Orleans' division which presumably had no casualties. This brings the grand total to approximately 23,000. Thus by four several lines of approach we get a grand total of slightly over 20,000.[1]

Until quite recently all chroniclers and historians have been in agreement that the French army outnumbered the English. But in 1946, Professor Ferdinand Lot in his *L'Art Militaire* attempted to show that the French were inferior numerically

[1] Delachenal computes the French as being twice as numerous as the English. As he puts the latter at about 10,000 he evidently agrees with our figure of 20,000 for the French.

to the English, or rather, he "suspects it". As the professor endeavours in this book to show that the French never had a numerical superiority at Crecy, Agincourt or Verneuil, or at least to throw doubt on the matter, it is desirable to examine his methods of calculation rather closely, for they constitute "the last word" and have never been answered from the traditional point of view.

He starts by arguing that King John cannot have had a large army because he was completely unable to turn the English position because of lack of men. This is a weak argument; especially when referring to a medieval battle where a frontal attack, when two armies were ranged in opposing lines, was almost a foregone conclusion. But he bases his main argument on the figures supplied by Jean le Bel, a foreigner writing hundreds of miles away, and not a particularly reliable authority. However, let us accept his figures for the sake of argument. Le Bel gives very low figures for the French cavalry, but adds: "The King had in his own division all the remnants of the men-at-arms and infantry, of whom there were such a large number that it was a marvellous sight." Lot accepts the first statement which supports his case, but rejects the second, which he explains away by the airy remark that "no doubt John sacrificed all to the desire to cut the Anglo-Gascon retreat to Bordeaux, and did not embarrass himself with a lot of infantry: they would have retarded his march. . . ."

As we have seen above, it is by no means certain that John tried on the Friday or the Saturday to cut the retreat of the English, but even if we allow that argument, King John was halted at Chauvigny for the best part of a day, and two whole days at Poitiers (thus allowing time for the infantry to come up) before the battle began. M. Lot also makes the assertion (copied from the German Lampe and not verified by him) that "there is no question of the presence of any crossbowmen . . . in the accounts of the action". This is not so: le Baker (p. 151, 1.6) refers to "a threatening body of crossbowmen" who made the sky dark with their arrows.

The professor concludes by asserting that the *Grandes Chroniques* says that the two armies were equal. What the *Grandes Chroniques* actually said was: "Although the king of France had as many men as the Prince . . ." which Delachenal describes as a statement made "très habilement, trop habilement" thus indicating that it was a *suggestio falsi*. But Ferdinand Lot seizes on it and twists it to his own purpose.

On such flimsy grounds and by such questionable methods does the learned historian seek to upset a hitherto universally accepted belief.

### THE HEDGE

We come now to the consideration of the exact location of the English position. The commentators are agreed that it was somewhere to the north of Nouaillé wood and near Maupertuis (La Cardinerie). Can we define it within narrower limits? Can we even aspire to discover the actual hedge, and the "*fameuse brèche*" in it? Let us see.

On grounds of inherent military probability we would naturally look for the position on a ridge facing toward Poitiers, and covering the road or roads by which the ultimate retirement to Bordeaux would have to be carried out. Now, the road running just west of La Cardinerie to Gué de l'Homme existed at the time of the battle, and would thus form a possible line of retreat. Maupertuis was a village or hamlet, and some sort of road connected it with the near-by abbey of Nouaillé, for a road crossed the river at that spot. Maupertuis lay in the direct line from the abbey to the city of Poitiers, another reason for the existence of this road. It seems natural that this road should take the approximate course of the present road, and that it would constitute a second possible line of retreat. Thus, we have two roads, both still in existence, to be covered by the English position. All accounts agree that this was a strong natural position. Looking at the ground to-day, there appear to be two possible positions and two only. The foremost lies on the ridge 400 yards to the north-west of La Cardinerie, which I call the North Ridge. The rear one is 400 yards south of La Cardinerie. Between the two runs the slight depression (which I call the "Depression") which joins the valley of the Moisson just south of Les Bordes, deepening as it descends.

Let us now see what light the study of place-names and discovery of relics may throw upon the subject. This study has been well summarized by Lettenhove in his edition of Froissart.

*Le Champ de la Bataille.* "Between Les Bordes and Maupertuis." Babinet puts it just south of the railway bridge west of Maupertuis. Broken swords and battle debris have been found here.

*La Masse Aux Anglais.* "A mound 500 metres from Maupertuis."

*L'Abreuvoir Aux Anglais.* "Further on." Probably the same as *Mare Aux Anglais*, a small pool at the head of the depression, at which the English watered some horses.

In addition, a silver coin of Edward III was picked up near Maupertuis; near the same place was found the "escarboucle" or jewel of the French king.

Finally, in Lettenhove's time "one still sees vestiges of field works constructed by the English", in the same locality. The cumulative effect of all these identifications is overwhelming; the inference is inescapable. The battle took place in the immediate vicinity of the present La Cardinerie.

Now the bulk of the fighting seems to have taken place slightly in advance of the English hedge; certainly the fight with King John's column was in front of it. Consequently the battle-field debris would be mainly in front of the hedge. This would point to the hedge being slightly to the south of La Cardinerie; *i.e.*, on the rearmost of the two positions I have suggested.

There are other considerations that point in the same direction. Here le Baker comes to our assistance. He describes an uncultivated hilltop, thick with scrub and undergrowth, bounded by a long hedge and ditch; beyond this hedge lay the cultivated land, partly vines and partly fallow at that season of the year. The first and third columns lay behind the hedge,

one end of which fell away into a marsh. Toward the other end
of the hedge, a good way from the marsh, was a large gap. The
position that I have indicated south of Maupertuis exactly fits
this description, if we allow the assumption that "marsh"
refers to my "Depression". Doubts have been expressed on
this point because of the words "wide and deep valley". That
description is true of the Moisson valley, but not of the depression near Maupertuis. I suggest, however, that the "marsh"
*does* refer to the depression. Though shallow at this point, it gets
deeper as it runs south, till on joining the Moisson valley south
of Les Bordes it is just as deep as that valley. It would be easy
for an absentee chronicler, relying on verbal accounts, to
confound the main valley with its tributary "marsh". Even this
assumption is not absolutely essential. Le Baker, in speaking of a
"wide deep valley and a marsh", may have intended, as I have
hinted above, to discriminate between them, the valley being
the Moisson valley, and the marsh being the Depression. But
what of the stream running through it? There is now no
stream, but it is probable that before the days of drainage
surface water trickled down it, especially as there was a
"reservoir" at its head. An alternative solution is that both
informants spoke of a marsh and le Baker incorrectly assumed
that they were referring to the same marsh, whereas there were
really two quite separate marshes—one in the Moisson valley,
and one in the Depression.

If my assumption is accepted, we can now fix the site of the
hedge within very narrow limits. It would face roughly north-
west; its left end resting on the "marsh", that is on the Depression, its right on the high ground near point 138 (see
Map 37.[1]

H. B. George says, "There is now no long hedge anywhere
*east* of the wood of Nouaillé," but it is to the *north-west* that we
must look. "Hedges and ditches disappear easily in fertile
soil," he continues, and certainly a visitor to the field nearly

---

[1] Hilaire Belloc favoured such a position, which he claimed extended for 1,000
yards "almost to a foot".

600 years later would scarcely expect the good fortune of
finding and identifying that famous hedge, but there are in
fact considerable portions of an old hedge exactly fitting the
requirements. In places it has disappeared and been replaced
by wire or fresh planting; but the line is marked by a continuous track which runs along in front of it (corresponding
to the ditch which we know lay in front of it). This hedge and
track start on the left at the Gué de l'Homme road, and run
north-east for 500 yards, crossing the Nouaillé road 300 yards
south-east of La Cardinerie. There is now no sign of the hedge
to the left of the Gué de l'Homme road, but if it indeed is the
actual hedge, we must picture it continuing another 200 yards
down to the Depression. Assuming that this is the veritable
hedge, where should we expect to find the equally famous
gap? The obvious spot would be where the road passes through
it. Now, we have seen that in all probability two roads, or
tracks, passed through it. Either of these might be the gap,
were it not that le Baker distinctly states that the gap was
"well removed from the marsh". This rules out the Gué de
l'Homme road, leaving only the Nouaillé road. The lower
gap would be barricaded[1] while the upper gap was left open.
This also we know from le Baker, who records that Warwick
held the lower part of the hedge, but that Salisbury kept back
"a stone's throw" from the gap.

We will now see how this identification of the position fits
in with a reconnaissance report[2] made by Marshal Ribaumont
just before the battle. We can picture him viewing the English
position from where the railway bridge now is. The intervening
ground, he reported, was partly planted with vines and partly
fallow. (This agrees with le Baker.) Since vines generally grow
on a southward-facing slope, the ground on his side of the
depression was probably covered with vines, with fallow ground

---

[1] An illustration in the copy of Froissart in the *Bibliothèque de l'Arsenal* in Paris
shows a gap barricaded with stakes interlaced with vine branches—a very natural
precaution.
[2] Delachenal describes this reconnaissance as "derisoire"—ridiculous—but I can
find nothing ridiculous in it—although Froissart is our only authority for it.

on the far side, immediately in front of the hedge. In his front was the hedge, pierced by the single obvious gap, through which a road ran.[1] To his right (English left) was a "petite montagne" on which he saw some horses. This would be Bernon, where the ground falls on three sides, and would have the appearance of a hill from the French side ("montagne" need mean no more than "hillock"). On his left was "ung petit plain", which is evidently represented by the flat-topped ridge about point 138. This was fortified, and a sort of laager of wagons was made to protect that flank, which was the most vulnerable of the two. No doubt this flank was "refused" and may have touched the extreme north edge of the Nouaillé wood.[2]

Thus Ribaumont's report is consistent with the site of the hedge suggested above. This site is satisfied by the other chronicles and is consistent with inherent military probability. In short, I believe the vestiges of hedge still visible are those of the famous hedge of Poitiers.

### THE BLACK PRINCE'S SPEECHES

I have already in the narrative suggested that the Prince of Wales attached great importance to the maintenance of morale. In this connection le Baker reports in great detail two speeches made by the Prince before the battle, the first to the whole army, the second to his archers. After the manner of his age, the chronicler uses *oratio recta*. Obviously the speeches cannot be literally correct, but I do not feel that they deserve the almost universal disregard that they have received from historians. Le Baker was not writing a panegyric, such as that of the herald, but sober history. So far as one can tell, in no single respect did he deliberately fabricate. Why should there be any difficulty in accepting the fact that le Baker received

---

[1] There is no foundation for the fable that it was a hollow road—any more than for the fable of the hollow road of Ohain at Waterloo; there is no trace of a hollow road now. Hollow roads tend to get deeper, not shallower, with the passage of time. Nor, of course, was there a double hedge.

[2] Luce, vol. v, p. vi, quotes from *Gallia Christiana* II, col. 1243, under date 1720, "*Saltus Nobiliacensis* (Nouaillé wood), *ubi etiamnum Anglorum castra fossis munita cernere est*". There are no visible signs now, but an air photograph might disclose something.

reports from various sources of what the Prince had said, and
of what a powerful impression his words had made on the
English host? It may certainly be accepted that he *did* address
his army. Villani, Froissart, and the *Eulogium* all testify to the
fact, and the account of the last named is in accord with
le Baker's as far as it goes. So also is that of Villani, two of
whose passages had their almost exact counterpart in le Baker.
Froissart adds the interesting point that the Prince caused his
words to be passed on by the leaders to their own units.
Obviously he could not address the whole army personally,
and the fact that he made a point of ensuring that his words
should reach all his troops shows that he attached considerable
importance to his utterance. Who can doubt but that these
speeches contributed to the glorious issue of the battle that
followed them? Indeed, they have every right to enjoy as much
fame as the speech put by Shakespeare into the mouth of
Henry V on the eve of Agincourt.

## MODERN WORKS

The chief modern works on the battle have been referred
to in this chapter. The two outstanding ones on the French
side are those by Roland Delachenal and Ferdinand Lot.
Colonel Babinet's researches are also essential. They are
printed in the *Bulletin des Antiquaires de l'Ouest* for 1883. The
most detailed account in English is Hilaire Belloc's *Poitiers*,
but it is difficult in this book to distinguish between what is
fact and what is inference.

# CHAPTER XIII

# EDWARD'S LAST CAMPAIGN

ON March 23, 1357, a two-year truce was signed at Bordeaux. But for unhappy, distracted France there was to be no peace. In fact the following two years were to be among the most miserable in her history. This for several reasons. The war in Brittany carried on as before; the Navarre war also smouldered; bodies of disbanded soldiers, later known as the Free Companies, roamed through France, seizing castles, living on the country and pillaging as they pleased, for there was no strong central authority or army to prevent them,[1] and France, deprived of her king, sank under the feeble government of the boy Dauphin into a state of chaos; peasants fought against nobles, fields were left untilled, and the king's writ practically ceased to run.

The Navarre war was kept alive largely by English soldiers. In June, 1347, the king of Navarre (well called "The Bad", for he was guilty of repeated treasons to the king of France and England in turn) obtained his freedom, and the Navarre war flared up once more; eventually nearly the whole of Lower Normandy—from Cherbourg to the Seine—was controlled by bands of Navarre and English soldiers. But only one event of great military interest occurred during those troublous two years and that was the siege of Rennes, to which we will now turn.

## THE SIEGE OF RENNES

When, at the conclusion of his Normandy campaign, the duke of Lancaster marched into Brittany to take up his post

---

[1] The most celebrated of these commanders was Sir Robert Knollys, whose "Company" was said to number 3,000. After assisting the king of Navarre, Knollys operated in the centre of France to the south of Paris, and no one dared to oppose him. All nationalities were in these free companies, but the English predominated.

as king's lieutenant, he at once appreciated that in order to get the whole duchy completely and firmly under English and Montfort control it would be necessary to take the capital Rennes and the county of Nantes.[1] But soon after his arrival, Charles de Blois, who had been released on payment of the bulk of his ransom, landed at Treguier and took up his residence at Guingamp. This could not be allowed, and Henry of Lancaster marched there himself. Charles, warned of the danger, made his escape to Nantes, and Henry took possession of Guingamp and recaptured Roche-Derrien.

No sooner was this effected than Henry learnt of the approach of the Black Prince from the south. Of his march *au grand galop* to join hands with his cousin we have already spoken. This attempt proving both abortive and unnecessary, Lancaster retraced his steps with his usual speed, covering the 100 miles in a few days, and he laid siege to Rennes on October 3.

The task was likely to prove a difficult one for the small Anglo-Breton army, for the circuit of the walls was large, and Lancaster possessed no siege engines. In several respects it resembled the siege of Calais. In both cases a direct assault was impracticable; blockade and starvation was the only obvious procedure, but was bound to be a lengthy one. Calais had held out for over ten months; could Henry of Lancaster better that? He determined to try, and, according to a French heroic poem the reliability of which, however, is no greater than the poem of the Chandos Herald, he swore that he would not desist till it surrendered.

During the autumn months, the siege, or rather blockade, took the usual dull course of all such blockades in their early stages. Then a youthful Breton leader, named Bertrand du

---

[1] The military historian of Brittany, la Borderie, pays this notable tribute to Henry of Lancaster: "An illustrious prince, renowned for his chivalrous courtesy, he enjoyed by his birth and his great reputation an almost regal authority. Such a general could not confine himself to a series of petty skirmishes and ambushes such as had, since the battle of Mauron, been the nature of the war raged in Brittany." The next sentence cannot be adequately rendered in English, "*Grand homme de guerre, il voulut faire la grande guerre.*"

Guesclin, appeared upon the scene. This young Breton was remarkable alike for his extreme ugliness and his martial virtues. At first he did not attempt to enter the city, but contented himself with harassing the besiegers from without.

This went on till the depth of winter, when Charles the Dauphin, duke of Normandy and now regent of France, sent two columns for the relief of the city. The first made a night attack on the besiegers but was completely cut up and its commander captured with 400 of his men. The other commander decided to proceed more cautiously, and settled down in the town of Dinan, 30 miles to the north. From there he harassed the besiegers to such an extent that Lancaster, without abandoning his grip on Rennes, took upon him the additional task of laying siege to Dinant, a town that had narrowly avoided being captured by Edward III 15 years before. Meanwhile du Guesclin was chafing to take a more active part in the defence of Rennes, and if we are to believe the poem, he effected his entry by the following stratagem. One of the garrison passed through the lines and pretended to give himself up as a deserter. Admitted into Lancaster's presence, he averred that a relieving army was approaching from the east, and was due to arrive that very night. The duke took the bait and marched out with his striking force to meet the relieving army. In his absence that night, Bertrand du Guesclin slipped in, and not only did so, but brought with him a captured train of supplies. Whatever the truth, du Guesclin did effect an entry, and is said to have heartened the garrison considerably.

Spring had now come, and more active methods of capturing the place were put in hand. The first was by mining—a slow process at the best of times, but particularly so in those days of primitive warfare. The essential technique of mine and counter-mine has not, however, altered through the centuries, and the French dug a successful counter-mine, and thus brought that line of attack to an end. The second method (indeed, the only other method possible, since the English possessed no breaching engines) was to employ a *beffroi*, or portable tower. This also was tried but met with the same method of defence as at La Réole: the French made a sortie by night and set it on fire.

The siege then relapsed into its old languid condition. On March 23 a truce was signed at Bordeaux between England and France to which Brittany was a party. Information of this was sent to Lancaster, but he anticipated Nelson by putting "his deaf ear to the trumpet" (if we may coin the phrase) and inflexibly carried on the siege for two months. Then in June, on receipt of a third order to cease operations, he entered into pourparlers with the garrison for surrender, not informing them that he must in any case give up the siege. The city was by this time suffering greatly from hunger, and "consented to be delivered from the siege on payment of 100,000 crowns". The siege thus came to an end on July 5, 1357, after exactly nine months, compared with the siege of Calais which lasted over ten months. Before departing the duke of Lancaster entered the town with ten knights carrying his banner which he placed on one of the city gates. Bertrand du Guesclin came forward and offered him a drink. The duke quaffed it and then departed. At once the banner was of course removed and thrown into the city ditch.

This qualified military success was seized upon by the French and broadcast through the country, no doubt "with advantages", as some solace for the recent disaster of Poitiers. But its real significance is the emergence of Bertrand du Guesclin into fame as the potential "saviour of France".

There seems now to have developed some coolness between the English king and his headstrong subordinate, and Henry asked to be allowed to return to England. To this the king consented when the duke had settled affairs in the following year, 1358. The truce was thenceforth observed in Brittany as elsewhere.

In glaring contrast to France, England was now enjoying

a period of peace and prosperity in spite of the Black Death. The king engaged in jousts and tournaments to his heart's content, and his royal prisoner, who was treated like a king and given almost complete freedom of person, seems to have found the time pass without undue tedium.

But Edward III now sincerely desired peace, and took advantage of a new approach by the persevering Pope, to come to terms with King John. Together they signed a treaty that may be called the First Treaty of London, by which the old duchy of Aquitaine was to revert to the English crown in absolute sovereignty, the king no longer being obliged to do homage to the king of France for it. In return, Edward agreed to abandon his claim to the French crown.

King John was also to return to France on payment of an immense ransom. There is no actual record of these terms, but the above gist of them was established by "the learned Dominican" Father Deniflé, and elaborated by Roland Delachenal.[1]

It is important to keep the terms of this treaty in mind if we are to understand the motives of Edward III in his next campaign.

The First Treaty of London was still-born. Parliament seems to have opposed it, being evidently more bellicose than the king himself, and Charles of Navarre also made objections. The two kings decided to try once more, and in March, 1359, actively encouraged by the Pope, they signed a second Treaty of London, more favourable to the English, for it included the return of the old Angevin possessions to England. But now it was the turn of the French government, despite their internal troubles, to demur. This intransigence, as he considered it, made Edward furious. He now lost all faith in peaceable negotiations and came to the conclusion that the only way to settle the matter for good and all was by force of arms; he must invade France once more.

---

[1] Professor Tout is the only English historian to notice this important treaty. See *E.H.R.* 1910.

But, he recollected, he had already invaded France five times, and each time he had expected it to be the last. This sort of thing could not go on; it had already lasted for 21 years. There must be no mistake about it; he would this time attain his object—"an honourable peace"—or die in the attempt. He made a solemn resolution and announced it in a speech to his army, that he would not return to England till peace had been secured.

He was prudent enough not to specify what sort of a peace, but it appears that he had two alternative objectives—"an optimum", the crown of France, and, failing that, one of the two Treaties of London. If nothing was to be left to chance this time prolonged preparations would be necessary, several months at least. That would involve an autumn, perhaps even a winter campaign. But that prospect did not affright or deter this iron-willed monarch. Preparations were methodically put in hand, and many of the measures may be read in Rymer's *Foedera*—but by no means all. We saw as far back as 1346 how far-seeing and provident the king was when preparing his Crecy campaign. But this time his problem was to be far more difficult and complex, for, instead of marching parallel to the sea-coast—the line that linked him with England—he would have to cut adrift from it, he must "burn his boats" almost literally; for months perhaps, he would be out of touch and communication with England, and consequently he must depend for all manner of war stores and weapons, ammunition, equipment, food, clothing and tentage, largely on what he could carry with him. For France was steadily becoming a desert. A few examples of his foresight are instructive. The stores included field forges and horseshoes, hand-mills for grinding "man-corn and horse-corn", and a large number of portable leather fishing coracles, in case the campaign should last into Lent, when fish would not be procurable from home. It is a remarkable fact that there is no record of cannons being taken on this campaign.

A vast train of wagons was therefore built and transported across the sea to Calais; numbers vary from 1,000 to 6,000,

each wagon drawn by four horses. No such baggage-train
had ever been seen in European warfare, nor was to be seen
again till the armies of Louis XIV lumbered across Europe.

Not only did the king prepare with much thought everything
requisite and necessary for a great army on a possibly long
campaign; he prepared also the plan of campaign referred to
above months ahead, a most unusual proceeding in the
fourteenth century when little attention seems to have been
paid to such things. We know this because the intelligence
service of the French government was good, and it obtained
possession of the outlines of this plan. It was a simple one, as all
military plans should be in their initial stages: the king of
England intended to march to Rheims, in the hopes that he
might be crowned and anointed king of France in that holy
city of Clovis, or if he failed in that object, that he might at
least induce the regent to come to its relief and thus to fight
him in the field. A shrewd plan, for the action of the archbishop
of Rheims had recently been suspect and he might be won over
to Edward's cause.[1]

Edward hoped to be able to open his campaign before
August was out, which should give at least two good campaigning months; but because of the usual and inevitable hitches and
delays, chiefly due to the shortage of shipping, it was not till
the beginning of October that the vanguard of the army
landed in Calais. The value of this port as a "pistol pointed
at Paris"—as it might truly be described—was now seen. The
king must have been thankful that he had persisted to the end
in the siege of Calais. Not only did it possess a nucleus of war-
stores useful for the campaign, but it was already the home of
English merchants and could speedily be turned into an arsenal.
It was also accessible to foreign volunteers and would-be
mercenaries, of whom a large number flocked to the town
during the late summer, for the king had made no attempt
to keep his expedition secret, and indeed encouraged volunteers.

[1] This is the view of H. Moranville (Bibliothèque de l'École des Chartes,
vol. LVI, p. 91.)

Flemings, Hainaulters, Brabançons, and Germans came to lodge in the town in large numbers–too large; they began to "own the place", and to eat up its victuals and drink up its drinks while waiting week by week for the English army to appear. Something had to be done to cope with this potential menace; a trusted subordinate must be sent ahead to cope with the situation before it got out of hand. Readers will have no difficulty in guessing on whom the king's choice fell. . . .

On October 1 Henry of Lancaster landed at Calais with 2,400 troops, and addressed himself immediately to the task of controlling the unruly band of foreigners. He explained to them that the king, with the main body of the army, could not arrive for a fortnight or more. There was meanwhile a growing shortage of food in the town and no money available for the troops. But, he pointed out, he was about to undertake a little chevauchée into the interior of France, to see what could be picked up. Would not they like to accompany him, instead of kicking up their heels aimlessly in Calais? The bait was taken, a little army formed, and the duke of Lancaster sallied forth on what may correctly be termed a raid.

Leaving St. Omer and Bethune on his left hand, he pushed on to the monastery of St. Eloi on the ridge a few miles north of Arras, where he halted for four days. Proceeding south, he struck the river Somme at Bray, where a strongly held castle barred the crossing. A fruitless attempt to storm it–the attackers wading up to their shoulders through the icy river–caused the army to swing to its right. Four miles on, a crossing was effected by the unbroken bridge of Cerisy.[1]

The army was now heading for Amiens, and within a dozen miles of it. Great was the consternation in that city. But it was saved from attack: for next day, November 1, a message was received from King Edward to the effect that he had landed at Calais on October 28, and that the duke of Lancaster was to return at once. It was clever of the messenger, who had a near-hundred-miles journey, to find the duke in only three days.

[1] Almost in the German front line during the summer of 1918.

The army returned to Calais without incident, and thither we also will now direct our attention.

\*       \*       \*

Before leaving England, the king, foreseeing that if he denuded the country of troops the French might be tempted to raid or even invade it in force, issued thorough-going regulations for such a contingency, the details of which we need not enter upon. It may have been these matters, in addition to shipping troubles, that caused the delay in opening the campaign. Walsingham's statement that no fewer than 1,100 vessels were collected must be an exaggeration; such a fleet could transport an army of over 30,000. But the king made use of a procedure adopted in the 1944 invasion of Normandy: he transported his army to Calais in several "lifts", having command of the sea in the Dover Straits. Thereby we see yet another advantage enjoyed by the possession of the Calais beach-head: the troops could be transported piecemeal, and in an unlimited number if there were unlimited time. The duke of Lancaster had taken part of his divisions with him, and possibly some of the Black Prince's crossed at the same time. The enormous train of wagons—necessary because of the denuded state of the country to be traversed—also required much time and tonnage to transport.

### THE RHEIMS CAMPAIGN

On October 28, 1359, very early in the morning, King Edward III set out upon his sixth and last campaign. The wind was favourable and strong, and he was enabled to land at Calais that same day. Seven days of strenuous staff-work followed, organizing and arraying the army, and on November 4, Lancaster's raiders having just returned, the army was ready to set out.[1]

---

[1] The view generally held (and adopted here) that Lancaster's army returned before the army set out is contradicted by le Bel, who may be right, as Lancaster must have made an extremely speedy return if he was back by November 4, but speed was natural to the duke. No doubt his wagon-train was left far in the rear.

The army that set out from Calais in a "do or die" attempt to end the war in a single winter campaign was in all probability the largest army that had ever left these shores, or was ever to do so again till the first campaign of Henry VIII in 1513. It can scarcely have been less than 15,000 combatants, with several thousand non-combatants. The names of the chief officers should be noted, for they were all names by now familiar to the reader. The Black Prince, accompanied by his brothers—the earl of Richmond (John of Gaunt)[1] and Lionel of Clarence—the duke of Lancaster, the earls of Warwick, Northampton, March, Salisbury and Stafford, Lord Burghersh, Sir Reginald Cobham, Sir John Chandos, Sir James Audley and, of course, Sir Walter Manny. A galaxy! One of the common soldiers also deserves naming, though his military career was inglorious—he was taken prisoner. His name was Geoffrey Chaucer.

The destination was, as we have seen, Rheims. Apart from the obvious reason for this objective—namely the hallowing of Edward Plantagenet as king of France—there were other considerations that favoured it, should the anointing project fail. The expedition, of which there was no attempt at secrecy, was of so menacing a nature that it might be assumed that the regent of France would oppose it by force of arms, if he had the power. Nothing would suit Edward's purpose better than to cross swords with his French opponent. Now, more than ever, he was confident of the result. If, on the other hand, the regent made no attempt to defend the sacred city, or to come to its assistance, the whole of France would draw the moral: namely, that the regent was impotent in his own dominion. His subjects would see and take note of the fact that not only was the country plunged into chaos and ruin, but that the English claimant to the crown was free to go wherever he pleased and do what damage he liked throughout the territories of a boy regent (dubbed by Ramsay "a sickly, timid lad of

---

[1] Who had just married the daughter of the duke of Lancaster, thus founding the "Lancastrian line".

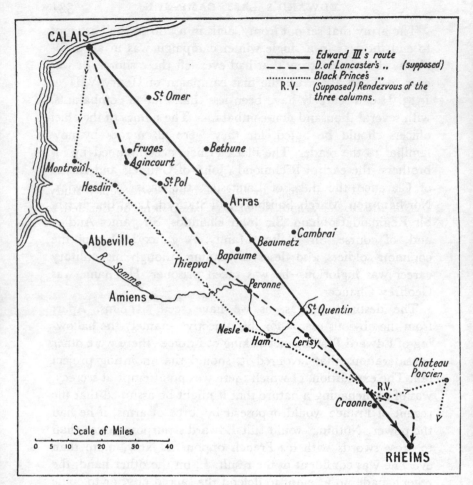

**CALAIS**

St Omer

Fruges
Agincourt
Bethune

Montreuil

Hesdin
St Pol

Arras

Abbeville

R. Somme

Cambrai

Beaumetz

Bapaume

Thiepval

Peronne

Amiens

St Quentin

Nesle

Ham
Cerisy

Chateau
Porcien

R.V.

Craonne

**RHEIMS**

——— Edward III's route
– – – D. of Lancaster's ,, (supposed)
·········· Black Prince's ,,
R.V. (Supposed) Rendezvous of the three columns.

Scale of Miles

0   5   10      20      30      40

17. THE RHEIMS CAMPAIGN

ninctccn"), and of an impotcnt govcrnmcnt. For 20 years the
iron-willed demi-Frenchman, Edward Plantagenet, had laid
claim through his French mother to the throne, and during all
those years France had steadily diminished in prosperity and
increased in misery. Might it not be as well, for the sake of
peace, to yield to the hard logic of events, and acknowledge the
ever-victorious Edward as their king? Such might very well
become the attitude of the country, thought Edward, as he
evolved his plan for a descent on Rheims.

Edward III's strategy in this campaign will repay study.
As in his Brittany and Normandy campaigns he decided to
advance on a broad front, by parallel columns, each marching
on a carefully planned route within supporting distance of its
neighbours, yet covering as wide a belt of country as possible.
There were to be three columns or divisions, one under the
Prince of Wales, one under the duke of Lancaster, and one
under the king himself. We know enough about these three
itineraries to draw certain conclusions. Fortunately a soldier,
who took part in the campaign, afterward wrote about it (not
Chaucer). His name was Sir Thomas Gray, and his chronicle
was called the *Scalacronica*. From it we are able to plot the
itinerary of the Prince's column (in which Gray served) with
some precision and certainty. From other sources we can also
plot the king's itinerary. The centre column, that of the duke of
Lancaster, can easily be interpolated. (See sketch map opposite.)

The route of the right-hand column was as follows: Montreuil,
Hesdin, Doullens, Albert, Nesle, Ham, just to the left of
La Fere and Laon, to Chateau Porcien and Rethel, 25 miles
north-east of Rheims.

That of the left-hand column was by St. Omer, Aire, Lillers,
Bethune, Arras, Beaumetz (midway between Bapaume and
Cambrai), then practically along what became the line of the
Hindenburg Line, by Epehy and Bellenglise to St. Quentin:
thence through country less familiar to English soldiers (though
known to many of Edward's army of 1339) to a general
rendezvous near Craonne.

The centre column must have passed near, if not over, the field of Agincourt, St. Pol, Acheux, Thiepval, Peronne (avoiding the river Somme), thence by Vermand and over what is now the St. Crozat canal, over the 1914 battlefield of Cerisy,[1] and so on to the rendezvous. From Agincourt to Peronne, this column, all unknowingly, trod in the footsteps-to-be (in the reverse direction) of Henry V's army en route for the immortal field of Agincourt.

If we plot these itineraries on a map carefully, we shall discover two striking facts, which go far to confirm the assertion that the marches were carefully plotted in advance. The first fact is that, once the flank columns had diverged from the common starting point to a distance of 20 miles, they kept to this distance, maintaining almost exactly parallel routes as far as St. Quentin. The second fact is that if one draws a straight line from Calais to Rheims, it passes exactly through St. Quentin, and also that the route taken by the king's column never diverges from this straight line by as much as five map miles. This can scarcely be a coincidence and we are sharply reminded of that very direct march of the king across Lower Normandy, followed by the almost geometrically straight one between the Seine and the Somme, as also of Lancaster's straight marches in his Normandy campaign. These four instances compel us to recognize that the English king must have been in possession of some primitive form of map, although there is no specific record of one. (My sketch map is designed to bring out these points.)[2]

This carefully charted itinerary of three parallel columns also calls to mind Napoleon's Ulm campaign. Is it too fanciful to picture Edward, like Napoleon, sprawling on the floor over his map with a primitive pair of dividers in his hand, plotting in advance his great *chevauchée*?

\*            \*            \*

[1] Where the 5th Cavalry Brigade smashed up a column of Uhlans (not to be confused with Cerizy on the Somme).

[2] Edward I had a map made of England, on which the Gough map of 1325 (c) is based, so there is no intrinsic improbability in the existence of a map of northern France.

The duke of Lancaster can have had only a few hours in which to re-shoe his horses and reorganize and refit his tired troops, who had just marched nearly 100 miles in three days, and whose transport was still on the move. He also had to sort out and disband those Germans who would not agree to serve in the coming campaign without pay. Indeed it is quite possible that he delayed his start by at least one day in order to carry out this task, and regained his position abreast of the other two columns by rapid marching. That should be an easy matter, for the rate of march was a leisurely one, being only six miles a day, halts included. If we exclude the halt days, it was still under ten miles a day. The unwieldy baggage train, together with the absence of any imperative need for haste, will account for this. Though Froissart waxes lyrical over the pomp and display of the expedition as it marched out of Calais, it soon degenerated into a dull and rather miserable march. For a steady downpour of cold autumn rain accompanied it and local provender was almost non-existent in the early stages, and the king had issued orders against damage and destruction. This was a welcome innovation; the usual course for an invading army at that epoch of warfare was to ravage and destroy, and the English army had certainly hitherto followed this course. But now, late though it might be, Edward realized that if he was to become the sovereign of the inhabitants through whose lands he was marching, it would be as well to keep on good terms with them. In fact this can be described as not so much a military invasion as a political procession with a military escort: the king was proceeding to his crowning—it was a coronation procession on a large scale.

In spite of the miseries of the march the discipline was of a high order. Straggling was sternly forbidden, and we read that they "did not leave a bag behind them". There was little opportunity for loot or destruction. The king's column was marching in the early stages along almost exactly the same route as that followed only a few days previously by Lancaster's hungry Germans. It was as when a unit occupies billets occupied the previous night by another unit that has bought up (or stolen) all the eggs, and drunk all the beer. Nor was any excitement to be obtained from military encounters, for the French troops had, in obedience to instructions, taken refuge in the walled towns along the route, the capture of which did not fall within the programme of the English king. It is perfectly clear that Edward intended his march to be as much a peace march as possible—unless the French regent dared to presume to cross swords with him.

After advancing for about 80 miles through towns and villages made familiar to English troops of 1914–18, the region between Cambrai and Albert was reached. Here provender was more plentiful and a halt of four days was made. But still it rained. . . .

The march was resumed according to plan, and under the walls of St. Quentin, which was not entered, Lord Burghersh had a satisfactory little fight with a few French knights who were rash enough to sally out of that city. The march was resumed, the king's column continuing on its dead straight route and the other two converging on it. The rendezvous or meeting point was a little to the east of Craonne. Here the army concentrated on November 29, and two councils of war were held. Experiences were exchanged, stock was taken of the situation and arrangements made for approaching the sacred city. The Prince's division was to hold the northern sector, the duke's the east, and the king's the south. This necessitated the columns crossing one another, the king's now being on the south.[1] No news had been heard of any move on the part of the regent, although he had had ample time to reinforce the city, or to advance at the head of the national army of France to encounter the invader outside its walls. Still, the possibility that this might yet occur had to be allowed for, and the march was resumed, with the divisions transposed, on December 1. It was a 30-mile march for the Prince and duke who passed

---

[1] There is no written authority for this, but the inference is as inescapable as the reason for it is obscure.

through Chateau Porcien, but somewhat less for the king. As the columns converged on the city the tall twin towers of the cathedral came in sight.

It must have been an exciting moment for Edward of Windsor when his eyes first beheld what must have been for months "the city of his dreams". After 21 years of effort, were these dreams at last to come true? Did he experience the feelings and excitement of his great ancestor, Richard Coeur de Lion, when he came in sight of the Holy City of Palestine? History does not relate; nor indeed have we a word from his own pen of this culminating point, as it must have seemed, in his life.

## THE SIEGE OF RHEIMS

On arriving in the vicinity of the city of Rheims on December 4 after a 170-mile march, King Edward made a reconnaissance of its walls and fixed the various headquarters. His own headquarters he established at the abbey of St. Basle, nearly ten miles to the south, while those of the Prince were half that distance to the north, and the duke's at Brimont to the east. These distances seem surprisingly large, and may be accounted for in two ways: in the first place the king required a commodious residence for his numerous retinue, and a sufficiently large abbey could not be found nearer the city: in the second place, it indicates that Edward did not intend to make the siege an active military operation, where his personal presence every day would be necessary. It was to be a passive affair; the active part in the proceedings was to be played by the citizens who, as soon as they saw that there was no hope of relief, would come out bearing with them the keys of the city. To mark this feature of the siege still more, Edward issued strict injunctions that the inhabitants were to be treated as if they were friends, and this unusual order was implicitly obeyed, such was the grip that the English king exerted over his army. As Knighton puts it, "the troops behaved as if they were on their own soil".

22

But it was all of no avail. The king did not know that the regent, or his council, being apprised months in advance of the danger to Rheims, had taken steps to strengthen the defences of the city both in material and men, and had issued strict instructions that it was to hold out, with hints of aid in such an event. Under the heroic archbishop and the count of Porcien the inhabitants responded nobly. The gates were kept closed and appeals for help were smuggled out of the city to Paris.[1]

Thus the days dragged on till Christmas. Most of the besiegers were billeted in the neighbouring villages, and it would be nice to know how these English soldiers spent their Christmas under arms in France. Did they, under the new relationship with the inhabitants, show that adaptability that their descendants did when Christmassing in France and Belgium five and a half centuries later?

Christmas came and went, and the conditions became most unpleasant. The weather was still abominable, and the horses, for the most part picketed out in the open, suffered severely. A static siege, opened and carried on in mid-winter, was until this war an almost unknown phenomenon in medieval warfare. The huts and quarters erected during the siege of Calais were lacking, and something had to be done soon, unless the army was to become immobilized in a foreign country, 200 miles from the coast. An attempt to breach and assault the town must have been a strong temptation to Edward, but he steadfastly set his face against it. Even though he might conceivably storm it without undue damage to materiel or inhabitants, he could not control the assaulters from "running amok" once inside—scarcely a propitious overture to his hallowing by the archbishop of Rheims. He could not hallow himself.[2] This was a quandary that seems to have been lost sight of by the historians.

---

[1] The assertion of *Les Quatre Premiers Valois* that an attempt was made to storm the walls must be dismissed.

[2] The hallowing, not the actual crowning, was the essential part of the ceremony —a king could place the crown on his own head—Napoleon did—but he could scarcely pour oil on himself.

During those anxious weeks of weary waiting, one thing became insistent: the troops must be employed. Unemployment in the field breeds indiscipline. There being as yet no sign of hostile activity in the direction of Paris, it seemed safe to send out minor expeditions on distant missions, and each division was instructed or allowed to carry out raids in its own sector. Four such expeditions at least were sent out. To the north-east Eustache d'Auberchicourt captured Attigny on the Aisne; to the east Lancaster, Chandos, and Audley, roaming wide, came to the strong castle of Cernay, near St. Menehould. This castle possessed two moats, one at least of which was wet. Henry, riding up to it, dismounted from his horse to conduct a recon-naissance on foot. The leading troops, on seeing this, also dismounted, and, if we are to believe Knighton,[1] such was their uncontrollable ardour that they incontinently rushed forward with a shout and after crossing both moats, scaled the walls and captured the town. Then they turned on the castle, but the garrison of this, apparently unnerved at the suddenness and vigour of the attack, surrendered at discretion. This was an affair after Henry of Lancaster's heart, but what military object it served it is difficult to descry. Indeed it has the appear-ance of being just "a lark" on the part of the delectable and, I think, dapper duke. The very next day he captured another walled town, and this was followed by others. It looks as if the prestige of the English troops was bringing down these fortified places just as in the eighteenth century in southern India the prestige of the English troops of Clive and Stringer Lawrence toppled over semi-impregnable fortresses like so many ninepins.

To resume the catalogue of raids: to the north-west Cormicy was stormed by the earl of March,[2] Lord Burghersh, and John of Gaunt, while to the west a raiding party penetrated right under the walls of Paris. Perhaps we should describe this as a reconnoitring rather than a raiding party, sent out for information about the attitude of the regent. But if so, the

[1] I would not trouble to repeat this improbable-sounding story if it came from Froissart.
[2] The earl died shortly afterwards.

party went about its work in a curious way. Walsingham describes rather humorously how they set up such a din in the suburbs that the garrison of the city thought an attack was imminent.

## TO BURGUNDY AND PARIS

By January 10, 1360, all the raiders had returned to camp, and King Edward had to come to an important decision. The Paris raiders had convinced him that the regent could not be coaxed out of his impregnable asylum, nor did the garrison of Rheims show any signs of weakening in their decision to hold out.

Rheims had been plentifully stocked with supplies in view of the siege, and to reduce it by starvation would probably take at least as long as had Calais. In this quandary only two possible courses remained: to take the city by storm, or to give up the siege and undertake some fresh project. The first course Edward still declined to take. His attitude commands admiration, though on wholly military grounds it was a surprising one: with his large and efficient army, with captains experienced in the arts of storming fortifications, and with the threat of outside intervention being now out of the question, it should have been possible to take the city by storm, though no doubt at high cost. Did the king shrink from the idea of high casualties, or was he merely remaining faithful to the course that he had laid out for himself–to secure his hallowing by peaceful persuasion? In view of his stern will-power and implacable resolution I think we may safely impute the latter motive to the English sovereign.

Be that as it may, the military policy of the French government, which was the best possible under the circumstances, presented a difficult problem to Edward.[1] It became necessary for him to frame a new policy. Such a policy may well have been

[1] Edouard Perroy gives the credit for this plan to the 19-year-old Dauphin. "Taught by experience, and influenced by his unwarlike nature, he went on war-strike. It was clever strategy, which was later attributed to du Guesclin's contrivance, but it was that of the Dauphin."

gestating in his mind during the past month, if not before (for we cannot forget those Lenten fishing-boats), and Edward now set it into operation. If the threat to Rheims could not goad the regent into intervention or negotiation, the capital itself must be threatened. But before doing so it would be prudent, seeing that the English army was now far from home and surrounded by potential enemies, to take preliminary steps to safeguard the move. Now the greatest potential danger came from Burgundy, whose duke was the most powerful vassal of France, and must be considered an enemy, although he had taken no active part in the war for many years. A descent upon Burgundy was therefore decided upon.

The nearest point in Burgundy to Rheims was 100 miles due south, and Paris was nearly 150 miles north-west of this point. To reach Burgundy it was necessary to pass through the province of Champagne from north to south. On January 11, 1360, Edward III set out on his new venture. Marching in the same formation of three divisions, each with its own vanguard, the army left Chalons on its right hand and crossed the Marne above it at Poigny on about January 26. Pushing south, the king punished the town of Bar-sur-Aube for some iniquity, and then turned west. Leaving unmolested the little town of Troyes –to become world-famous in 60 years' time–he crossed the Seine at Pont and Mery and pushed southward into Burgundy. The young duke had collected his army at Montréal, but here it remained, for he dared not draw upon himself the formidable English army. The latter therefore roamed his country at will. Various towns were captured, notably Tonnerre, where a welcome stock of Burgundy wine was found–and drunk. The injunctions against ravage and pillage seem to have become a dead letter, whether explicitly or not.

It was in all probability of set policy, intended to cow the duke into submission. But for the moment nothing happened, and Edward seemed in no hurry that it should. February and Lent had arrived. It was the close season for warfare. Fishing took the place of fighting and all the pious knights were enabled to keep the season as laid down, though the common soldiers, we are told, had to fend for themselves. Hunting and hawking were, however, allowed, and the king settled down at Guillon, 40 miles west of Dijon, to a pleasant season of sport. Occasionally a walled town was taken or a monastery pillaged, but in the main Lent was placidly and piously observed. During this period there were some changes among the higher officers. The earl of March died, but we are not told the cause. Most of the German knights departed for their not very distant homes in Lorraine, but their place was more than filled by knights of the Free Companies who had been operating in that part of France for the past 12 months, and who now took regular service in the royal army. Sir Robert Knollys must have been one of these, and there were many others. Also some Gascon lords, including the Captal de Buch of Poitiers fame, in their desire to serve under the banner of the Black Prince, made their way right across France by a devious route which took them through Beauvais, and joined him in Burgundy. What with internal dissension in the country, the Free Companies and the de-predations and exactions of the army of England, all northern Burgundy was now in a deplorable state, and the duke at length sent emissaries to sue for peace. Edward was, of course, in a position to demand any terms he desired. These were that there should be a three-year truce, that Burgundy should remain neutral in the war between Edward and the regent, and that it should pay a large indemnity. These humiliating terms were signed on March 10, and five days later the English army set out with its face turned toward Paris.

All was now going according to plan: Lent was nearly over, the spring grass, which would provide fodder for the horses, was beginning to sprout, and if the regent desired to fight for his father's crown, he would now be given the opportunity.

In mid-March the army moved away in a westerly direction toward the county of Nivernais, of which Nevers was the capital. This county promptly compounded against invasion as Burgundy had just done. All danger to flank and rear being now at an end, Edward turned north, and descended the valleys of the Cure and the Yonne,[1] heading for Paris.

An event now occurred on the English shore that had repercussions upon the campaign in France. The offensive is the best form of defensive; and some of the regent's advisers were aware of the fact. Seeing what a very large army the English king had brought with him to the Continent, they supposed that England had been denuded of defenders and that a lodgement of some days, at least, would be possible—sufficient to bring the king hurrying home to the defence of his own land. But they had misjudged their man and forgotten history only 14 years old. For when the Scots had invaded England in 1346 Edward had left its defence to those to whom he had entrusted it before setting out. It was the same again. The far-seeing monarch had made what proved to be ample measures for the defence of the realm when on March 15 a French fleet suddenly appeared off Rye. An actual landing could not be prevented, nor the dreadful atrocities committed at Winchelsea by the French troops (possibly in revenge for the ravages of their native land). But within 24 hours reinforcements were speeding to the spot according to plan, and after a sharp fight the French were driven back to their ships, suffering very heavy casualties.

The outcome was satisfactory, but the stories of atrocities that reached the king (no doubt exaggerated) so stung him and his army to anger that he hastened his march towards Paris, and resumed the old policy of devastation.[2]

On the Tuesday in Holy Week, March 31, the army halted in a line 20 miles south of Paris, between Corbeil and Longjumeau, the royal headquarters being established at Chante-

---

[1] Passing through the little town of Cravant, to be the scene of a remarkable English victory 63 years later.

[2] Delachenal asserts that the news of Winchelsea dictated Edward's strategy, he having up till that time been uncertain what to do. But Delachenal does not seem to have fathomed, or even suspected, the depth of the English king's strategy throughout the campaign. The Winchelsea raid was repulsed on March 16. Four days later, before the news can have reached him, the King resumed his advance on the French capital.

loupe, near Arpajan, where they remained till the Easter feast was over. The smoke of some burnings carried out at Long-jumeau was visible from the walls of Paris and created a panic in all the suburbs of the city, the terrified inhabitants crowding into the city for refuge in those long melancholy streams that have become too familiar in recent wars. A short, abortive truce conference was held at Longjumeau, to which reference will be made later.

On the Tuesday in Easter week the advance was resumed, and the army came to a halt on the line of heights a few miles to the south-west of the city between Issy and Beaugirard, the king lodging at Montrouge. Walter Manny now led a party right up to the walls and tried to exasperate the garrison by his taunts into making a sortie. In addition, the whole English army deployed into line and advanced within sight of the walls, challenging battle. Edward had some reason to believe that the challenge would be accepted. Froissart speaks of heralds being sent forward and Knighton says that some arrangement to engage in a fight was made by the regent but not kept. What-ever be the truth, the French made no more. Strict orders to this effect had been issued, and they were obeyed by the garrison, whether willingly or not. However, on April 10 a deputation treating for peace came out of the city. A conference, at which the Pope's legates were present, took place at the abbey of Cluny on the Orleans road, but it led to no conclusion. The sequel to this conference must have surprised the French manning the city walls, for 48 hours later a long line of English troops deployed and advanced close up to the walls. Once again the garrison did not budge. A few hours elapsed and the English army had vanished. It was in fact well on its way to Chartres. The demonstration had been merely a covering force—a skilful rearguard posted to screen the with-drawal. The English king had made another of his surprise moves.

Edward III did not commit to paper the motives and reasons that inspired his various actions throughout this puzzling campaign, and we are reduced to guessing at them in practically every case. In most cases, and pre-eminently in this one, we are obliged to form our conclusions largely by the logic of subsequent events. We will therefore narrate these events in brief and then come back to the reasons for this abrupt withdrawal from the second "city of his dreams" before scarcely a shot had been discharged by either side.

On Sunday April 12, 1360, the withdrawal began, the general direction being south-west toward Chartres. The French made no attempt to follow it up. On Monday there was a terrible storm, hailstones as large as pigeons' eggs raining down on the long column and killing several men and horses. According to the London Chronicle the day became known as Black Monday.[1] The march was continued by easy stages past Chartres into the region of Bonneval and Chateaudun, 20 miles south of that city. One might suppose that the French government and the people of Paris heaved a sigh of relief at the retreat of their formidable enemy, perhaps even singing a Te Deum in Notre Dame. What, in fact, they did was surprising. Though the danger now appeared to be past, the regent sent emissaries hurrying after the retreating army to treat for peace! They caught up with the army near Chateaudun and asked for the negotiations, broken off on April 10, to be resumed. To this the king of England agreed, and within eight days a treaty of peace, based on the terms offered by Edward in the first Treaty of London, had been drawn up and signed.

That is the outline of the extraordinary story. It presents a double problem, first the reason for the English abrupt retreat (if it was a retreat) and second, the anxiety of the French to come to terms with a retreating opponent approximately on terms dictated by him. A besieged army that wishes for or is reduced to suing for terms normally does so as the result of starvation, of threat of being stormed (when no quarter is

[1] Froissart asserts that king and army were frightened and that Edward was induced to make an immediate peace, but according to Walsingham the storm had little effect on the march, and Delachenal discredits Froissart's story. Edward was too tough a man to be diverted from his aim by a bad hailstorm.

given), or of an actual assault. I know of no case in the whole medieval period similar to the one we are considering.

## THE TREATY OF BRETIGNY

Let us first consider the English case. Henry Knighton gives no reason for the move; Gray, in his *Scalacronica*, asserts that the move was made in order to find fodder for the horses, it being lacking outside Paris. Froissart states that the king intended to pass down the Loire valley into Brittany, where he would rest and recuperate his army till the late summer and then return to besiege Paris. Was this one of Froissart's reckless statements based on guesswork? It certainly was an obvious guess, for the English army was heading in that direction, and as all prudent commanders keep two or more possible plans in mind, in case things go wrong, Edward probably considered such a course. But it is hard to believe that he had such a design, involving a tame retreat when within sight of his goal, or that his troops, who must have been keyed up with hopes of a spectacular and profitable victory, would have acquiesced in this disappointment—which apparently they did. So the mystery deepens the closer we look into it.

Another assertion of Froissart may lead us toward the solution. He states that the duke of Lancaster, ever avid for battle and adventure, now suddenly became an ardent advocate of peace. The last thing we should expect of this fire-eater! Now, Henry of Lancaster had been English leader in the two abortive peace conferences of April 3 (Good Friday) and April 10. No record exists of the discussions on those occasions, but it is reasonable to suppose that they narrowed the ground between the two parties, and enabled each side to see on which subjects the other side was adamant. Now, Henry of Lancaster had always been *persona grata* with the French, who genuinely admired this dashing and chivalrous soldier. Is it too far-fetched to imagine that at these conferences he gained the confidence of the French delegates, and that in the course of the proceedings of the second conference the French leader, the constable Robert de Fiennes, took Henry aside into an alcove and explained "off the record" (as we might now express it) that *amour propre* prohibited the regent from accepting any terms of duress on the part of a threatening army outside his gates, but that if the English army would be so kind as to move off a few days' march, he knew the regent would jump at the opportunity to accede to the English demands, at least as far as the First Treaty of London? In order to "save face" for the French, secrecy would be essential, and Lancaster on his return would prevail upon the king to give the plan at least a trial. No doubt the English leaders would be let into the secret, under a pledge of secrecy, and a confused story would get about to the effect that Lancaster, who had been seen closeted with the king on his return from the peace conference, had prevailed upon the king to make peace. This in time would come to the ears of Froissart, who then put into the mouth of Lancaster the well-known words of the chronicle.

The above solution is, of course, purely conjectural, as must be any solution, in view of the paucity of recorded facts; but it, and it alone, seems to explain the otherwise curious attitude and actions of both sides in the matter. The one stark and arresting fact is that, as soon as the English "retreated" from Paris, a peace favourable to them was brought about.

If the above is the true explanation, it shows King Edward to be what the French chroniclers and historians are always so ready to call him, an astute diplomat whether in council or in the field.

\* \* \*

On April 27 the French delegates arrived at Chartres.[1] The king was now established at Sours, five miles east of the city, and he fixed on a hamlet named Bretigny between that village and the city for the peace conference.[2]

On May Day, 1360, this historic conference assembled.

---

[1] The Black Prince may have had his quarters there: it is stated in Chartres that the name of the Prince appears at the head of a subscription list for the construction of one of the towers of the cathedral.

[2] A stone monument now marks the spot.

There were 16 French and 22 English delegates. It is as well to record the names of the leading delegates to this famous meeting. The leader of the English party was the duke of Lancaster, and he was supported by the earls of Northampton, Warwick, Salisbury, Stafford, Sir Reginald Cobham, Sir John Chandos, Sir Frank Halle (of Auberoche fame), the Captal de Buch, and the inevitable Sir Walter Manny. With what curiosity must the French delegates have gazed on these men whose names had been so prominent throughout the land for nearly a generation.

The French leader seems to have been a priest, the bishop of Beauvais, and many of the members were also priests or civilians.

Of the deliberations we unfortunately have no record, but it appears that the main heads were agreed upon with singular speed, two days sufficing for this purpose. This lends weight to my supposition that much unsuspected headway had been made at the two previous conferences, in spite of their short duration. The terms of the Treaty of Bretigny were slightly, but only slightly, more hard for France than those of the First Treaty of London. The English territorial gains were enlarged by the county of Rouergue (about the same size as that of Kent). The ransom for King John was reduced by one quarter, probably because Edward had the sense to recognize that the original sum was beyond the country's capacity to pay—especially now that no money would be forthcoming from Rouergue.

It followed that since Edward had signed the First Treaty, which he must have considered "an honourable peace",[1] the same honour was satisfied by the Bretigny Treaty, and his vow not to leave France till he had obtained such a peace was carried out.

A further five days were devoted to thrashing out and drafting the numerous and complicated details—another example of expeditious work. The exact nature of these details

[1] Technically it was not a peace, for it had to be ratified at Calais in the autumn, under a separate Treaty of Calais.

is not relevant to this book, but it must be noted that they were drawn up with the greatest care, every effort being made by both sides to reduce to a minimum the chance of disputes or conflicts arising from differing interpretations.

The main effect of the Treaty was to return to the English crown her old dominion of Aquitaine, but with this all-important difference that this time it was to be held in absolute right of ownership, the French king abandoning his suzerainty. Thus the main stumbling block to good relations between the two countries – the fact that the king of England was also the vassal of the king of France for his French possessions – was abolished. From now onward there could be permanent peace between the two countries. Edward was to abandon his claim to the French throne, and John was to be released on the payment of an enormous ransom. Calais and Ponthieu were ceded to England.

Great importance was attached to swearing to, and signing, the Treaty.[1] Since King John could not sign it, neither did King Edward, and the two chief signatories thus became the regent and the Prince of Wales.

Leaving the earl of Warwick as Guardian in Normandy and the duke of Lancaster to lead the army home *via* Calais, the king, accompanied by his sons, made straight for home. Setting sail from Honfleur on May 28, he made a speedy crossing, arriving at Rye the same day. Then, without losing a moment, he mounted a horse and rode straight to London, scarcely stopping for rest or refreshment en route. Thus he reached Westminster at 9 o'clock next morning after a journey from France of little over 24 hours. Arrived at Westminster, he met and embraced John de Valois, exclaiming: "You and I are now, thank God, of good accord!" For Edward had acquired a real liking for John, and as long as both kings lived, peace between England and France was, humanly speaking, assured.

Both countries now gave themselves up to thanksgivings and rejoicings. Te Deums were sung and church bells were

[1] The Treaty was cited in the dispute regarding some Channel Islands in 1954.

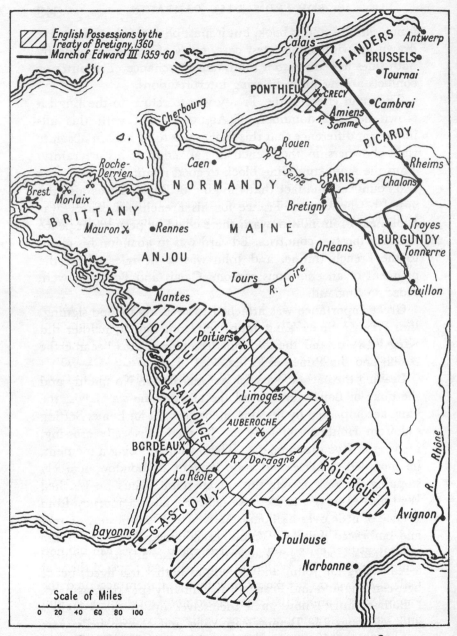

**18. FRANCE AFTER THE TREATY OF BRETIGNY, 1360**

rung: the roots of antagonism and discord had been rooted up and the seeds of perpetual peace between the two great countries sown. Overhead was the blue sky of heaven–but on the far horizon might be seen a little cloud, no bigger than a man's hand.

# APPENDIX

### THE NUMBERS OF EDWARD III'S ARMY

All the chroniclers are agreed that the English army was of exceptional size. This was to be expected in view of the king's grim determination this time to leave nothing to chance. Villani gives the figure of 100,000, which is merely another way of saying that it was very large, but that he does not know the figures. Le Bel, writing not long after the event, gives detailed figures for two of the divisions, which bear the impress of being based on some precise information, even though perhaps exaggerated. His total for the king's and Prince's division is 18,500. Froissart adopts le Bel's figures in his first edition, but scales them down in a combination of the Amiens and Abrégées editions by 2,500, bringing the total to 16,000. These figures exclude the division of the duke of Lancaster, so that the grand total cannot well be less than 20,000.

The Dauphin, in a letter dated October 11, stated that at the time of writing, 12,000 troops had landed at Calais. But this does not help us for we do not know what proportion of the army had then landed, nor was the Dauphin likely to have accurate information himself. However, if the divisions of Lancaster and the Black Prince were by then landed, a grand total of 20,000 would not be far from the mark.

The above figures do not take into account the foreign volunteers that eventually marched under the English banner. Knighton states that Walter Manny collected 1,500 of them at Calais, but we do not know how many of them accepted the king's terms, namely that they could not expect any pay, but only booty. The number was probably almost negligible.

The fact that the king did not seem anxious for their presence imparts veracity to his statement that he already had a large enough army for his purpose.

Taking everything into consideration the indications are that the army was at least equal in combatant strength to that of the Crecy campaign, and vastly superior in non-combatants, who must have numbered several thousands. Hence the number of men, armed and unarmed, who set out from Calais in the last expedition of Edward III may have exceeded 20,000.

It is true that Rymer's *Foedera* only records 3,474 infantry as being summoned in England and Wales, but there clearly must be some omissions in this collection of *Foedera*. Ramsay, however, assumes that it is complete and on the strength of it he calculates that the total was under 6,000 combatants. Even so, he fails to take into account any foreign element, or English troops already in Calais or other parts of France.

Moreover, it is probable that Sir Robert Knollys' Grande Compagnie, about 3,000 strong, joined forces in the centre of France where they were operating. Delachenal contents himself with the observation that the figure 20,000 is "probably too high". Ferdinand Lot, another apostle of the low numbers school, follows Ramsay.

## SOURCES

The only eye-witness's account we have (for Chaucer wrote nothing) is Sir Thomas Gray, so his *Scalacronica* must take first place. Unfortunately it is all too short. Apart from this, Henry Knighton is our main source. Walsingham, writing later, adds a few facts of his own. Rymer's *Foedera* is essential for the king's measures before setting out to France, and it gives the text of the Treaty of Bretigny, the original of which does not exist in complete form.

Of the neutral writers, le Bel is useful; Froissart copies him, and gives some interesting details of his own about the army; Villani gives a few facts which appear nowhere else.

For the early stages, the French chroniclers are almost valueless, but as the campaign progresses, so they become progressively more useful. The *Grandes Chroniques* is the best, and it prints the Bretigny Treaty. The continuator of de Nangis was in Paris during the siege, so his details are here reliable and to the point. The *Chronique des Quatre Premiers Valois*, though it gives a certain amount of information of its own, is not to be depended upon, and the *Chronique Normande* is no longer of much help.

The only modern works of real assistance, apart from Ramsay's *Genesis of Lancaster*, are of French origin. Two of these, supplemented by some papers in the *Bibliothèque de l'École des Chartes*, Henri Deniflé's *La Désolation des Églises . . .* and Roland Delachenal's *Charles V*, cover the ground between them.

### EDWARD III'S STRATEGY

There were significant changes in the strategy of the king during the war. He started by amassing allies, but soon learnt to distrust them. He then turned to the strategy of exterior lines, which was rendered possible to an island power in control of the sea.

But absence of communication between his armies caused so many disappointments that in his last campaign he reverted to the strategy of concentration, together with an absence of reliance on allies. This proved to be the correct policy for his times and procured him complete victory.

# RETROSPECT

IT was stated in the preface (which may have been skipped by many readers) that the dominant feature of the Crecy War was the person of Edward III–the central figure of the war. Around this remarkable man events pirouetted like dancers round a maypole, or concentrated upon him like filings upon a magnet. That the war was won was due almost entirely to the personality and persistence of a single man, the king of England. Kings, rulers and generals of France came and went during the course of the war, but not the English commander. Throughout a war lasting 22 years–precisely the length of the Napoleonic Wars–Edward pursued relentlessly his main objective: the freeing of the English crown from the vassalage of France, and thereby the termination of a centuries-old conflict.

If the commander changed not, neither did his chief captains. There is a remarkable, perhaps a unique continuity in the high command of the English army. In his first campaign Edward selected as his senior officers Henry of Derby, Warwick, Northampton, Suffolk, Reginald Cobham, and Walter Manny, while Sir John Chandos served as a junior. In his last campaign, 21 years later, he took with him the same six commanders, the only newcomers of note being the Prince of Wales and Lord Burghersh. It is incontestable that the king possessed in a high degree the gift of selecting the right leaders, and it is quite remarkable that, unlike Napoleon's marshals, Edward's generals did not quarrel and fall out among themselves; there is no record of personal feuds or jealousies: all were merged into a veritable "band of brothers", united in devoted service to their king and leader. To this homogeneity in the senior ranks must be attributed much of the English success in the field. Search where I may in the pages of military history, I can find nothing quite to match it.

Now these captains were rugged, masterful soldiers, of differing temperaments, who would not have shown such marked fidelity and devotion to a weakling king: they were the sons of the nobles who had dealt otherwise with his father Edward II. It follows that King Edward must have possessed a dominant yet attractive personality of his own, and that he added to this a natural talent for war and a proficiency in its execution that inspired in them confidence and implicit obedience. This attitude towards their king and commander must have been passed down to the rank and file, for *tel chef, telle troupe*. The confidence thus engendered inspired the whole army with a vibrant morale, without which no army can achieve great things. This in turn reacted upon its discipline, which steadily improved until it attained a high pitch in the final campaign of the war, where privations and frustrations were alike extreme. The army as a whole had also, by dint of much campaigning, reached a high standard of professional ability, and it had been well armed and supplied by a far-seeing commander. There can be no doubt that by the time of the signing of the Treaty of Bretigny the English professional soldier was easily the finest in the world. This is the fundamental reason why a small country like England was able to defeat one several times as large as itself. It follows from this that the English army was then the finest in the world; and this position of pre-eminence it owed to its king—the architect, the *fons et origo* of the whole vast machine.

England was, on military grounds, fortunate in her king. Whether she was equally fortunate on moral grounds it is not within the province of this book to enquire. I will only observe that it must be easy to condemn him on these grounds—to judge by the attitude of most English historians who castigate the king unmercifully. But it is permissible to wonder whether, had the critics lived at that epoch, they would have regarded the matter in the same light. Edward III was a product of his time, a child of his generation, and from all accounts a very likeable child in the period with which we are dealing. Moreover he was genuinely, if narrowly, religious, and it was not a mere formality that he bespoke the prayers of the two archbishops before setting out on his campaigns. Most human actions are the resultant of two or more impulses or motives, and Edward's action in fighting the king of France was no exception to this principle. He was no doubt influenced by the lust for power, and attracted by the glamour and excitement of adventure; but I believe that his dominant motive in so persistently maintaining the struggle was the one given above. He was, according to his lights, doing the right thing, and I will leave it at that.

Whether on material grounds England was fortunate is a fairly easy question to answer, but that also does not strictly appertain to this book. I will therefore confine myself to two observations. During the period covered by this war the internal state of the country was at least as peaceful and undisturbed as in any period of our medieval history: and toward the end, in spite of the ravages of the Black Death, it was rapidly increasing in material prosperity: it really did look as if it paid to go to war. The second observation is that the impact of the series of victories abroad seems to have stoked up the fires of national consciousness and pride in the hearts of this essentially young nation, and it was no mere coincidence that the signing of the Treaty of Bretigny practically coincided with the introduction of the English tongue into Parliamentary proceedings. The Crecy war was responsible for much.

# INDEX

# INDEX

359